WILEY

FASTCOMPANY

READER SERIES

LEADERSHIP

WILEY

FAST**COMPANY**

READER SERIES

LEADERSHIP

GRETCHEN M. SPREITZER, EDITOR

University of Michigan

KIMBERLY HOPKINS PERTTULA, EDITOR

University of Southern California

www.wiley.com/college/spreitzer

Acquisitions Editor   *Jeff Marshall*
Marketing Manager   *Charity Robey*
Editorial Assistant   *Jessica Bartelt*
Managing Editor   *Lari Bishop*
Associate Production Manager   *Kelly Tavares*
Production Editor   *Sarah Wolfman-Robichaud*

This book was set in 10/12 Garamond by Leyh Publishing LLC and printed and bound by Courier Corporation. The cover was printed by Phoenix Color Corp.

This book is printed on acid free paper. ∞

ISBN: 0-471-45805-8

Printed in the United States of America

10 9 8 7 6 5 4 3 2 1

CONTENTS

SECTION 1: LESSONS OF LEADERSHIP   7

SECTION 4: LEADING OTHERS IN A GLOBAL, DIVERSE WORLD 137

SECTION 5: LEADERSHIP OF THE FUTURE 161

ACKNOWLEDGEMENTS

What a great time we've had sifting through back issues of *Fast Company,* reading articles on contemporary issues in leadership. We thank Kim Jaussi for insights on the use of *Fast Company* in the classroom, as well as members of the Organizational Behavior Teaching Society. We also thank Jeff Marshal, our editor at Wiley, for his vision of the Wiley/*Fast Company* Reader Series: Leadership. We were thrilled when he sought us out to lead this project. We thank the journalists and editors at *Fast Company* for having the courage and insight to create a business periodical that is so radically different. Through their writing, they inspire us to think differently about our own role as educators. And of course, we thank the authors of these twenty-four articles who make this leadership reader possible.

Gretchen M. Spreitzer
Ann Arbor, Michigan

Kimberly Hopkins Perttula
Santa Monica, California

ABOUT THE EDITORS

GRETCHEN M. SPREITZER

Gretchen M. Spreitzer is an organizational behavior and human resource management faculty member at the University of Michigan Business School (UMBS) and a faculty affiliate of the Center for Effective Organizations (CEO) at the University of Southern California. She joined the Michigan faculty in 2001 after spending nine years on the faculty at the University of Southern California Marshall School of Business.

Gretchen's research focuses on employee empowerment and leadership development, particularly within a context of organizational change and decline. Based on extensive field research, she has authored a number of articles on contemporary issues in organizational behavior in leading journals, such as the *Academy of Management Journal,* the *Academy of Management Review,* and the *Journal of Applied Psychology.* She is the co-author of three books: *The Leader's Change Handbook: An Essential Guide to Setting Direction and Taking Action* (1999) with Jay Conger and Edward Lawler; *The Future of Leadership: Speaking to the Next Generation* (2001) with Warren Bennis and Thomas Cummings; and *A Company of Leaders: Five Disciplines for Unleashing the Power in Your Workforce* (2001) with Robert Quinn. Gretchen has been awarded the Western Academy of Management's Ascendant Scholar award for early career contributions.

Gretchen is a section editor of the *Journal of Management Inquiry* and also serves on the editorial boards of *Organization Science* and the *Journal of Organizational Behavior.* She serves on the executive board of the Organization Development and Change Division of the Academy of Management and the executive board of the Western Academy of Management.

Prior to her doctoral education, Gretchen worked with the management consulting group at Price Waterhouse's Government Services Office and with Partners for Livable Places, a not-for-profit urban planning firm in Washington, D.C. She has a bachelor of science in systems analysis from Miami University (in Ohio) and completed her doctoral work at the Michigan Business School.

KIMBERLY HOPKINS PERTTULA

Kimberly Hopkins Perttula is a Ph.D. candidate at the University of Southern California (USC). Prior to her doctoral work, she attended San Jose State University, where she received her master of science degree in industrial/organizational psychology. While in the master's program, Kimberly worked in organization development and human resources at Applied Materials, a technology company in Silicon Valley.

At USC Kimberly teaches an undergraduate course in organizational behavior. Her research focuses on leadership development, employee development, and employee motivation. She has authored an article in the *Journal of Management Inquiry* and is active in several professional organizations, including the Academy of Management and the Western Academy of Management. Kimberly has also completed the Presidential Fellows Program, a 12-month leadership development and community service program at the USC Leadership Institute.

Prior to her graduate education, Kimberly worked in Washington, D.C. as a legislative assistant to Vice President Al Gore and with the Council on Competitiveness, a not-for-profit, nonpartisan association. She has a bachelor of arts degree in psychology from Wake Forest University.

INTRODUCTION

Warren Bennis, in his introduction to the book entitled, *The Future of Leadership,* ponders whether the future of leadership has any "shelf life." By "shelf life" he means, do any of the ideas about leadership developed over the last century have staying power as we begin the 21st century? Bennis is right to wonder about the staying power of traditional leadership theories. Most were developed around the time of World War II and have their roots in a military model of organizational effectiveness. In these models, leadership is apt to be located at the top of a hierarchical organization with a clear chain of command and division of labor. Leadership is heroic and visionary, and the rest of the organization falls in line as directed.

But a quick look at the business environment prevalent in the beginning of the 21st century tells us that today's business world brings challenges that are fundamentally different from those addressed by traditional models of leadership:

- Competition is keen. Leadership has to be results-oriented. Wall Street demands that public companies meet their short-term performance goals, but effective leadership also recognizes the need for long-term development of people, products, and services. Leaders must learn to make the appropriate tradeoffs between short-term and long-term performance.

- Change is a constant. Leaders must learn to transform their organizations to meet the changing needs of their environments. Vision is key, but implementation of the vision is even more important. Leaders must gain the commitment and buy-in of their workforces.

- More and more organizations are becoming networked and virtual— everything but core competencies are outsourced so that organization's can focus on their strengths. Leaders are less likely to be co-located with their followers as telecommuting and global teams become more common. Consequently, traditional management models focused on visual monitoring are inadequate in this context.

- Balancing life and work is increasingly difficult and stress abounds. The number of dual career and single parent families are on the rise. New technologies have all but erased the barriers between work and personal time. Fierce competition demands that more organizations offer services and products twenty-four hours a day, seven days a week. Leaders must learn to not only manage their own work-life issues, but to also support their employees' need for balance.

- The business world is increasingly global. Not only are organizations serving a wider customer base than ever before, but workforces are also becoming internationalized. Leaders must learn to manage in an environment where customers and employees bring different and sometimes conflicting cultural values.

- Organizations are becoming more diverse than ever. Organizations that can harness the benefits of their diversity are apt to gain more creativity and innovation. But diversity, whether it is based on gender, nationality, race, sexual orientation, personality, or socioeconomic background, also brings profound challenges for how people work together.

- Structures are becoming flatter and more participative. Employees are more likely to be empowered to voice their opinions about how they do their work and how the organization should be run. Teams are replacing hierarchies. Leadership capability is being moved to lower levels of the organization. And consequently, rewards such as stock options are increasingly being offered to employees at all levels of the organization to compensate them for their leadership orientation.

These are just some of the challenges that face contemporary leaders—challenges that require radically different approaches than the command and control orientation of traditional leadership theories. Unfortunately new theory often lags behind practice, and approaches to leadership development become quickly outdated. So where can practicing leaders find solutions for effectively leading in this new age? Enter *Fast Company*.

LEADERSHIP: *FAST COMPANY* STYLE

Alan Webber and Bill Taylor, two former *Harvard Business Review* editors, launched the business magazine *Fast Company* in November 1995. Its aim was to be different from traditional business periodicals, such as *Fortune* or *Business Week*. A global revolution was taking the business world by storm at the same time that business was also changing the world. *Fast Company* entered the scene with intentions to seek out new business practices, chronicle how companies develop and compete, and showcase the best and brightest leaders who are inventing the future and reinventing business.

In less than ten years, and with dozens of prominent awards for its creativity and insight, *Fast Company* has become more than a magazine—it's become a movement. It has been called a "handbook for the business revolution" and a "manifesto for change." It captures the spirit of the new workplace and the people who are leading the revolution. Millions of people in the new economy depend on *Fast Company* for the tools, techniques, and tactics they need to succeed at work and life.

Every issue of *Fast Company* screams, "This is a different kind of magazine!" Articles are often short, even just a few paragraphs in length. At the end of each article is the email address of the protagonist, with the idea being that the reader can begin a dialogue with that particular individual, using the article as a starting point.

Fast Company is also full of action photos that bring its stories alive. And the leaders in those pictures look different than the typical CEO or executive in a pinstriped suit. *Fast Company* brings to light influential voices on the future of business, regardless of where they sit in organizations or what kinds of organizations they are part of. The magazine showcases real people with real solutions driven by innovative ideas. They are just as likely to be members of Generation X or Generation Y as they are to be Baby Boomers.

Fast Company tends to highlight the change efforts of emerging leaders, in emerging companies, often in nontraditional industries or contexts. The focus tends to be less on those at the top of the Fortune 500 and more on fast growing start-ups, not-for-profits, or nonbusiness contexts. Witness recent *Fast Company* articles that have highlighted leadership lessons from a leaderless orchestra, a dance company, and a Navy ship. These alternative contexts provide stimulating analogies for learning about effective leadership in a new age. They move toward innovative thinking on leadership and change.

Since it's inception, *Fast Company* has published more than 2,200 articles on the topic of leadership alone. It has become the first place people go when they want the latest thinking on leadership.

THE BIRTH OF A WILEY/*FAST COMPANY* READER ON LEADERSHIP

As the readership of *Fast Company* has increased over the past five years, more and more teachers are requiring a subscription to *Fast Company* as part of their leadership courses or are including *Fast Company* articles in their course readers. The idea is to supplement textbooks that tend do a great job of describing established theories on leadership with dynamic examples of contemporary leaders facing 21st century challenges. We've used *Fast Company* articles in our undergraduate and MBA coursepacks for several years, and our students single them out as their favorites. The *Fast Company* articles resonate with students because they reflect their own opinions about what makes organizations great places to work. For those without much work experience, the *Fast Company* articles also bring to life the leadership theories introduced in their textbooks.

In producing this leadership reader, we've sifted through the more than 2,000 leadership-oriented articles in *Fast Company* since 1995. Our goal was to identify the most hard-hitting, insightful pieces on leadership. We wanted to represent a wide range of leadership issues—from different leadership styles to managing diversity to the future of leadership. We looked for articles that offered an interesting analogy for leadership or a contrasting or unique viewpoint. We sought to tap a wide range of industries, contexts, and organizational settings. We looked not only for established experts on leadership, but also for new voices from which to learn—voices that might not be represented in leadership textbooks. And of course, we wanted articles with substance. Through an iterative process, we narrowed down the list of possible articles from 2,000 to 450 to 50. We both reread these final 50, looking for the optimal set of readings that together would form a cohesive and comprehensive perspective on effective leadership in contemporary organizations. The final product is this set of twenty-seven articles, grouped into five topic areas.

OVERVIEW

The Wiley/*Fast Company* Reader Series: Leadership is organized into five different sections. The first section we entitled "The Lessons of Leadership." It includes seven articles that describe the essence of leadership in contemporary organizations. The second section we have titled "Leading Amidst Change." These seven articles provide insights about how to envision and implement significant strategic and organization change. Often the changes are not the traditional top-down driven change efforts but more grass roots efforts initiated at all levels of the organization. The third section we labeled "The Leader as Learner (Especially from Failure)." Together, these four articles articulate the importance of a leader's ability to grow and develop as they learn from their every day experiences. They also highlight important lessons of experience, especially experiences of challenge, crisis, and failure.

The fourth section is entitled "Leading Others in a Global, Diverse World." The three articles in this section describe the real challenges leaders face as they lead in a global business world made up of an increasingly diverse workforce and customer base. The final section of the Wiley/*Fast Company* Reader Series: Leadership is entitled "Leadership of the Future." While all *Fast Company* articles look toward the future, these three articles emphasize the elements of leadership that are expected to be critical in coming years. They push the envelope on traditional ideas about leadership effectiveness.

HOW TO USE THIS LEADERSHIP READER

This Wiley/*Fast Company* Reader Series: Leadership could be used as the primary textbook or as a supplementary coursepack for both undergraduate and MBA courses. The reader would be appropriate for introductory courses in organizational behavior or general management but also, obviously, for teaching courses in leadership. It could also be used for courses on organizational change, given the large selection of articles on change in the second section of the reader.

We recommend that specific articles from the Reader be assigned for each class period. Then students should come to class prepared to discuss the article(s) of the day. Professors can have students review the articles in a given section for best practices in contemporary leadership. Students can debate whether and how the approaches used in alternative leadership contexts, such as the captain of the racing yacht, introduced in the reader apply to leadership in business environments. They can then begin to build their own contingency theories of leadership, outlining leadership similarities and differences across different types of contexts.

Professors might also assign to each student one article for which they serve as the discussion facilitator. The discussion leader can prepare five to eight discussion questions provoked by the article. Students might take a few minutes to formulate their own answers to the questions, then break into small groups to discuss the articles, and finally report on their answers to the whole class. It's also possible to have students write one-page responses to particular articles that catch their attention or to those with which they disagree.

If the leadership reader is a supplement to a coursepack, students may compare and contrast the leadership approaches exemplified in the reader with the theories of leadership outlined in the textbook. Such an exercise can provoke students to think about new directions for leadership in a netcentric, global business world.

Some of the articles in the reader showcase leading edge leadership books, such as *Tempered Radicals* by Deborah Meyerson. We find that these readings often pique students' interest in these books, and book reports and presentations on these materials may be a natural follow-on. In advanced courses, professors may even want to assign one of these trade books for more in depth coverage.

Clearly, these are just some starting points for professors to think about when integrating *Fast Company* into their course materials. Hopefully, these ideas will stimulate other ideas for the use of *Fast Company* in the classroom.

LESSONS OF LEADERSHIP

This section includes articles that introduce different approaches or styles of leadership. It begins with two thought pieces. The first highlights Harvard Business School Professor Michael Porter and the importance of strategy for effective leadership. The second showcases Marcus Buckingham and his two best selling books. The article introduces his "strengths-based" approach to leadership, in which leaders work to capitalize on their unique talents while compensating for their weaknesses. The remaining six articles offer exemplars or profiles of effective leaders in action. Two of the leaders, Andy Pearson of Tricon and Donald Winker of Ford Motor Company, come from traditional business organizations. But the other four articles are based on alternative leader contexts, including a racing yacht, the Navy's USS Benfold, and the leaderless Orpheus orchestra. These profiles provide different viewpoints for better understanding the challenges of effective leadership across contexts. Commonalities across these wildly divergent contexts are likely to be robust qualities of effective leadership.

BY KEITH H. HAMMONDS   FROM *FAST COMPANY* ISSUE 44, PAGE 150

Michael Porter's Big Ideas

THE WORLD'S MOST FAMOUS BUSINESS-SCHOOL PROFESSOR IS FED UP WITH CEOS WHO CLAIM THAT THE WORLD CHANGES TOO FAST FOR THEIR COMPANIES TO HAVE A LONG-TERM STRATEGY. IF YOU WANT TO MAKE A DIFFERENCE AS A LEADER, YOU'VE GOT TO MAKE TIME FOR STRATEGY.

Here is how Michael E. Porter regards the business landscape: Beginning in the mid-1980s, he more or less left the strategy world to its own devices, focusing his attention instead on the question of international competitiveness. He advised foreign governments on their economic policies and headed a U.S. presidential commission. He wrote books and papers on industry dynamics—from ceramics manufacturing in Italy to the robotics sector in Japan. He spoke everywhere. He was consumed by understanding the competitive advantage of nations.

Then, in the mid-1990s, he resurfaced. "I was reading articles about corporate strategy, too many of which began with 'Porter said … and that's wrong.' Strategy had lost its intellectual currency. It was losing adherents. People were being tricked and misled by other ideas," he says.

Like a domineering parent, Porter seems both miffed by the betrayal and pleased by his apparent indispensability. I can't turn my back for five minutes. Well, kids, the man is back. Porter seeks to return strategy to its place atop the executive pyramid.

Business strategy probably predates Michael Porter. Probably. But today, it is hard to imagine confronting the discipline without reckoning with the Harvard Business School professor, perhaps the world's best-known business academic. His first book, *Competitive Strategy: Techniques for Analyzing Industries and Competitors* (Free Press, 1980), is in its 53rd printing and has been translated into 17 languages. For years, excerpts from that and other Porter works have been required reading in "Competition and Strategy," the first-year course that every Harvard MBA student must take. Porter's strategy frameworks have suffered some ambivalence over the years in academic circles—yet they have proved wildly compelling among business leaders around the world.

This is the paradox that Porter faces. His notions on strategy are more widely disseminated than ever and are preached at business schools and in seminars around the globe. Yet the idea of strategy itself has, in fact, taken a backseat to newfangled notions about competition hatched during the Internet frenzy: Who needs a long-term strategy when everyone's goal is simply to "get big fast"?

With his research group, Porter operates from a suite of offices tucked into a corner of Harvard Business School's main classroom building. At 53, his blond hair graying, he is no longer the wunderkind who, in his early thirties, changed the way CEOs thought about their companies and industries. Yet he's no less passionate about his pursuit—and no less certain of his ability. In a series of interviews, Porter told Fast Company why strategy still matters.

BUSINESS KEEPS MOVING FASTER—BUT YOU BETTER MAKE TIME FOR STRATEGY.

It's been a bad decade for strategy. Companies have bought into an extraordinary number of flawed or simplistic ideas about competition—what I call "intellectual potholes." As a result, many have abandoned strategy almost completely. Executives won't say that, of course. They say, "We have a strategy." But typically, their "strategy" is to produce the highest-quality products at the lowest cost or to consolidate their industry. They're just trying to improve on best practices. That's not a strategy.

Strategy has suffered for three reasons. First, in the 1970s and 1980s, people tried strategy, and they had problems with it. It was difficult. It seemed an artificial exercise. Second, and at the same time, the ascendance of Japan really riveted attention on implementation. People argued that strategy wasn't what was really important—you just had to produce a higher-quality product than your rival, at a lower cost, and then improve that product relentlessly.

The third reason was the emergence of the notion that in a world of change, you really shouldn't have a strategy. There was a real drumbeat that business was about change and speed and being dynamic and reinventing yourself, that things were moving so fast, you couldn't afford to pause. If you had a strategy, it was rigid and inflexible. And it was outdated by the time you produced it.

That view set up a straw man, and it was a ridiculous straw man. It reflects a deeply flawed view of competition. But that view has become very well entrenched.

The irony, of course, is that when we look at the companies that we agree are successful, we also agree that they all clearly do have strategies. Look at Dell, or Intel, or Wal-Mart. We all agree that change is faster now than it was 10 or 15 years ago. Does that mean you shouldn't have a direction? Well, probably not. For a variety of reasons, though, lots of companies got very confused about strategy and how to think about it.

OF COURSE STRATEGY IS HARD— IT'S ABOUT MAKING TOUGH CHOICES.

There's a fundamental distinction between strategy and operational effectiveness. Strategy is about making choices, trade-offs; it's about deliberately choosing to be different. Operational effectiveness is about things that you really shouldn't have to make choices on; it's about what's good for everybody and about what every business should be doing.

Lately, leaders have tended to dwell on operational effectiveness. Again, this has been fed by the business literature: the ideas that emerged in the late 1980s and early 1990s, such as total quality, just-in-time, and reengineering. All were focused on the nitty-gritty of getting a company to be more effective. And for a while, some Japanese companies turned the nitty-gritty into an art form. They were incredibly competitive.

Japan's obsession with operational effectiveness became a huge problem, though, because only strategy can create sustainable advantage. And strategy must start with a different value proposition. A strategy delineates a territory in which a company seeks to be unique. Strategy 101 is about choices: You can't be all things to all people.

The essence of strategy is that you must set limits on what you're trying to accomplish. The company without a strategy is willing to try anything. If all you're trying to do is essentially the same thing as your rivals, then it's unlikely that you'll be very successful. It's incredibly arrogant for a company to believe that it can deliver the same sort of product that its rivals do and actually do better for very long. That's especially true today, when the flow of information and capital is incredibly fast. It's extremely dangerous to bet on the incompetence of your competitors—and that's what you're doing when you're competing on operational effectiveness.

What's worse, a focus on operational effectiveness alone tends to create a mutually destructive form of competition. If everyone's trying to get to the same place, then, almost inevitably, that causes customers to choose on price. This is a bit of a metaphor for the past five years, when we've seen widespread cratering of prices.

There have been those who argue that in this new millennium, with all of this change and new information, such a form of destructive competition is simply the way competition has to be. I believe very strongly that that is not the case. There are many opportunities for strategic differences in nearly every industry; the more dynamism there is in an economy, in fact, the greater the opportunity. And a much more positive kind of competition could emerge if managers thought about strategy in the right way.

TECHNOLOGY CHANGES, STRATEGY DOESN'T.

The underlying principles of strategy are enduring, regardless of technology or the pace of change. Consider the Internet. Whether you're on the Net or not, your profitability is still determined by the structure of your industry. If there are no barriers to entry, if customers have all the power, and if rivalry is based on price, then the Net doesn't matter—you won't be very profitable.

Sound strategy starts with having the right goal. And I argue that the only goal that can support a sound strategy is superior profitability. If you don't start with that goal and seek it pretty directly, you will quickly be led to actions that will undermine strategy. If your goal is anything but profitability—if it's to be big, or to grow fast, or to become a technology leader—you'll hit problems.

Finally, strategy must have continuity. It can't be constantly reinvented. Strategy is about the basic value you're trying to deliver to customers, and about which customers you're trying to serve. That positioning, at that level, is where continuity needs to be strongest. Otherwise, it's hard for your organization to grasp what the strategy is. And it's hard for customers to know what you stand for.

STRATEGY HASN'T CHANGED, BUT CHANGE HAS.

On the other hand, I agree that the half-life of everything has shortened. So setting strategy has become a little more complicated. In the old days, maybe 20 years ago, you could set a direction for your business, define a value proposition, then lumber along pursuing that. Today, you still need to define how you're going to be distinctive. But we know that simply making that set of choices will not protect you unless you're constantly sucking in all of the available means to improve on your ability to deliver.

So companies have to be very schizophrenic. On one hand, they have to maintain continuity of strategy. But they also have to be good at continuously improving. Southwest Airlines, for example, has focused on a strategy of serving price-minded customers who want to go from place to place on relatively short, frequently offered flights without much service. That has stayed consistent over the years. But Southwest has been extremely aggressive about assimilating every new idea possible to deliver on that strategy. Today, it does many things differently than it did 30 years ago—but it's still serving essentially the same customers who have essentially the same needs.

The error that some managers make is that they see all of the change and all of the new technology out there, and they say, "God, I've just got to get out there and implement like hell." They forget that if you don't have a direction, if you don't have something distinctive at the end of the day, it's going to be very hard to win. They don't understand that you need to balance the internal juxtaposition of change and continuity.

The thing is, continuity of strategic direction and continuous improvement in how you do things are absolutely consistent with each other. In fact, they're mutually reinforcing. The ability to change constantly and effectively is made easier by high-level continuity. If you've spent 10 years being the best at something, you're better able to assimilate new technologies. The more explicit you are about setting strategy, about wrestling with trade-offs, the better you can identify new opportunities that support your value proposition. Otherwise, sorting out what's important among a bewildering array of technologies is very difficult. Some managers think, "The world is changing, things are going faster—so I've got to move faster. Having a strategy seems to slow me down." I argue no, no, no—having a strategy actually speeds you up.

BEWARE THE MYTH OF INFLECTION POINTS.

The catch is this: Sometimes the environment or the needs of customers do shift far enough so that continuity doesn't work anymore, so that your essential positioning is no longer valid. But those moments occur very infrequently for most companies. Intel's Andy Grove talks about inflection points that force you to revisit your core strategy. The thing is, inflection points are very rare. What managers have done lately is assume that they are everywhere, that disruptive technologies are everywhere.

Discontinuous change, in other words, is not as pervasive as we think. It's not that it doesn't exist. Disruptive technologies do exist, and their threat has to be on everyone's mind. But words like "transformation" and "revolution" are incredibly overused. We're always asking the companies we work with, "Where is that new technology that's going to change everything?" For every time that a new technology is out there, there are 10 times that one is not.

Let's look again at the Internet. In Fast Company two years ago, we would have read that the Internet was an incredibly disruptive technology, that industry after industry was going to be transformed. Well, guess what? It's not an incredibly disruptive technology for all parts of the value chain. In many cases, Internet technology is actually complementary to traditional technologies. What we're seeing is that the companies winning on the Internet use the new technology to leverage their existing strategy.

GREAT STRATEGISTS GET A FEW (BIG) THINGS RIGHT.

Change brings opportunities. On the other hand, change can be confusing. One school of thought says that it's all just too complicated, that no manager can ever solve the complex problem that represents a firmwide strategy today. So managers should use the hunt-and-peck method of finding a strategy: Try something, see if it works, then proceed to the next. It's basically just a succession of incremental experiments.

I say that method will rarely work, because the essence of strategy is choice and trade-offs and fit. What makes Southwest Airlines so successful is not a bunch of separate things, but rather the strategy that ties everything together. If you were to experiment with onboard service, then with gate service, then with ticketing mechanisms, all separately, you'd never get to Southwest's strategy.

You can see why we're in the mess that we're in. Competition is subtle, and managers are prone to simplify. What we learn from looking at actual competition is that winning companies are anything but simple. Strategy is complex. The good news is that even successful companies almost never get everything right up front. When the Vanguard Group started competing in mutual funds, there was no Internet, no index funds. But Vanguard had an idea that if it could strip costs to the bone and keep fees low—and not try to beat the market by taking on risk—it would win over time. John Bogle understood the essence of that, and he took advantage of incremental opportunities over time.

You don't have to have all the answers up front. Most successful companies get two or three or four of the pieces right at the start, and then they elucidate their strategy over time. It's the kernel of things that they saw up front that is essential. That's the antidote to complexity.

GREAT STRATEGIES ARE A CAUSE.

The chief strategist of an organization has to be the leader—the CEO. A lot of business thinking has stressed the notion of empowerment, of pushing down and getting a lot of people involved. That's very important, but empowerment and involvement don't apply to the ultimate act of choice. To be successful, an organization must have a very strong leader who's willing to make choices and define the trade-offs. I've found that there's a striking relationship between really good strategies and really strong leaders.

That doesn't mean that leaders have to invent strategy. At some point in every organization, there has to be a fundamental act of creativity where someone divines the new activity that no one else is doing. Some leaders are really good at that, but that ability is not universal. The more critical job for a leader is to provide the discipline and the glue that keep such a unique position sustained over time.

Another way to look at it is that the leader has to be the guardian of trade-offs. In any organization, thousands of ideas pour in every day—from employees with suggestions, from customers asking for things, from suppliers trying to sell things. There's all this input, and 99% of it is inconsistent with the organization's strategy.

Great leaders are able to enforce the trade-offs: "Yes, it would be great if we could offer meals on Southwest Airlines, but if we did that, it wouldn't fit our low-cost strategy. Plus, it would make us look like United, and United is just as good as we are at serving meals." At the same time, great leaders understand that there's nothing rigid or passive about strategy—it's something that a company is continually getting better at—so they can create a sense of urgency and progress while adhering to a clear and very sustained direction.

A leader also has to make sure that everyone understands the strategy. Strategy used to be thought of as some mystical vision that only the people at the top understood. But that violated the most fundamental purpose of a strategy, which is to inform each of the many thousands of things that get done in an organization every day, and to make sure that those things are all aligned in the same basic direction.

If people in the organization don't understand how a company is supposed to be different, how it creates value compared to its rivals, then how can they possibly make all of the myriad choices they have to make? Every salesman has to know the strategy—otherwise, he won't know who to call on. Every engineer has to understand it, or she won't know what to build.

The best CEOs I know are teachers, and at the core of what they teach is strategy. They go out to employees, to suppliers, and to customers, and they repeat, "This is what we stand for, this is what we stand for." So everyone understands it. This is what leaders do. In great companies, strategy becomes a cause. That's because a strategy is about being different. So if you have a really great strategy, people are fired up: "We're not just another airline. We're bringing something new to the world."

Keith H. Hammonds (khammonds@fastcompany.com) is a *Fast Company* senior editor based in New York. Contact Michael Porter by email (mporter@hbs.edu).

BY POLLY LABARRE — FROM *FAST COMPANY* ISSUE 49, PAGE 88

Marcus Buckingham Thinks Your Boss Has an Attitude Problem

MARCUS BUCKINGHAM TEACHES CEOS HOW TO GET THE MOST OUT OF THEIR PEOPLE AND THEIR ORGANIZATIONS. HIS FIRST LESSON: FORGET EVERYTHING YOU THINK YOU KNOW ABOUT BEING A LEADER.

There is a noble promise at the heart of the new world of business: Everyone has the right to meaningful work, and people who do meaningful work create the most value in the marketplace. Even as the talent wars have fizzled into pink-slip parties, few senior executives would dispute the vital importance of finding, engaging, and developing the best people. Ask any CEO, "What's your company's most precious asset?" Without hesitation, the answer will be, "Our people." Ask the same CEO, "What's the primary source of your competitive advantage?" Chances are, the reply will be, "Our unique culture."

This kind of talk drives Marcus Buckingham nuts. It's not that he disagrees with the sentiments—he's spent his 15-year career as a pioneering researcher and a global-practice leader at the Gallup Organization, making the link between people, their performance, and business results. What troubles him is the lack of rigor behind the rhetoric. "There's a juicy irony here," says the 35-year-old Cambridge-educated Brit. "You won't find a CEO who doesn't talk about a 'powerful culture' as a source of competitive advantage. At the same time, you'd be hard-pressed to find a CEO who has much of a clue about the strength of that culture. The corporate world is appallingly bad at capitalizing on the strengths of its people."

Buckingham, on the other hand, is remarkably good at communicating his subversive message. He has produced two best-selling books: *First, Break All the Rules: What the World's Greatest Managers Do Differently* (Simon & Schuster, 1999), with coauthor Curt Coffman, and *Now, Discover Your Strengths* (The Free Press, 2001), with coauthor Donald O. Clifton. Meanwhile, Buckingham has helped build a ballooning consulting practice at Gallup, with more than 1,000 clients, including Best Buy, Disney, Fidelity Investments, Toyota, and Wells Fargo.

His mission, as he describes it, sounds almost quaint: "to create a better marriage between the dreams of workers and the drive of companies to win." His methodology is anything but quaint. Buckingham has led an effort inside Gallup to crunch three decades' worth of data on worker attitudes into actionable insights on human performance and productivity. First, he and his team tapped into a database of more than 1 million Gallup surveys that focused on workers from around the world. Although these workers had been asked many questions, there was one big question behind the interviews: "What does a strong and vibrant workplace look like?" Buckingham eventually distilled 12 core issues (called the "Q12" in Gallup-speak) that represent a simple barometer of the strength of any work unit.

Next, Buckingham's team ran massive number-crunching studies to analyze how answers to the Q12 shaped hard-core business results. The link between people and performance was vivid. The most "engaged" workplaces (those in the top 25% of Q12 scores) were 50% more likely to have lower turnover, 56% more likely to have higher-than-average customer loyalty, 38% more likely to have above-average productivity, and 27% more likely to report higher profitability.

Buckingham and his colleagues made one other finding that startled them: There was more variation in Q12 scores *within* companies than *between* companies. That is, in each of the more than 200 organizations that he analyzed, Buckingham found some of the most-engaged groups and some of the least-engaged groups. His conclusion: There is no such thing as a corporate culture. Companies are made up of many cultures, the strengths and weaknesses of which are a result of local conditions.

"It's staggering," he says. "Few of the CEOs in our study could say which work units in their company were engaged effectively and which weren't. They didn't know where their culture was strong and where it was weak, whether it was getting better or getting worse—or how much this variation was costing."

Talk about speaking truth to power. CEOs don't understand what makes their employees tick. They don't know how to get the best performance out of the most people. They can't say where their companies are strongest or weakest—or why. And that's just the first of Buckingham's series of assumption-busting messages. "The major challenge for CEOs over the next 20 years will be the effective deployment of human assets," he declares. "But that's not about 'organizational development' or 'workplace design.' It's about psychology. It's about getting one more individual to be more productive, more focused, more fulfilled than he was yesterday."

In several conversations with Fast Company, the tireless Buckingham offered an overview of his pathbreaking research and identified five attitude adjustments that redefine the essence of leadership in business.

ATTITUDE ADJUSTMENT #1

Measure what really matters. (By the way—the numbers you're using now *don't* matter.)

Numbers are crucial to running a company, and CEOs love them. Yet the numbers that most leaders use to manage the people who are part of their business are mostly off target. The CEOs who come to us are almost always fixated on two questions: How is our average performance improving over time? and How do we stack up against our competitors?

Both of those questions obscure what's really important. Averages hide the fact that within any company are some of the most-engaged work groups and some of the least-engaged work groups. But this range is what is most revealing.

You can divide any working population into three categories: people who are engaged (loyal *and* productive), those who are not engaged (just putting in time), and those who are actively disengaged (unhappy and spreading their discontent). The U.S. working population is 26% engaged, 55% not engaged, and 19% actively disengaged.

In essence, then, the CEO's job is to improve the ratio of engaged to actively disengaged workers. But here's the problem: Few of the CEOs in our study could say which work units in their company were effectively engaged and which weren't. They didn't know where their culture was strong and where it was weak, whether it was getting better or getting worse.

That's where the Q12 comes in. Survey the workforce every six months, and the result will be a vivid picture of which work units are engaged in a way that leads to the best performance and which workers are not.

I work closely with Best Buy, the big electronics retailer. When they started surveying their employees in 1997, they were in the 45th percentile of our Q12 database. By the end of last year, they were in the 70th percentile. More important, in those four years, 99 stores improved their Q12 scores significantly, while just 18 stores had scores that fell. The 99 stores that improved their engagement level dramatically improved their P&L budgets. The stores whose engagement level fell missed their P&L budgets. These are the numbers that matter.

ATTITUDE ADJUSTMENT #2

Stop trying to change people. Start trying to help them become more of who they already are.

CEOs hate variance. It's the enemy. Variance in customer service is bad. Variance in quality is bad. CEOs love processes that are standardized, routinized, predictable. Stamping out variance makes a complex job a bit less complex.

There is, however, one resource inside all companies that will hinder any attempt to eliminate variance: each individual's personality. Human beings are the one irreducible complexity in every company. And you can't eliminate that complexity by forcing people to become more like one another. You can't standardize human behavior. Of course, that's precisely what most leaders attempt to do. That goal—standardizing human behavior—is the driving force behind most executive-training programs and leadership-development courses. What's the quickest way to build a coherent culture? Get everyone to manage the same way.

Not only is that approach psychologically daft, it's hugely inefficient. It's fighting human nature, and anyone who fights human nature will lose. The best managers don't even try to fight that fight. We studied 80,000 of them from 400 different companies—people who excelled at getting great performance from their people. These managers followed the same basic set of principles: People don't change that much, so don't waste your time trying to rewire them or trying to put in what was left out. Instead, spend your time trying to draw out what was left in. When it comes to getting the best performance out of people, the most efficient route is to revel in their strengths, not to focus on their weaknesses.

Let me give you an example from my company. Our senior VP of marketing, Larry Emond, doesn't have a lick of empathy. It was surgically removed at birth. He also lacks a quality that I call "developer": getting a kick out of seeing someone else grow. Now, I could spend my time admonishing Larry. I could try to explain to him why that blistering email he dashed off had a crushing effect on several people. But he still wouldn't get it.

You might think that Larry is doomed to be a poor manager. Absolutely not. Larry's strength is that he has the qualities of self-assurance and a strategic mind-set. He doesn't need to have empathy to achieve results. People feel that Larry encourages their development, because he keeps thinking about how they can be part of this future he's describing.

Now Larry's approach seems obvious—why would you do anything else? And yet, in most organizations, Larry would be confronted by some nice, well-intentioned HR person—probably going off of feedback from a 360-degree survey—who would say, "Larry, as a leader, you need to be more responsive to your direct reports." There would be a lot of, "Tone that down, Larry." Well, how about, "Dial that up, Larry"?

If you are clear about the outcome that you want, instead of standardizing the qualities and steps that you think are required to get to that outcome, you should honor the fact that Larry's nature is irreducibly unique—rather than wasting time and money wishing that it weren't so. What goes for Larry goes for all kinds of people in companies. The best strategy for building a competitive organization is to help individuals become more of who they are.

ATTITUDE ADJUSTMENT #3

You're not the most important person in the company. (Believe it or not, your middle managers are.)

American culture is CEO obsessed. We celebrate the hard-charging heroes and mythologize the iconoclastic visionaries. Those people are important. But when it comes to getting the most productivity out of everyone in the company, they're not the most important people. Our research tells us that the single most important determinant of individual performance is a person's relationship with his or her immediate manager. It just doesn't matter much if you work for one of the "100 Best Companies," the world's most respected brand, or the ultimate employee-focused organization. Without a robust relationship with a manager who sets clear expectations, knows you, trusts you, and invests in you, you're less likely to stay and perform.

I admit, it seems like the most obvious point in the world. But do we revere the role of the middle manager? Hardly. We don't even like the term! We'd rather transform everyone into grassroots leaders, change agents, intrapreneurs. We look at managers as costs to be cut—or, at best, as leaders-in-waiting, people who are putting in time before they get the big job.

So what exactly do great managers do? First, the best managers start with a radical assumption: Each person's greatest room for growth is in the area of his greatest strength. It goes back to my last point. Good managers believe that each person is wired in a unique way—and these managers are fascinated by this individuality. Rather than seek to round it out or fill it in, the best managers do everything they can to sharpen and amplify that uniqueness. And then those managers work with people to help them understand their strengths, to build on them, to give them the confidence to be different.

ATTITUDE ADJUSTMENT #4

Stop looking to the outside for help. The solutions to your problems exist inside your company.

Talent is a multiplier. The more energy and attention you invest in it, the greater the yield will be. That's why the best leaders are relentless at seeking out, shadowing, studying, and highlighting the lessons of their own top performers.

The funny thing is that most CEOs spend their time benchmarking best practices in other companies. They want to know how they're doing relative to their peers. I tell my clients, Don't go on a tour of Disney, Southwest Airlines, or Discover Financial Services. You have some of the world's best managers working inside your own company. Look to them first. Learn from your own people first.

At Gallup, we've spent years documenting the simple, charming secrets of these extraordinary people. In the corners of every big company that we've studied, there are hundreds or thousands of them toiling away in relative obscurity. If you find them and shine a light on them, they will point the company's way to the future.

Take another look at Best Buy. It's like a controlled laboratory that is devoted to understanding the power of local managers and local work groups. In a sense, the company's strategy is built on uniformity—everything from store layout to product positioning to uniforms to operations manuals are standardized across the country. Yet even across 400 nearly identical environments, there's an amazing range of employee engagement and business performance. In the Best Buy store that has the highest Q12 scores, 91% of employees strongly agreed with the statement, "I know what's expected of me at work." In the store with the lowest score, just 27% agreed.

Not incidentally, the store with the highest Q12 score ranks in the top 10% of Best Buy stores as measured by P&L budget variance—and the store with the worst Q12 score falls in the bottom 10%. To improve overall corporate performance, Best Buy's leaders don't need to look outside the company. They just need to figure out how to build on the strengths of its best stores.

Building on these strengths means identifying internal best practices and shining a light on your best managers—people like Ralph Gonzalez. Ralph is a store manager who was charged with resurrecting a troubled Best Buy in Hialeah, Florida. He immediately named the store the Revolution, drafted a Declaration of

Revolution, and launched project teams, complete with army fatigues. He posted detailed performance numbers in the break room and deliberately over-celebrated every small achievement. To drive home the point that excellence is ubiquitous, he gave every employee a whistle and told them to blow it loudly whenever they "caught" anybody—whether coworker or supervisor—doing something "revolution-ary." Today, the whistles drown out the store's soundtrack, and, by any metric—sales growth, profit growth, customer satisfaction, employee retention—the Hialeah store is one of Best Buy's best.

But here's what really impressed me. Most companies would take a best practice like Ralph's whistle and say, "That's a great form of recognition. Let's give out whistles in every store." Best Buy did something much smarter: It extracted and spread the core lesson from Ralph's best practice, rather than institutionalizing the practice itself.

ATTITUDE ADJUSTMENT #5

Don't assume that everyone wants your job—or that great people want to be promoted out of what they do best.

There are two myths about talent that feed the conventional—and misguided—approach to career tracks and leadership development in most companies. The first myth: Talent is rare and special. Wrong. We all have talent. What's rare and special is a worker who finds a role that suits his or her talents. The second myth: Some roles are so easy that they don't require talent. Wrong again. We hear a lot about developing more respect for frontline workers and customer-facing employees, but peel the onion and you run into a rigid hierarchy of jobs. The compensation system evolves out of that hierarchy. So do titles and careers.

We say that we want to build world-class organizations. That's meaningless if we don't value world-class performance in every role. Yet the people who touch customers the most—hotel housekeepers, outbound telemarketers—get the least respect and the lowest paychecks. The assumption is that anyone can do that job and that nobody would want to do it if they were given a choice to do something else. Frontline talent has a prestige problem, and it's turning into a corporate-performance problem.

We studied the 3,000 housekeepers of a 15,000-room luxury-hotel chain. It turns out that great housekeepers are not beaten down by the relentless grind of cleaning rooms. On the contrary, they seem to be energized by doing the work. In their minds, the work they do asks that they be accountable and creative and that they achieve something tangible every day.

Unfortunately, the only way we have to reward excellence on the front lines is to promote people out of the very roles that they do best. We turn great housekeepers into supervisors, virtuoso shelf stockers into salespeople, and managers into leaders. A major challenge for CEOs is to define excellence in every role—and pay on it, award titles on it, distribute prestige on it, and make it a genuine career choice.

Satisfaction at work depends on nothing more than self-knowledge. And that gets leaders right back to their main task of engaging their employees at every level. What are you doing to turn your people's talent into the kind of performance that thrills customers, whether those customers are internal or external? The beautiful thing about a culture that is built by focusing on individual strengths is that no one can steal it. And any advantage that's hard to steal is an advantage that lasts.

Polly LaBarre (plabarre@fastcompany.com) is a *Fast Company* senior editor based in New York. Contact Marcus Buckingham by email (mbuckingham@gallup.com).

12 QUESTIONS THAT MATTER

If you want to build the most powerful company possible, then your first job is to help every person generate compelling answers to 12 simple questions about the day-to-day realities of his or her job. These are the factors, argue Marcus Buckingham and his colleagues at the Gallup Organization, that determine whether people are engaged, not engaged, or actively disengaged at work.

1. Do I know what is expected of me at work?
2. Do I have the materials and equipment that I need in order to do my work right?
3. At work, do I have the opportunity to do what I do best every day?
4. In the past seven days, have I received recognition or praise for doing good work?
5. Does my supervisor, or someone at work, seem to care about me as a person?
6. Is there someone at work who encourages my development?
7. At work, do my opinions seem to count?
8. Does the mission or purpose of my company make me feel that my job is important?
9. Are my coworkers committed to doing quality work?
10. Do I have a best friend at work?
11. In the past six months, has someone at work talked to me about my progress?
12. This past year, have I had opportunities at work to learn and grow?

BY DAVID DORSEY   FROM *FAST COMPANY* ISSUE 49, PAGE 78

Andy Pearson Finds Love

TWENTY YEARS AGO, AS CEO OF PEPSICO, ANDY PEARSON WAS NAMED ONE OF THE 10 TOUGHEST BOSSES IN AMERICA. NOW AT TRICON, PEARSON HAS FOUND A NEW WAY TO LEAD—ONE BASED ON PERSONAL HUMILITY AND EMPLOYEE RECOGNITION.

High above Tennessee, the leaders of Tricon Global Restaurants Inc., the largest restaurant chain in the world, are having a casual but strategic conference in one of their corporate jets. Andy Pearson may be sitting in front—but you'd never know he is one of the two men who run this company. Like all of the others, he wears a golf shirt that bears the logos of their three restaurants: KFC, Pizza Hut, and Taco Bell. He comments lightheartedly on the ideas that the others are advancing about partnering with another food chain—multibranding in their restaurants for variety. Maybe they'll put a Baskin-Robbins inside Taco Bell. At 30,000 feet, all ideas are good: Pearson isn't about to bring anyone down to earth from up here.

And that in itself is a huge change in Pearson's leadership style. This is the new Andy Pearson, a man who, now in his mid-70s, has transformed himself into a new kind of boss. The old Andy Pearson ran PepsiCo Inc. for nearly 15 years, driving revenues from $1 billion to $8 billion. Back then, he was known for his skills at bringing people down to earth, from any altitude. His chief weapons at the time were fear, surprise, and a fanatical devotion to the numbers. In 1980, *Fortune* named him one of the 10 toughest bosses in the United States. Pearson was singled out for the relentless demands that he put on his people. As one employee put it, Pearson's talents were often "brutally abrasive."

He was an effective CEO: His style worked. Pearson raised the bar for even the most outstanding performers. Nothing was ever quite good enough for him—even in situations where results were better than projected. One PepsiCo manager, for example, agreed to increase the volume of his unit's business by 12% that year. Instead, he racked up a 15% gain—and came to his performance review expecting at least a smile from his boss. Instead, Pearson pointed out that the market had grown even faster than this manager's operation and suggested that his performance had better improve.

Twenty years later, Pearson is still proud of having been included in the *Fortune* article. And he's still unapologetically tough. Over the years, he earned a reputation for his relentless, Socratic, two-word interrogation in meetings: "So what?" Every year, without hesitation, he fired the least productive 10% to 20% of his workforce—and he still thinks it's a good idea to let go of a certain layer of the company's lowest performers. But now he's learned to demand high standards in a different way.

"There's a human yearning for a certain amount of toughness," Pearson says. "But it can't be unmitigated toughness."

These days, Pearson is focused on a different, more positive emotional agenda: "You say to yourself, If I could only unleash the power of everybody in the organization, instead of just a few people, what could we accomplish? We'd be a much better company."

You can see this new attitude in the way that he speaks and listens, even up here, at this altitude, in a cushioned swivel chair. Pearson presides over this brainstorming session, tossing pithy cautionary asides into the air. He points his words with barbs of humor to make them stick. Tricon's chairman and CEO, David Novak, is the official leader of this group, this meeting, and this company. Yet Pearson's wisdom holds everyone in thrall. At the age of 76, he's been doing this sort of thing twice as long as anyone else on the jet. Everyone listens, over the drone of the turbines, when Pearson speaks. Even Novak listens, often leading the company by following Pearson's line of thought. Pearson just offers up what he knows and lets it sink in.

Someone suggests opening an all-night restaurant. Pearson doesn't think it would work, but he doesn't say so, at least not directly. He finds some nugget of intelligence in the idea and offers what he sees as "the challenge." "For Kinko's, being open all night is a big thing," he says. "But you would have to preempt the category. You can't share it." The suggestion is, if people want to tackle the challenge, he won't stop them. But they've been warned.

Pearson guides—but he doesn't control. He used to make a living running companies. Now he *governs*. The shift is more radical than it may sound.

PERFORMANCE FROM THE HEART

As founding chairman and former CEO of Tricon (Novak took over the post in January), Pearson feels that he has arrived at a personal inflection point that has universal significance—although he can't pin down any particular moment when the change occurred. He has learned some of his new leadership skills by watching Novak inspire the company with warmth, energy, and charisma. Yet the roots of his change go deeper.

Pearson has had several different careers. He spent 14 years as president and chief operating officer at PepsiCo, learning the business of soft drinks, snack foods, and restaurants. Before joining PepsiCo, he was a senior director at McKinsey & Co., the global consulting firm, where he rose from associate to senior director and was in charge of the firm's marketing practice.

After PepsiCo, he taught at Harvard Business School, where he wrote many articles for the *Harvard Business Review,* such as "Muscle-Build the Organization" and "Tough-Minded Ways to Get Innovative"—aggressively Pearson-esque articles that summarized the elements of his macho leadership style. He joined the leveraged-buyout firm Clayton Dubilier & Rice in 1993, then joined Tricon at Novak's insistence. "I told him it would be really meaningful if he would join me at Tricon," Novak recalls. "He could call himself anything, do anything."

At Tricon, Novak has established a culture that elevates the common worker in a way that brings out the emotional drive and commitment that is at the heart of good work. As a result, Pearson has seen employees weep with gratitude in reaction to nothing more than a few simple words of praise. Where before he might have dismissed that kind of display as sentimentality, he now recognizes emotion for what it is: the secret to a company's competitive edge.

It's a new way of thinking, as much as a new way of feeling. When Pearson came to Tricon, he absorbed what he saw in Novak's style—and realized it was more than a style. It was a *method.* Almost overnight, Pearson saw how the human heart drives a company's success—one person at a time—and how this kind of success can't be imposed from the top but must be *kindled* through attention, awareness, recognition, and reward.

The logic was clear: If the need for recognition and approval is a fundamental human drive, then the willingness to give it is not a sign of weakness. It's a lesson that has changed Pearson's own definition of leadership. "Great leaders find a balance between getting results and how they get them," he says. "A lot of people make the mistake of thinking that getting results is all there is to the job. They go after results without building a team or without building an organization that has the capacity to change. Your real job is to get results and to do it in a way that makes your organization a great place to work—a place where people enjoy coming to work, instead of just taking orders and hitting this month's numbers."

THE SMARTEST GUY IN THE ROOM

Not that there's anything wrong with hitting—or exceeding—your numbers. Under the leadership of Pearson and Novak, Tricon has increased its store-level margins from 11% to 15%, boosted operating profit by 32%, and cut its debt in half, to $2.5 billion. Tricon's leaders credit those numbers directly to their new culture of employee recognition. All of this has made Tricon a $22 billion retail operation with more than 30,000 restaurants and 725,000 employees worldwide. (It opens a new restaurant somewhere around the world every 10 hours.) Spun off of PepsiCo in 1997, Tricon's brands have worked their way into the fiber of people's lives. In China, there is a life-size statue of Colonel Sanders outside almost every KFC, and families there actually have to reserve their Thanksgiving bucket of chicken. (KFC imported the American holiday as a marketing ploy.)

When Novak invited Pearson to join the team, Pearson agreed, with one stipulation: "You are going to run this company. You will answer to me, but everyone else will answer to you."

"We'll do this together," Novak replied. "We can learn from each other."

When Pearson showed up at Tricon's corporate offices in Louisville, Kentucky (also the headquarters of KFC), the staff had a little surprise waiting for him. When he drove up, he saw hundreds of employees cheering. There was even a band playing to celebrate his arrival.

"All the time I was at Pepsi, nothing remotely like this had ever happened," Pearson says. "It was overwhelming. I knew something was going on that was fundamentally very powerful. If we could learn how to harness that spirit with something systematic, then we would have something unique."

Pearson's mission was manifest: to refine the new soul of this old machine into something rigorous, systematic, and shrewd—without destroying the generosity and warmth at the heart of it. The awe that he felt eventually became a profound respect for Novak's achievement. For Pearson, Novak has become something of a guru over "soft-side" issues, just as Pearson remains Novak's mentor on the "hard side."

This change of heart for Pearson—this stance of humility as a management style—became immediately apparent to everyone around him. Those who already knew him saw the transformation right away. Pearson had always been known as the quickest study around; he could learn a lesson in a matter of seconds. But he used his mental quickness as a weapon to see through the faulty logic of the people who reported to him, enabling him to prove how smart he was—particularly compared with *them.*

"I proved that I was smart by finding fault with other people's ideas," Pearson says. "I remember bringing one of our market-research women to tears because I told her that the information she was gathering wasn't producing anything. I could just see the breath come out of her. I realized that in today's world, you can't treat people that way. First, people have so many more options than they used to. They can leave—and you can't find more talent just by turning over the next log. Second, that kind of treatment demoralizes people. I don't think that woman was ever the same. If you're not careful, you might discard a very good person. There are a lot of ways to ask tough questions without killing somebody." The result of Pearson's new awareness: "I think I've gone from making my way by trying to be the smartest guy in the room to just asking questions and insisting that the answers be reasonable and logical."

Aylwin Lewis, Tricon's chief operating officer, started working with Pearson three years ago, before the new Andy had completely emerged. He's the first to point out that, even after his change of heart, Pearson has lost none of his business acumen—nor his ability to be blunt. But the old Andy was often known to be, well, a little too blunt.

"I used to read his stuff in the *Harvard Business Review,*" Lewis says. "But Tricon was the first time I had personal contact with him. He was brutal. He'd just beat the crap out of us. I remember one time he told us, 'A room full of monkeys could do better than this!' That was only three years ago."

Pearson had a powerful influence in Lewis's own career development. Lewis had become disgruntled with the way that Tricon was working. He felt overlooked. And although he believed that he was totally committed to the company, others saw only his discontent.

"He was constantly threatening to leave," Pearson says. "One day we were driving from one store to another, and I told him, 'The problem I've got with you is that if something happened to you and you died, I don't think I could get two people in top management to carry your casket. We all want you to succeed. But you're making it impossible.' He asked me why. I told him, 'You don't come to meetings, and you're constantly bitching.' That was a year and a half ago. Now he is the most productive guy we have in top management."

In retrospect, it may sound like a throwaway line. But in fact, the key sentence that Pearson said to Lewis was, "We all want you to succeed." When he said it, Pearson *felt* it—and Lewis knew it. Pearson may have been blunt, but he was reaching out to Lewis to help him, rather than to browbeat him.

Later, when they were by themselves, Lewis approached Pearson with a few words: "Andy, you changed my life."

LETTERS THAT BRING TEARS

Pearson's new leadership style is more than a way of relating to people. It involves the nuts and bolts of what he does from day to day, the processes that define the company's operations. Where before, Pearson would have dealt with only a small team of direct reports, he now seeks contact with people at all levels. It's his responsibility to motivate people across the company. He now believes that it's less important to issue orders than it is to *seek* answers and ideas from below. His job is to listen to the people who work for him and to serve them. He believes in firing those who don't perform. But more important, he's committed to making a strenuous effort to find a proper place for the talented ones who, for whatever reason, aren't living up to their potential.

"My old mantra was to influence the direction and behavior of a relatively small circle of direct reports," Pearson says. Now he and Novak move their values and ideas across the organization through programs such as CHAMPS, which rewards employees for recognizing the best practices of fellow workers, and through regular visits to the restaurants, during which they study those practices and reward people for good work.

"We need to make an enormous effort so that people feel that their individual contribution is vital to our success, starting with the store manager," Pearson says. Doing that requires a relentless sacrifice of shoe leather. "I was out in stores twice in the past two weeks," Pearson says. "I had a chicken burrito and a chicken taco the last time I was out. They didn't have any taste! Couldn't we put something in there? Salsa or something? You need a product that sends people into orbit. Retail is detail. Little ideas and details parlayed over the course of the year make a huge difference. Set the example. That's leadership."

Pearson has become a mentor to a group of leaders inside Tricon. "I spend a day with them, like a playing lesson with a golf pro," he says. "They talk to me about how they're doing. It's friendly. I get one or two letters a week from people saying, 'I can't believe that the founding chairman of the company would come and spend an hour just to talk with me.' I get letters that would just bring tears to your eyes."

HOW DO YOU SPELL "YUM"?

In Dallas, at the headquarters of Pizza Hut and Tricon International (a division of Tricon that handles the company's overseas business), 1,000 people have assembled in the long, high-ceilinged atrium for Tricon Founders' Day 2000. For Pearson and Novak, this is what the business is all about: a celebration of numbers hit and cultural commitments kept. Today, the leadership duo will honor four outstanding general managers in front of thousands of people who will watch both here and in other cities via satellite.

Overhead, a banner reads, "The Customer Is Why." Novak is already into his speech: "Our same-store sales will go up, not down. You never go down when you're satisfying customers. We're a company of customer maniacs."

People shake noisemakers built from two paper plates pasted around popcorn kernels. Up front sit the general managers, the four with the company's highest CHAMPS scores. Novak launches into a cheer: "Gimme a *Y!* Gimme a *U!* Gimme an *M!* What's that spell?"

"YUM!"

"What's that spell?"

"YUM!"

"What's that spell?"

"YUM!"

The audience screams and does a wave, like spectators at a football game. "This is the loudest Founders' Day welcome in history," Novak says. He shouts out the glowing numbers: Earnings per share are in the double digits and growing, and debt has been reduced by more than half. "You can count on one hand the number of companies that generate that kind of cash," Pearson adds.

It's quite a show. As the two of them play off of each other, it becomes clear how warmly the corporation has embraced Pearson, who has assumed an almost iconic persona: the Big Bad Guy. He's the gatekeeper, the guy who throws ice water on the coach *before* the game. But with Novak by his side, with the endorsement of the feel-good CEO, Pearson becomes loveable. His employees trust him. The new Andy can make fun of his own toughness—and be tough at the same time. He is tough love.

"Our same-store sales were down a percentage point," Novak says. "We need to bring that up."

It's the only bad number, but it's a big one, a key measure. You can keep increasing overall revenue by opening new stores around the world, but if you aren't increasing productivity and sales per store, at some point you run out of places to expand.

"We've got to get maniacal," Novak tells the crowd. "I'm talking about satisfying our customers every day. In 30,000 stores, we have to make that happen every day. It's all about motivating through recognition and celebration. We will be the biggest restaurant developer in the world."

It's time to call up the four winning managers. Awaiting them is the YUM award: a huge set of false teeth that walks when wound up. The managers are humble and moved as they accept their award. They are being singled out for recognition in front of the entire company. It means a lot.

Novak does what all great leaders do: He pays homage to these four managers as leaders. "They have created a work environment where they can come to work and be excited about what they do," he says. "The work environment that these leaders have created is the best I've ever seen."

As the event winds down, Novak asks Pearson to reflect on his career so far at Tricon. And it's Pearson who gets the loudest cheer of the day when he tells the crowd, "My experience at Tricon represents the capstone of my career."

In person, without the cheering crowd around him, Pearson is even more appreciative of the change that he's gone through. In his Connecticut office, on the table near his couch, is KFC rubber chicken number 227—the one that Novak gave him in 1997 when he joined the company. On the side of the chicken, Novak had written a note: "Congratulations on being the first chairman and CEO of what is sure to be the best restaurant company in the world. You are clearly our Big Chicken around the world."

What's the lesson for other CEOs? "Ultimately," Pearson says, "it's all about having more genuine concern for the other person. There's a big difference between being tough and being tough-minded. There's an important aspect that has to do with humility. But I've been modestly disappointed at how hard it is to get leaders to act that way. I think it's going to take a generation of pounding away on this theme. We've got a half-dozen or so real leaders in our company, but we don't have 20 or 30. You know what it takes? Role models."

David Dorsey is a frequent *Fast Company* contributor who lives in Rochester, New York. Contact Andy Pearson by email (andy.pearson@tricon-yum.com).

How Do We Break Out of the Box We're Stuck In?

DONALD WINKLER IS PROFOUNDLY DYSLEXIC. HE IS ALSO A STARTLINGLY EFFECTIVE LEADER AT ONE OF THE WORLD'S BIGGEST COMPANIES. THE TWO ARE RELATED. HE SEES THE WORLD IN WAYS WE CAN'T OR WON'T.

It was early in the morning, and Donald Winkler's office telephone was not accommodating his distinctive view of the universe. That is, the freaking voice mail wasn't working. Winkler punched numbers in an order he thought was right, but the system rejected them each time. Growing more and more agitated, he finally yelled at the recalcitrant device, "Goddamn it to hell!"

At that, the chairman and CEO of Ford Motor Credit Co. caught himself. He jumped from his desk, spun around, and dug into a cabinet drawer. Winkler is rummaging through the same drawer right now, reenacting the moment in an interview. He turns and presents himself—transfigured! A red latex ball adorns his nose. "That morning, I looked at myself in the mirror with this on, and I asked, What did I accomplish by getting mad at the telephone? I felt like a fool," Winkler says.

Here is what we take away from that episode, in the words that Winkler himself espouses.

Donald Winkler is profoundly dyslexic, and he is a startlingly effective leader. Donald Winkler doesn't fail. Events fail.

You don't see many guys with red latex noses roaming the top floor of Ford Motor's world-headquarters building. Up until now.

Mark Turner, 34, vice president, corporate risk, Ford Credit: "We were meeting with a group of managers from Ford Motor. On the first day, one of the Ford Motor guys piped up, 'If you guys in credit would just do this.' Don said, 'Hang on. I'm an officer of Ford Motor Co. We're all part of Ford. If you're going to sit in this room and work on this team, you've got to drop this 'we' and 'they.' And if you have a problem with that, let's step outside.' Don didn't realize what 'stepping outside' meant in the manufacturing world. It was just his way of engaging. The whole meeting went quiet. He came back after a break and apologized. He said, 'I'm just trying to make the point that this is a collective effort.' People got the message, and this has turned into one of the most high-performing teams that I've worked on at Ford."

Don Winkler, 52, is a dominating man. It is not just his weight, which, through lack of exercise, has ballooned to 250 pounds in the past year. Winkler talks straight, he talks often, and he enjoys monopolizing a room. Colleagues acknowledge, with both amusement and annoyance, that they must battle him in meetings for control of the microphone. For relaxation outside work, he lectures at schools and universities—wherever there's an audience.

Winkler's publicity handlers warn that he tends to wander during conversations. He does, egregiously, though where he strays typically is at least as compelling as whatever point he may have left behind. They mention his need to focus his gaze on something—which is why, if you don't offer constant eye contact, he requires a mirror, a picture, or a window reflection behind you to avoid being distracted. Talking on the telephone, he sometimes stares at himself on a TV monitor or in a small mirror by his phone. He scribbles constantly in a little notebook to help track and synthesize what happens around him.

Winkler, in other words, struggles to process the world in the way that the rest of us do. On the other hand, he often sees that world in ways that we can't or won't. That a man of such disjointed perception was hired a year ago to run Ford's huge finance arm (with more than 10 million customers and $165 billion in receivables) speaks to his productive harnessing of something that most people reckon is a disability. It also says something about how business today must be done and how we must think to survive. The complex, the chaotic, the unexpected—that is reality. Companies and their managers who steer straight-line courses do so at their own peril. Paths must be continually flexible and constantly recharted.

So it is for Ford. The company provides financing for more of its customers, more profitably, than anyone else in the industry. Yet late last year, Ford Credit was losing business in the United States to banks. And while truck sales were strong, sales growth for many of Ford Motor's cars was weak. "When you're best in class," Winkler observes, "you risk standing still. It's easy to be too content. You need to take the paradigm that you're in and turn it upside down."

That is to say, you slap on a red nose in meetings to show you don't take yourself too seriously. You launch "Cato attacks" (after the hyperkinetic character of Pink Panther films) on the people who report to you, calling them out of the blue and demanding that they immediately recite their strategic priorities. You tweak the organizational language. Winkler, for example, won't allow the word "but" to be spoken in his presence. "And," which is more inclusive and more constructive, is the accepted conjunction. "People don't fail," he says. "Events fail." People learn. His unfailing response to any statement that has even a hint of negativism: "Up until now."

It sounds like bad ad copy. And it isn't how folks in Dearborn, Michigan are accustomed to talking to one another—until now, that is. Rapidly, almost comically, since his arrival last October, Winkler's stock phrases have infused the deepest reaches of Ford Credit.

Greg Smith, 49, president, Ford Credit North America: "We have a small subsidiary, AMI Leasing, in Worcester, Massachusetts. It's not at all in the corporate mainstream. I visited last month for a business review, and every person in the room was wearing a button with one of the language tools: 'But to and.' 'Up until now.' Not only had they heard and grasped them all, they each had embraced the specific tool that he or she was having trouble with. At our Fairlane operation in Colorado Springs, there is a jar sitting on a table. Every time someone says, 'but,' that person puts a dollar in the jar."

Winkler's language is the language of "breakthrough leadership." It is the strategy for organizational change that he has developed and preached, in one form or another, for nearly three decades. It is a way of thinking that was born of his need, as an engineer and as a dyslexic, for extreme systemization—and, too, of his need for perpetual reexamination and continual improvement. It is the lever that he hopes will revolutionize Ford Credit and, in a perfect world, Ford Motor Co. as well.

Breakthrough leadership began, essentially, in 1972 at a General Instruments factory. Winkler was a newly minted electrical engineer designing new microelectronic circuits. Compelled to ask questions, to understand everything completely, he was constantly on the production floor, schmoozing with the people on the prototype line. Together, they set up a "white room," a place where his designs could be critiqued and tested. The result: Winkler's projects came in far faster and yielded far higher productivity than those of his colleagues. General Instruments made him its worldwide-operations manager when he was 26 years old.

Winkler began writing about everything, taking meticulous notes to help him visualize his thoughts. He thought a lot about purpose—and then about how his personal mission drove his goals. "If it works for me," he realized, "it should work for the business too." The organization should produce a statement of purpose, he thought. It should work together to map its goals and its strategy. It must harness the energy of every individual.

In 1976, Winkler took such nascent thinking to Citibank, which had recruited him as vice president for its corporate-trust business. He took over an operation of 1,000 people who were pushing around massive piles of paper—with a rework rate on that paper of 20%. He took one group of workers aside and told them to invent their own ideal environment. He told them to ask themselves, "How do we break out of the box we're stuck in?" The workers figured it out. Productivity soared.

Alan Weber, 51, vice chairman, Aetna Inc.: "Don worked for me in operations at Citibank. He's not motivated by money but by success. He wants to accomplish and to get recognition for what he accomplishes. Maybe it's because when he was a kid he had to sit in the back of the classroom. But accomplishment and recognition are what really turn him on. He'll work 24 hours a day to get that. He always views himself as the underdog. He likes to surface from out of nowhere and win."

Winkler refined breakthrough leadership at Bank One Corp., which hired him in 1993 to build its Finance One credit subsidiary. He thrived, according to people who worked with him then, by embracing the unconventional: He fused together the indirect-lending units of roughly 70 Bank One affiliates; sold home-equity loans to the less-than-creditworthy customers whom Bank One itself had turned away; and launched an online auto-lending program with CarsDirect.com Inc. Before leaving the company amid a mass exodus of top executives last year, he had turned a humdrum organization with $10 billion in assets into a $45 billion leviathan that enjoyed nearly 30% annual earnings growth.

Breakthrough leadership, Winkler says, is about creating "something that would not have happened otherwise and something that will never go back to the way it was. Leadership is about taking people to places that they wouldn't have gotten to by themselves."

The process begins with an annual reevaluation of strategic vision, purpose, and values. Put people in a room together, and get them to question themselves and one another. Why are we here? What will it look like when our purpose has been realized? What do we see when we imagine a successful end? "We need to establish the vision," Winkler says, "so that we can share it with others in the organization. You can tell when chisel has met wood in a purpose statement. It actually becomes the working surface for everything that follows. It allows you to set direction. It's the rudder on a sailboat."

(Winkler has a purpose statement of his own. So bent is he on reexamination and improvement that he refines the thing 20 to 30 times a year. But over a quarter of a century, the basic conceit hasn't changed much: "To get people to think smarter, *His* in such a way that, through intellectual conversation and larger question asking, *Mission* growth occurs, so that mankind will benefit.") *Statement*

The goal of this initial exercise is to start people thinking in new ways, to challenge their old ideas, and to inspire in them some innovative new approaches. In any business situation, Winkler argues, there is a "current view" and there is a "better view." The current view reflects the status quo, the road most often traveled. The better view says that the often-traveled road is just one path in a world of infinite possibilities.

"A paradigm," Winkler tells employees in many of his frequently held breakthrough-leadership seminars, "is a box that limits thinking and constrains growth. There are lots of reasons why we stay in the box, but the number-one reason is fear of failure. To break out of the box, you have to ask questions—power questions."

Barrett Burns, 55, executive vice president, global risk management, Ford Credit: "I was chief operating officer at Finance One's biggest division. There was one part of the business that really was falling apart. So Don and I visited, and they gave us a presentation. It was the usual stuff. All of a sudden, Don stopped the show and said, 'Give me all the petty cash you have. Let's have a town meeting.' No one said a word; this hadn't been done before. Don said, 'Come on, just ask me questions.' Finally, someone did, and he gave her $5. Someone asked another question, and he gave another $5. A guy asked, 'How come the phones don't work every day?' Don gave him $25. 'Why doesn't the computer refresh our information daily?' $30. He was using the cash as a technique to break down barriers. When it was over, the site manager was upset. Don told him, 'You probably think that I'm going to get mad. Well, I am mad, but not because you have problems. I'm mad because if you don't tell me what your problems are, I can't help you.' And word got around: If you tell Don what's wrong, he'll help you fix it."

What comes after you break out of the box? You translate vision into strategy. "That is the hardest thing to do," Winkler says. It's hard, he says, because the exercise forces people to align vision with practice, to decide what truly is important. What strategic issues prevent growth? How do you begin to address them? Which projects do you set in motion?

Winkler starts a ball in motion by asking everyone in the room to decide, individually, which five strategic issues are the most important. That's difficult enough for most managers. Once that's done, though, the floor is open for discussion and negotiation. Suddenly, individual strategies become the group's concern. Do they jibe with one another? Do they duplicate? Which ones best support the organizational statement of purpose? Which ones are most important?

At Ford, Winkler began gathering his top 100 executives for three or four days each month. At the onset, members of the group identified 1,800 or so projects that had been deemed important enough—by someone, somewhere, at some time—to merit attention and resources. 1,800 projects. "I thought, Holy mackerel, no wonder we've got some issues here," Winkler says. "We were doing 50 projects on the Internet alone, and none of the people working on those projects were talking to one another." After four months, the executives had distilled the 1,800 projects to the 84 that were most important.

Winkler's most impressive strategic victory at Ford (indeed, he says, the biggest win of his career) was born of a similar "family meeting," as he calls them. Both Ford Credit and Ford Motor were looking for ways to address cooperatively their slipping share of auto financing and their anemic overall car sales. Winkler and Lloyd Hansen, Ford Motor's controller for North America, gathered a task force off-site.

Lloyd Hansen, 52: "This meeting started differently from most. Don had the room set up like a party, with hats and whistles and a banner that read, 'Congratulations! 2002 Reunion.' As people came in, Don and I shook their hands and congratulated them. This was a reunion, two years from now, of our group, and we were celebrating our success. Then we started talking to one another about what we had accomplished. And, of course, that led to ideas about what it was we really wanted to accomplish now. When it was done, there was a pretty clear vision statement. Then we asked, 'If we're going to accomplish this, what four or five key areas do we need to go after?'"

The team agreed to rationalize dramatically a complex lease-pricing schedule that had been confusing and aggravating to dealers and their customers. The new schedule also simplified categories of customer creditworthiness, which had been yet another source of dealer angst. Most importantly, Winkler agreed to change the way that Ford Credit calculated lease residual values, which allowed for lower monthly lease payments. Ford Credit would take a lower margin—but Ford Motor would sell more cars, which in turn would allow Ford Credit to make more loans.

Many of the changes were put into place within 48 hours. Ford Motor's U.S. car sales rose almost instantly. And Ford Credit's lending contracts went up as well. In June, Ford Credit financed 54% of all the cars Ford Motor sold—up from 46% a year earlier. In practice, it is nearly impossible to finance a higher percentage. In large part because of that performance, Ford Credit's operating profits in the first six months of this year totaled $741 million—up 17% from the first half of 1999.

As stunning as the company's financial performance has been, Winkler is forging something even more remarkable at Ford Credit. He is changing the way that people talk, think, and behave. He is creating a place, he hopes, where people are accountable for their work; where openness and honesty dictate communication; where respect and trust determine relationships; and where "everyone," as he says, "is on the same level." Every idea counts.

After every meeting, after every transaction, Winkler sends an email message to the people involved: "Here's what just happened, this is what we did right, this is what we could do better next time." He expects members of his executive team to do the same after their meetings. He writes regular "love letters" to the people who report directly to him. The dispatches detail the people's strengths, their weaknesses, and their strategies for personal improvement; the messages are the start of a dialogue to move those people to the next level—from good to great.

"You'll know that you've got a real breakthrough when the values change in a place," Winkler says. "Sure, you won't see it overnight. You may see some numbers come up positive. But you have to look at the culture of a place over three to five years to see if you've really made anything happen."

Elizabeth Acton, 49, executive vice president and chief financial officer, Ford Credit: "Don has made me more sensitive to my role as a leader, more aware of the shadow that I cast. Lots of people watch us, so my behavior is elevated out of the day-to-day. I think more strategically about it. What signals am I sending? What's my body language saying? Where am I on the mood elevator, and how does that affect people around me? Don has sensitized me to that."

Every morning, Don Winkler wakes at 3 AM. He begins each day with 20 minutes of mental calisthenics: simple exercises that help point his brain in the right direction. It is not something he particularly enjoys, yet he requires himself to keep at it. He feels that he cannot be effective otherwise.

"When I did my warm-ups this morning," he says, "I was teary-eyed. I thought, There are people who don't have to do all this. My productivity could be so much higher. Other people wouldn't do it this way.

"But that's good and bad. I'll do something outrageous, and people will think that I'm a bit strange. But then, that's okay. That's good. Let's be a little outrageous."

Keith H. Hammonds (khammonds@fastcompany.com) is a *Fast Company* senior editor. Contact Donald Winkler by email (don@cyberwink.com), or learn more about him on the Web (http://www.cyberwink.com).

WHAT'S FAST

Donald Winkler, chairman and CEO of Ford Motor Credit Co., never misses a chance to preach the virtues of "breakthrough leadership." For much of his career, he has been breaking the rules for what business leaders do. Here are his 10 principles for effective leadership.

1. Set real priorities and real commitments.
2. Grab hold of tough problems, and don't delegate them.
3. Don't let the guy below you make the hard decisions.
4. Set and demand standards of excellence.
5. Create urgency! It's always better to do something than it is to do nothing.
6. Pay attention to details. Getting all of the facts is the key to good decision making.
7. Be committed, and show it. Concentrate on possibilities.
8. Be willing to see failure as a stepping-stone to success.
9. Be tough and be fair with people. Avoid compromise when choosing coworkers.
10. Last but not least: Play! You can't accomplish anything unless you're having fun.

I Can Only Compete through My Crew

OF ALL THE ENVIRONMENTS FOR TESTING ONE'S ABILITY TO BE A LEADER, ONE OF THE TOUGHEST IS THE DECK OF A RACING YACHT, A PLACE WHERE SIMON WALKER HAS SPENT MUCH OF HIS ADULT LIFE.

"I won't do it. I've got a bad back." When Simon Walker recalls his most difficult challenges as a leader, those words of resistance light up like a theater marquee. In his first command of a large sailing yacht, Walker endured every leader's nightmare: A member of his own team called him out.

The year was 1994, and Walker was a skipper in the Spitsbergen sailing expedition, a seven-week-long journey from Plymouth, England to Svalbard, an island halfway between Norway and the North Pole. A native of Shrewsbury, England, Walker was 26 years old, just five years removed from the University of Manchester, where he had graduated with a degree in computer engineering. Some of the crew members were twice his age.

At 8 AM one day, Walker and his crew lined up on the boat's foredeck and prepared to take in the 100-pound anchor. "There was one particular guy who probably drank a few too many beers the night before. Suddenly, he says he's got a bad back—right in front of the entire crew," Walker recalls. "Everyone knows his back is fine. So all eyes turn to me to see what I'm going to do. Do I confront him? Do I let him get away with it? I had a split second to decide."

Walker decided to be "unreasonably reasonable." He'd play the guy's game. "The only way to hold on to my authority was to make him look stupid. I told him to trade places with this little woman, Kirsten, who was at the wheel. Now, this big hulking fellow has just lost his place to someone barely 5 feet tall. The next day, I didn't let him take the anchor or the helm. I had him go below and make tea. 'The lads will need a cup after their hard work,' I told him, 'and we don't want to put a strain on your bad back.' Wouldn't you know, his back magically healed—and he went on to become one of the stars of the expedition."

Of all the environments for testing one's ability to build a winning team and to be a leader, one of the toughest is the deck of a racing yacht, a place where Walker has spent much of his adult life. He's sailed across the Atlantic Ocean seven times. He's led two expeditions to the Arctic Ocean. He won the first Teacher's Whiskey Round Britain Challenge race in 1995. But in the world of sailing, the toughest race of all is the BT Global Challenge, a 30,000-mile marathon "the wrong way" around the planet—that is, against prevailing winds and currents. More people have traveled in space than have circumnavigated the globe the wrong way. Walker has done it twice, the first time as a first mate. The second time, at age 28, he was the youngest skipper ever to compete in the event.

Now, instead of leading a crew of 14 people, Walker heads an organization of 120. As the managing director of Plymouth-based Challenge Business, Walker is the point man for a massive undertaking: vetting the crews, selecting the skippers, lining up the sponsors, and shotgunning the logistics for sailing's toughest races. As you read this, the 12 yachts competing in the BT Global Challenge 2000 are racing furiously down the coast of South America, bound for Buenos Aires by mid-November.

The concept behind the Global Challenge is straightforward and ultrademocratic: to give ordinary people—many of whom have no sailing experience—a chance to take on the challenge of their lives and sail around the globe. The lessons that the race imparts are rich and universal. If you want to learn what it really takes to be a leader, then spend some time navigating the challenges of this race.

The BT Global Challenge serves up a big-time test on several fronts. First, it is physically daunting. Crews must battle violent weather, mind-numbing fatigue, injuries, 100-degree heat in the tropics, and lacerating cold in the Southern Ocean. Andrea Bacon, 32, who crewed on the yacht Group 4 during the 1996-1997 BT Global Challenge, recalls that on the first night out they hit gale-force winds, and 10 members of the crew became violently seasick. "That meant that four people were left to manage the boat," Bacon says. "They couldn't go off watch. They had to keep working around the clock. Then we went to another extreme: We hit incredibly high temperatures as we approached the equator. The steel boat just heats up, and down below it's like an oven. There's no air, and you lie in your bunk just saturated in sweat. You can't sleep. You can't eat. But every six hours, you've got to go back on deck and take your shift."

Even as the race physically drains you, it tests your mental agility. Both skipper and crew must cope with equipment failure, make complex tactical decisions on the fly, and stay nimble enough to keep up with weather and ocean conditions that are forever changing. But above all, the race tests a leader's ability to lead. Recognizing that, such companies as British Airways, Microsoft, and Xerox have joined with the UK consulting group Inspiring Performance Ltd. and Oxfordshire's Henley Management College to study team and leadership dynamics during this year's race.

"In the last race, we discovered that each boat's performance had very little to do with sailing," says Walker. "It had much more to do with the leadership that we as skippers were exhibiting, and with our ability to develop the full potential of our teams. All of the skippers were extremely good yachtsmen. All of them excelled at managing the boat. But ultimately, the race is all about managing people."

During a midsummer sail across the San Francisco Bay, Walker looked back at the 1996–1997 BT Global Challenge, when he skippered the Toshiba Wave Warrior. He recounted some of the leadership lessons that he took from a flat-out race around the planet.

TO FINISH FIRST, FIRST YOU MUST FINISH

Nine months before the starter's pistol fired for the 1996–1997 challenge, race founder Sir Chay Blyth announced the crew lists for each yacht. For the 14 skippers, the race before the race—to build a fast crew—had begun. Most of the skippers took their crews to the water to log as many training miles as possible. Simon Walker headed for high ground. He led his crew to a large holiday house in Wales, where they spent two days talking about the race. His reasoning: You can't build a team before you've agreed on the goal.

"I'm pretty competitive, but I can only compete through my crew," says Walker. "So first I had to learn each crew member's agenda. One guy wanted to win at all costs. Another guy wanted simply to make it around the world. The key was to avoid agreeing to the lowest common denominator. So I said to the guy who just wanted to have an adventure, 'You aren't competitive in your sailing, but you're certainly competitive in your work life. And I think you'll enjoy the race more if we're sailing fast and if we're doing things professionally.'

"But I also had to be realistic—and setting a goal like 'win the race' just isn't credible," says Walker. "So I said to the all-or-nothing guy, 'To finish first, first we have to finish. We have to sail smart. If we go for broke, sooner or later we'll blow up.'"

After much discussion, the team worked out a statement of strategic intent: to build a campaign that is capable of winning the BT Global Challenge. They chose the words carefully. "To build a campaign" meant that the work started now, nine months before the race; "that is capable of winning" meant that all of their planning and preparation was devoted to one goal: to make the boat go faster.

The crew members would do more than steer quickly or trim the sails like speed demons. Sailing fast meant adding value to every task. They'd clean the head like pros, to lessen the chance that they'd all come down with a stomach virus. They'd use an Excel spreadsheet to plan out four meals a day for what would be 163 days at sea—because the way they ate through 800 kilos of food would affect the trim of the boat. The commitment to be fast even affected the way they slept. To help balance the boat, they'd switch bunks whenever the conditions dictated. Even in the mayhem of the Southern Ocean, where they sailed through six gales and three storms, the Wave Warriors "hot bunked."

"There's a watch change at two in the morning," Walker explains. "So seven people who have been on deck for four hours in immense waves and windchill get to go down below. They're covered in sleet. They're bruised. They're exhausted. And they've got four hours before they're due back on deck. They clamber out of their dry suits. They lay out their moldy sleeping bags on the bunks on the high side of the boat, and they get in. They've already used up 30 minutes. After another half hour, the wind shifts, and the guys on deck need to tack the boat. That means the guys down below have to wake up, grab their sleeping bags, walk across the boat, and lay out on the other side. Now they've lost even more sleep."

Watch in, watch out, for 30,000 miles, the Wave Warriors hot bunked. "If I had come up with this idea in the middle of the race, I could have been the most charismatic leader in the world, and I never would have gotten them to agree to it," Walker continues. "It all goes back nine months, to when we sat in that house in Wales. After that, we didn't talk about it—we did it. That was our life."

KNOWLEDGE DISPELS FEAR

There's an old mariner's expression: "No law, no God." Go beyond 40 degrees south latitude, and you're in the Southern Ocean. Figuratively, you're beyond the reach of all nations. Go past 50 degrees south, and you're beyond the limits of civilization itself and into a world that is utterly alien. At its southernmost extreme, the 6,600-mile leg from Rio de Janeiro to New Zealand took the fleet to 60 degrees south. No law, no God—and for the crew members, big fear.

Walker and his crew sailed from Rio de Janeiro down the coast of South America, turned west at Cape Horn, and hit the ferocity of the Southern Ocean. Cape Horn is feared for its bad weather and its big seas. The reasons are geographical. Westerly winds shriek across the earth's surface, unimpeded by any major landmass. The winds, storms, and currents combine to whip up huge seas, driving rough waves on top of massive swells. If that weren't enough, the seabed at Cape Horn shelves dramatically from around 10,000 feet up to several hundred feet. Like waves breaking on a beach, the shallower seabed forces waves to pile up on themselves, compressing them and making them even steeper, sharper, and uglier.

Andrea Bacon of the Group 4 recalls trying to steel herself in the safety of the companionway before climbing onto the deck and into the maelstrom. "The yacht was heeling over at 35 degrees, and the effort to get up the steps was beyond belief," she says. "Terrified and speechless, I huddled low, clipped on my safety harness, and held on to the nearest secure objects as waves crashed over my head. The one thing that I dreaded was having to let go and do something."

Still, to survive, the crews had to sail. That meant changing sails in 60-knot winds and massive seas—as towering sheets of water surged over the yacht's bow. Walker used several tactics for tamping fear. The first was a simple one: He gave his crew members a real-world account of what to expect. "Knowledge dispels fear," he says. "So we talked through every scenario: what we'd encounter when we rounded Cape Horn, what we'd do if we hit an iceberg or had our rig damaged. If you told them that Cape Horn would be easy, and then they got the shit knocked out of them, they'd never trust you again, would they? Still, you stay positive. You tell them that it's going to be tough, but we're prepared for it, and that the boat is strong. It's about saying what you can do, not what you can't."

Walker doesn't flinch from admitting that he, too, was scared. What then? On a racing yacht at sea, a leader can only confide in his team—if he chooses to confide at all.

"If I shared all of my worries and woes with one person, he'd think that I was completely losing it. So my strategy was to choose a number of people, and share one element of my worries with each of them—but just that one element. So, for example, I'd go to Spike, our doctor, and tell him that I'm worried about Jo's broken arm. Or I'd go to our engineer and tell him that the rig doesn't look so good.

"No one was getting the whole picture, thank God," laughs Walker. "But confiding in each of them was the only way for me to handle the loneliness of command, which is very, very real."

He was right to worry about the rigging. They were deep in the Southern Ocean, halfway between Cape Horn and New Zealand, when the standing rigging failed. Someone would have to climb 60 feet up the mast and replace a steel fitting that joined the rigging to the mast—a job that entailed slackening an entire side of the rigging. It was here that Walker's third tactic for handling fear kicked in: In a high-risk situation, a leader chooses the best person for the job. In this case, it turned out that the best person was the leader himself.

"We were out there in the Southern Ocean, feeling very insignificant in a big part of the planet," recalls Walker. "At any minute, another storm would sweep in. We hatched a plan: Spike and I would climb up and jury-rig the fitting. As we started the climb, I told the crew that they must helm the yacht very carefully on the opposite tack, as the rigging was only holding up one side of the mast. If the helmsman made a mistake while we were up on the mast, we'd crash down over the side with the entire rig on top of us."

If that were to happen, the crew quite possibly would have lost both its skipper and its rig to the world's harshest seas. Why take on such a risk? "Because I was young, I was fit, but most importantly, I was a member of the team," Walker says. "And sending me up there was the best use of the team's resources. So I did it."

IT'S TOUGHEST WHEN THE GOING GETS EASY

The most challenging sailing was in the Southern Ocean. But the leadership challenge was comparatively easy. "It was muck and bullets—battleground leadership," recalls Walker. "These guys were hanging on by their fingernails. As long as I was technically competent, leading was pretty straightforward."

In terms of leading, it was toughest when the going got easy. That would be the race's "Paradise Leg," from Cape Town to Boston. At 7,000 miles, it is the longest leg of the race. But the crews are sailing downwind with the spinnaker up. They're cruising through the tropics, and their biggest worry is whether to use SPF 20 or 30 sunscreen. Forget fear. Now downtime takes a toll. There's gossip. And the skipper starts to earn his paycheck.

The crew's morale bottomed out when the Wave Warrior hit the Doldrums, an area near the equator that is notorious for its calms and its light, shifting winds. As they approached the equator, all of the data on weather, wind, and currents pointed toward taking a westerly route. But they were in second place, about one day behind the leader, the Group 4. Gambling to make up time, Walker and his navigational gurus plotted an easterly route instead.

They turned east and, soon after, lost the bet. The wind dropped, they missed the most favorable position to cross the Doldrums, and they slipped to eleventh place. Fed up with the conditions, members of the crew began to lose faith in their strategy. One crew member complained that he had wasted three years of his life training for the race. The solution was to reset the goal. "I called the crew up on deck, and we discussed what had happened," says Walker. " 'We're in the eleventh position,' I told them. 'We can't think about winning. We're going to set ourselves new targets to beat as many boats as we can, one boat at a time.'"

The first goal: Pass the tenth-place boat, which was five miles ahead of the Toshiba Wave Warrior, within the next 12 hours. The crew members did it. Then, they overtook the next boat and the one after that. Some 1,000 miles later, the Wave Warrior stormed into Boston in third place. "The race was all about learning: The team that learned the fastest would win," says Walker. "My ambition was for the crew to learn so well that they wouldn't need me. I really feel that a leader's goal should be to make himself redundant."

Walker believes that the crew achieved his ambition when they sailed into Boston Harbor. It was quite a challenge. After 7,000 miles at sea, the prospect of suddenly coming into land is daunting. Nevertheless, the crew raised the boat's big red spinnaker—4,000 square feet of sail—and raced hard. They piloted around rocks and through reefs outside the harbor, past navigation lanes, lighthouses, and buoys inside it. To alter course, they jibed. That is, they changed the sail from one side to the other—a complicated maneuver on such a large boat. When the boat was closer to the wind, the crew had to peel, or raise a new spinnaker on the inside and trip the large spinnaker away. In all, they did seven jibes and two peels sailing into Boston. Every move was flawless.

As for Walker, he stood on the deck and took photos. "I thought, What an achievement. These so-called amateurs have transformed themselves into one of the most professional crews I've ever sailed with." Walker had made himself redundant.

BUILT TO LAP

The learning never stopped, even on the last day of the race. Two miles from the finish line at Southampton, England, the Toshiba Wave Warrior had to double back around one last buoy. For the final time, the crew took the spinnaker down and raised the headsail—without a hitch.

"But then I noticed two of the guys standing on the foredeck," says Walker. "They were pointing up at the mast, discussing something. It turns out that one of them had noticed some small thing, and they were talking about a better way to take the spinnaker down. It was absolutely incredible. Here they had done this sail change a thousand times before, and they were never going to do it again. But the culture of continuous improvement, of reviewing and revising everything, was so ingrained in them that they were still looking for a better way—even when the race was all but over.

"Some of the other boats did everything exactly the same way, from start to finish. On our boat, there wasn't a single operation at the end of the race that we did the same way as in the beginning. You were learning, changing, and evolving all the time. If you weren't, you were dead."

The crew learned fast, but not fast enough. In the end, the Wave Warrior never did catch the Group 4. After 30,000 miles, the two boats finished second and first, respectively. But the Wave Warriors drubbed the rest of the fleet.

Andrea Bacon, who coauthored a book on the 1996–1997 race, says the reason that the Group 4 and the Toshiba Wave Warrior performed as well as they did had little to do with yachting and everything to do with the leadership that their skippers exhibited—the teams they built, the cultures they helped create. And it turns out that Simon Walker and Group 4 skipper Mike Golding are different leaders.

The Group 4 crew was a team of highly focused specialists—each crew member had one, and only one, clearly defined primary role. On the Toshiba Wave Warrior, crew members traded among several responsibilities. Golding was independent and very much his own boss. Walker was more collaborative and accessible.

"Mike and I barely talked during the race," Walker recalls. "But afterward, we went out for some beers and we learned something: He aspired to be more like me, and I aspired to be more like him.

"I wanted my team to specialize in particular areas and stick with particular functions, but that wasn't me. And Mike wanted to be more sensitive to his team and be more collaborative, but that wasn't him. Ultimately, it's not a matter of which style works better than the other. It all comes down to which style works best for you."

Walker is a competitive man, and you can sense behind his big smile the disappointment over finishing second. But, while his team failed to win, it's clear that they succeeded. "At the end of the race," he says, "when we knew that we wouldn't take first, one of the guys said, 'Finishing second isn't bad for the first lap. What are we going to do about the next one?' And it really hit me: We'd created something with longevity. We had built something that would last."

Bill Breen (bbreen@fastcompany.com) is a *Fast Company* senior editor. Contact Simon Walker by email (simonwalker@challengebusiness-box.com), or follow the BT Global Challenge 2000 on the Web (http://www.btchallenge.com).

WHAT'S FAST

A few years ago, as a crew member of the yacht Group 4, Andrea Bacon raced against Simon Walker—and her boat beat his. Now she is the research director of Inspiring Performance Ltd., a Southampton, England-based consulting company. Working in partnership with the UK's Henley Management College and with the support of such organizations as Cap Gemini Ernst & Young and Microsoft, Inspiring Performance is studying team dynamics during this year's round-the-world race.

It's an event worth studying. In the BT Global Challenge, almost all things are equal. The boats are identical, the members of every crew are evenly matched by ability, and everyone is put through exactly the same training regimen. So what separates the speedsters from the laggards? According to Bacon, it all comes down to a skipper's ability to lead and a crew's capacity to team. Looking back at the last race, Bacon cites three lessons for leading teams to victory at sea.

Celebrate a success. "Taking the time to celebrate an achievement—whether it was passing another boat, rounding Cape Horn, or finishing the first leg—made a huge difference in people's morale. But we could have been better at that. For example, we spent Christmas day in the Southern Ocean, and we did a radio linkup with the other boats. All of them had done something special to celebrate—one crew had written a Christmas play, another had drinks—but we did nothing. The conditions were horrible down there, and we all needed a lift. But the fact that everyone around us was celebrating, and we weren't, made it that much harder to take."

Never, ever hesitate. "You can't put off a decision, especially when you're sailing in extreme conditions. When we were in the Southern Ocean, we logged the wind speed every 10 minutes. As soon as we started to see a pattern of wind increases, we'd think about making a sail change early. It's really dangerous to get into a big wind with too much sail up. Now, the last thing you want is a skipper who puts off a decision just to see what the wind does. Because the longer that decision is delayed, the more the fear builds up inside you that things will turn really nasty—and you will still have to change that sail."

If you have to, fake it. As a leader, you have to keep the team's confidence up—even when your own confidence is in the toilet. "When the boat has plowed into a gale, and the waves are thundering against the hull, the last thing you want to hear from the skipper is 'This isn't normal, but we'll be fine.' The skipper has to exude 100% confidence at all times—even if his knuckles are turning white as he grips the chart table."

Contact Andrea Bacon by email (andreabacon@inspiringperformance.com).

Leadership Ensemble

HOW DO THE MUSICIANS OF ORPHEUS GET TO CARNEGIE HALL? THEY PRACTICE—NOT JUST THEIR MUSIC, BUT A RADICAL APPROACH TO LEADERSHIP THAT HAS BECOME A COMPELLING METAPHOR FOR BUSINESS.

The second week of January at Baruch High School in Manhattan: Teenagers are noisily making their way to and from class. On the street below, a siren blares through Union Square. And in a classroom on one of the floors of the high school, musicians are sight-reading a piece of music. After several frustrating attempts, cellist Melissa Meell finally stops and shrugs her shoulders. "We're a long way from Carnegie Hall," she quips.

That kind of wisecrack would be typical of a clever 12th-grader who's struggling through her first Mozart symphony, hoping to ace her audition for all-city orchestra and get a crack at playing on the stage of that revered concert hall. But, in fact, Meell is 44, a professional musician, and a member of Orpheus—a Grammy-nominated chamber orchestra that's widely considered one of the best of its kind on the planet. Although she and her fellow musicians are just 19 days away from their next Carnegie Hall performance, they still sound as if they're playing rubber bands.

With such an imposing deadline at hand, why is this prestigious group of musicians rehearsing in such noisy surroundings? The school, it turns out, is its home. Orpheus has been the orchestra in residence at Baruch High School for more than three years and at Zicklin School of Business, which is affiliated with New York City's university system, since September 1999. Orpheus is a conductorless orchestra, and it was for that very reason that Baruch wanted the orchestra to take up residence there—so that students could watch Orpheus rehearse and observe firsthand how it uses collaboration and consensus building to settle its creative differences. High-school students would get a living lesson in conflict resolution. And business students, who would soon be working in a world where few people believe that a CEO has—or should have—all of the answers, would learn that self-governance makes a worthwhile model and that leadership is most effective when all levels of an organization have input.

Its self-governing and leadership abilities have made Orpheus more than just a group of gifted musicians. Orpheus has actually become a metaphor for structural change—the kind of change that has bedeviled so many big companies and exasperated so many big-company CEOs. Orpheus's founder, Julian Fifer, 49, first became aware of the group's metamorphosis when a chairman of a large Japanese publishing company approached him several years ago. "He told me how much he had enjoyed our concert," Fifer recalls. "But then he confided that he didn't want his employees to discover us." Fifer was amused—and intrigued: If old-line business leaders resisted their self-governing process, presumably there were corporate mavericks who would find it compelling. That assumption proved to be correct: During the past two years, several large companies, including Kraft Foods and Novartis AG, have hired Orpheus to demonstrate its process to their executives. This spring, the orchestra will be sharing its lessons with hospital trustees and directors in Dallas and with PR executives in New York City. Within the next year and a half, the group is scheduled to make presentations to international business leaders in Berlin, Paris, and Tokyo.

What do these executives find so compelling about Orpheus's sound and system? To them, the group is a radical, ongoing experiment to find out whether grassroots democracy and commitment to consensus can lead to transcendental performance—or whether it will all end in organizational chaos and muddled results. So what is the key to the orchestra's continued success? A set of insights about motivation, decision making, performance, and work that are as relevant in conference rooms as they are in concert halls.

MOTIVATION: THE SWEET SOUND OF SATISFACTION

Those who aspire to a career as a classical musician and who are studying at a top conservatory have a few obvious career paths: Clearly, the more talented you are, the more options you have. Those who win or place well in big competitions can go on to sign recording contracts and to enjoy solo careers. They can also choose to join chamber-music groups, as do many of their other colleagues. Virtually all—no matter how successful or well-known—teach. Some, however, are forced to do so to support themselves financially. Most orchestra musicians who want to perform full-time join symphony orchestras.

Those jobs offer relative stability and a decent income, but they are hard to come by. Even so, back in the early 1970s, when Orpheus's founding members were trickling out of music schools and into the New York freelance scene, taking such a job was not high on their list of career goals. "Many of us believed that joining a traditional orchestra would lead to a creative dead end," says Ronnie Bauch, 47, a violinist with Orpheus since 1974, "because you'd be under the thumb of its conductor for the next 30 or 40 years."

"Ironically, your conservatory training leaves you ill-equipped to play in large orchestras," adds Frank Morelli, 49, a bassoonist who joined Orpheus in the late 1970s but sometimes also plays in conductor-led groups. "Presumably, you've devoted so much time to studying music because you have a need for self-expression. If you've studied at a top school for the past four or so years, you've also got a certain amount of pride and ego invested in your career. And you're self-motivated because the competition is so steep. But all of those things can get in the way when you're sitting in an orchestra with a conductor telling you what to do."

Some observers of the orchestra scene today believe that the moral righteousness of Orpheus's early members was prophetic. "The climate in most conductor-led orchestras is appalling," says Harvey Seifter, 46, Orpheus's executive director, who left the theater world about two years ago to take on the delicate task of administering to the needs of this self-governing enterprise. "Orchestras take a lot of very smart people, many of whom learned to read music before they learned to read words, and, if they're violinists, sit them in the last row of the second-violin section, where they must unquestioningly follow someone who's waving a stick at them. Success is defined as how good you are at getting your bow to leap off your violin at the exact same nanosecond as all of the other violinists' bows."

That interpretation is in keeping with the results of a study conducted by Harvard psychology professor Richard Hackman. In the early 1990s, Hackman looked at job satisfaction among symphony musicians in 78 orchestras in four countries and found widespread discontent. Indeed, in this now well-known study, symphony members experienced the same levels of job satisfaction as the federal prison guards whom Hackman had studied earlier. Symphony musicians were, however, happier than professional hockey players.

"Most of them adapt," explains Hackman. "But they often do that by finding other ways to develop musically. One person said that he had to be very careful not to let his symphony job get in the way of making music."

For Fifer, the inspiration for Orpheus came from his chamber-music experiences back at Juilliard. He found the sense of intimacy and connectedness that he felt with other musicians in those groups exciting and inspiring, and he longed to find a way to re-create that experience on a larger scale. "I loved chamber music's clarity of sound and flexibility of temperament," he says. "I wanted to bring that camaraderie and spirit into a larger setting. And in order for everyone to be able to communicate more effectively, it seemed necessary to do without a conductor."

So Fifer invited a select group of musicians to that first rehearsal, carefully choosing among those who he knew could take—as well as give—criticism. He named the group Orpheus, for the Greek god who created music so powerful that stones rose up and followed him. "We had no particular method for presenting interpretations and ideas on a piece, but our spirits were high, and we had a great deal of enthusiasm," he recalls. "It was as if we were calling out to anyone who would listen, 'Look Ma, no hands!'"

DECISION MAKING: EVERYONE'S A LEADER (JUST NOT ALL AT ONCE)

But could they do it? When Fifer's idea first took shape, he knew of no preexisting model for a conductorless group of Orpheus's size—anywhere. So his idea was an ambitious one: assembling a number of renegade musicians and building a sustainable enterprise fueled only (at least at first) by idealism and satisfaction. Still, the group pressed on, meeting at Chinese restaurants, rehearsing in churches, and performing at public libraries and housing projects, because city-owned property cost nothing to rent. Eventually, the group got a few annual grants from New York's arts commission, created a demo tape, and, in 1974, booked a small hall at Lincoln Center for its debut performance. In 1979, Orpheus made its first concert tour of Europe, and five years later, it signed a recording contract with the prestigious Deutsche Grammaphon label.

Even as performances gained recognition and attracted larger audiences, rehearsals remained a work in progress. At first, all 27 members of the group participated in every decision that had to be made for each piece—hundreds of tiny details involving dynamics, phrasing, and tempo. So that Orpheus wouldn't sound like dueling stereos, each decision had to be unanimous. And that could take a while, especially when 27 strong-willed musicians were involved, and the buck stopped with all of them. "Rehearsals were becoming free-for-alls," says Martha Caplin, 48, a violinist with the group since 1982. "We needed twice as many rehearsals just to try all of the ideas."

Any organization that operates on consensus risks the possibility of arriving at utterly wishy-washy decisions. If the agreement process is itself chaotic, that risk is even greater. To combat that problem, Orpheus decided to experiment with a new rehearsal method. Instead of just giving the floor to anyone who had an interpretation to offer, Orpheus formed smaller core groups, whose members would change regularly, that would rehearse each piece before the entire group began working on it.

"These core groups formulate one interpretation of a piece," Bauch emphasizes. "It's not necessarily the interpretation. Sometimes it's just a starting point." A core group does the same sort of preparation that a good conductor would do—researching the composer's other works, learning the history of the particular work that will be performed, and listening to recordings of that piece of music. Then the core group presents its ideas to the entire ensemble during the first read through.

Another unusual aspect of Orpheus is the role that its concertmaster plays. In conductor-led orchestras, the concertmaster is usually more of a team captain. But in Orpheus, that function (which rotates regularly) is similar to that of a player-coach on a soccer team. Orpheus's concertmasters are responsible for actually running its rehearsals, moderating debates among members, suggesting resolutions to those debates, and making sure that such discussions don't get too bogged down. Although the core group exerts its influence mostly in the early stages of rehearsing a piece, the concertmaster has more influence as performance dates near.

According to Fifer, having different people be concertmaster seemed the only logical way to run a group fueled by 1960s idealism. The decision to rotate core-group members was, however, more pragmatic: "That rotation method actually alleviates some of the pressure to try to get your way all of the time," admits Bauch. "Having to modulate our personalities and to take on different roles gives us an opportunity to develop leadership skills as well as a chance to be supportive." At first, the entire group voted on who would be the concertmaster for each piece. Eventually, Orpheus elected an executive committee that appoints a concertmaster according to an individual's particular musical expertise.

Not only do core groups and concertmasters change from concert to concert, but they also change from piece to piece. Such frequent changes in leadership require some preperformance planning. At the conclusion of every piece, Orpheus musicians bow and walk off stage. When they return for the next selection on the program, they take different seats, according to their part in that piece. This maneuvering is similar to that of the small chamber groups that Fifer envisioned when he formed Orpheus.

And also like those small chamber-music groups, different members of Orpheus give one another musical cues. Alert audience members will notice a musician use a nod of a head or a gesture of a bow, in a way inviting a fellow musician to join the "conversation" by offering that person a chance to pick up a musical thought. "At any time, you can be leading or following. 'Supporting' is the word that we like to use," says Bauch. "When I'm about to get a cue, I often find myself moving with the musician who's playing." That physical style of playing is usually not experienced in a standard symphony orchestra. It's as if members of Orpheus are all breathing with the same set of lungs.

For performances, Orpheus sits in a semicircle, with the center space (which is normally reserved for a conductor) empty. As a result, casual observers and some critics have erroneously referred to the ensemble as being "leaderless." In fact, "Orpheus exerts more leadership than any other orchestra I've examined," says Harvard's Hackman.

PERFORMANCE: PRACTICE RANDOM ACTS OF LEADERSHIP

Soloists often adjust how loud they play a piece and how long they hold a note to the acoustics of a particular recital hall. Orpheus does the same. Those who have never worked with the group may find its methods fascinating. "One of the neatest things about Orpheus is that one of its musicians will go down and sit in the audience to hear how each piece sounds to a concertgoer's ears," says Susan Botti, 38, a singer and composer who wrote a piece that Orpheus premiered during its series of concerts in late January. "I come from the theater, so I'm used to having people out where the audience sits taking notes and giving feedback during a run-through, but I've never seen that happen in an orchestra before."

Whether or not the concertmaster for a piece is particularly vocal, or the core group unusually opinionated, Orpheus's members all demonstrate great faith in the feedback from the colleague who's doing a sound check. "It's a crucial part of what we do," says Bauch. "On stage, you can't hear how a piece of music sounds to an audience, so you have to trust your colleague's ear. We used to vote on that kind of stuff at the last minute. Now that our listening skills are more refined, I think we trust one another more." (Bauch also has had an opportunity to hone another of his senses—just in case he'll need it on the concert stage: He's helped taste-test New York Super Fudge Chunk ice cream for his childhood friends, Ben and Jerry.)

Bauch notes that changing core-group participants and the concertmaster position has given each orchestra member an intensive course in leadership training. "I've always been a quiet person, but in this group, speaking up is a matter of survival," says Susan Palma-Nidel, 53, a flutist with Orpheus since 1980. "This experience has allowed me to discover strengths that I didn't know I had. Not only have I helped lead the group, but I've also been interviewed by the media—something I never thought I'd do. If I hadn't been forced to do those things, I'm not sure that I ever would have."

WORK: MUSICAL CHAIRS IN THE TALENT MARKET

Making great music without a conductor is challenging on its own. Imagine doing that with a rotating group of musicians. Despite performing music at the highest levels of excellence, Orpheus has no dedicated full-time members. Actually, it would be impossible for the 27 members of Orpheus to work for the group full-time and make an adequate salary. The most anyone can earn performing with Orpheus is about $35,000 a year. There are many reasons for this challenging financial environment, including a general decline in the popularity of classical music and a crowded, competitive landscape in the group's home city. But when you're in a profession where the tools of your trade (your musical instruments) can cost more than a house, it's no wonder that Orpheus's musicians must take on additional freelance opportunities so that they can support themselves financially.

Bassoonist Frank Morelli leads a life that's typical of a freelance musician. Besides participating in Orpheus, he teaches at Juilliard, Manhattan School of Music, and Yale. He's principal bassoonist in the New York City Opera Company's orchestra and in the American Composers Orchestra, and he also plays regularly with other well-known orchestras. In addition, he has his own woodwind quintet that tours regularly, and he performs as a guest with chamber ensembles. Orpheus requires that each of its full members plays at least 35% of its concerts each year; Morelli figures he performs at least that often. Although Orpheus provides only about 10% of his yearly performance-related income, he says that artistically, it may be the most rewarding work he's ever done.

When Morelli and other full members can't make a performance, Orpheus uses ringers to fill in for them. The cast keeps changing, but the performances must cohere. "It's like a wedding band," says an exasperated Harvey Seifter, who's trying to find a way to boost attendance and compensation. "You get a bunch of musicians together for one gig, and then they disband."

During any given year, about 75 different musicians will perform with the group, and sometimes substitutes perform more often than Orpheus's permanent members. Last year, at one Carnegie Hall performance, only about 40% of the full members were present, even though family and professional obligations have them clamoring for more in-town engagements.

With those statistics, it's only natural to wonder at what point Orpheus is no longer really Orpheus. How many members have to be absent before audience members are hearing some group other than the one that they're expecting? It would be easy to say that as long as a performance meets the standards that the group has become known for, then it doesn't matter who's filling those seats.

But to ensure that consistency of performance and to maintain its stellar reputation, the orchestra has adopted some rough guidelines that are somewhat similar to those that the Chicago Bulls used in the 1990s: When Michael Jordan and Scottie Pippen were on the court, it almost didn't matter who else was out there with them. As long as the other three players were solid, Jordan and Pippen could lead their team to a championship performance. Likewise, Orpheus takes great pains to make sure that at least one member from each instrument section who's fluent in the group's leadership process performs at each concert.

Fortunately, New York City is filled with hundreds of high-quality freelance musicians and Juilliard graduates eager to perform with this unique chamber orchestra. Among that large group, Orpheus has a dozen or so regulars who perform so frequently with the group that they have become part of its extended family of musicians. Freelancers who are familiar with the Orpheus process are crucial, especially because newcomers are often reluctant to speak up, and full members can't carry the entire responsibility of shaping how a piece of music will be performed.

"I remember the first time I subbed, I felt as if I were entering a private club," recalls cellist Melissa Meell, who became a full member of the group in 1991. "At the time, I didn't clearly understand how much I was expected to contribute, so it was easy to feel odd about making my opinions heard. Now I know that all of the musicians need to participate as if they were members. Hearing fresh, new voices is always good." To help ensure that everyone is heard, members and subs in many sections participate equally over the course of a performance cycle, dividing the principal roles among each section member.

Sheer longevity in the business helps a lot too. Not only do you become familiar with a classical repertoire, but you also get to know other musicians, even if some of them aren't always around. "I remember reading a story about Bill Russell many years ago," says Bauch. "He said that when the intensity of the game of basketball reached its highest level, everything seemed to slow down so much that he could almost predict what each player would do and what each move would be. To me, that best describes the experience of playing chamber music with people whom I've known for years. Time stands still, and you can anticipate one another's every move. Nothing outside that moment seems to exist."

Nothing, that is, until the last note of Brahms's Serenade No. 2 resonates through Carnegie Hall. Then the silence is broken by enthusiastic applause from audience members, among whom are a large group of Baruch students who have come to see for themselves what collaboration and consensus building can do.

Ron Lieber (rlieber@fastcompany.com), a *Fast Company* senior writer, is based in New York City. For more information on Orpheus, contact Harvey Seifter by email (hseifter@orpheusnyc.com), or visit Orpheus on the Web (http://www.orpheusnyc.com).

The Agenda—
Grassroots Leadership

NAVY COMMANDER D. MICHAEL ABRASHOFF USES A LEADERSHIP MODEL THAT'S AS PROGRESSIVE AS ANY IN BUSINESS.

You expect to be awed by the view from the deck of the USS *Benfold*. The $1 billion warship is one of the U.S. Navy's most modern, most lethal fighting machines: 8,300 tons of steel armed with the world's most advanced computer-controlled combat system; revolutionary radar technology; a stock of missiles capable of taking out precise targets on land, sea, or air; and a crack crew of 300 highly skilled, totally committed sailors. In 1997, a year and a half after its commission in the Pacific fleet, the guided-missile destroyer spearheaded some of the most critical missions in a confrontation with Iraq. Now tethered to a dock on San Diego's sprawling naval base, the *Benfold* gleams with power. When eating up the sea at full throttle, she generates a plume of froth that's two-stories high.

What you don't expect to find on board the *Benfold* is a model of leadership as progressive as any celebrated within the business world. The man behind that model is Commander D. Michael Abrashoff. His career includes a sterling service record, combat experience, and prestigious posts in Washington, DC. He has won dozens of medals. He is also credited with building the *Benfold*'s reputation as the best ship in the Pacific fleet. Last year, in fact, the ship won the prestigious Spokane Trophy for having the best combat readiness in the fleet—the first time in at least 10 years that a ship of its class had received that honor. Yet Abrashoff doesn't quite look the part: Think of a military leader, and you may envision George C. Scott's depiction of General George S. Patton. Abrashoff, however, has an easy smile and electric-blue eyes.

Behind Abrashoff's relaxed confidence is his own brand of organizational zeal. Settling into his stateroom, Abrashoff, 38, props his feet on a coffee table, sips a soda, and says, "I divide the world into believers and infidels. What the infidels don't understand—and they far outnumber the believers—is that innovative practices combined with true empowerment produce phenomenal results."

That the ranks of the nonbelievers include most of his superiors and fellow commanding officers doesn't deter Abrashoff one bit. "I'm lucky," he says. "All I ever wanted to do in the navy was to command a ship. I don't care if I ever get promoted again. And that attitude has enabled me to do the right things for my people instead of doing the right things for my career. In the process, I ended up with the best ship in the navy—and I got the best evaluation of my career. The unintended benefit? My promotion is guaranteed!" After completing his 20-month tour

49

of duty as commander of the *Benfold* this past January, Abrashoff reported to a top post at the Space and Naval Warfare Systems Command.

Abrashoff continues to see his mission as nothing less than the reorientation of a famously rigid 200-year-old hierarchy. His aim: to focus on purpose rather than on chain of command. When you shift your organizing principle from obedience to performance, says Abrashoff, the highest boss is no longer the guy with the most stripes—it's the sailor who does the work. "There's nothing magical about it," he says from his stateroom on the *Benfold*. "In most organizations today, ideas still come from the top. Soon after arriving at this command, I realized that the young folks on this ship are smart and talented. And I realized that my job was to listen aggressively—to pick up all of the ideas that they had for improving how we operate. The most important thing that a captain can do is to see the ship from the eyes of the crew."

That perspective provided Abrashoff with two insights about change: First, there's always a better way to do things. In the first few months of his command, Abrashoff took apart every process on board and examined how each one helped the crew to maintain operational readiness. "I pulled the string on everything we did, and I asked the people responsible for—or affected by—each department or program, 'Is there a better way to do things?'" Most of the time, he discovered that there was.

Abrashoff's second insight about change: The more people enjoy the process, the better the results. Spending 35 days under way in the Persian Gulf is anything but enjoyable—but Abrashoff managed to lead his sailors through their missions and to have fun in the process. An ingenious supply officer procured pumpkins—not an easy task in the Middle East—thereby allowing the *Benfold* to sponsor a pumpkin-carving contest for the fleet in October 1997. During replenishments alongside supply tankers, the *Benfold's* crew became known throughout the Gulf for projecting music videos onto the side of the ship. The crew took its entertainment detail a step further during Christmastime, when K.C. Marshall, the ship's highly skilled Elvis impersonator (and chief navigator), serenaded the admiral's ship with a rendition of "Blue Christmas."

Abrashoff first developed his inclination to skirt standard operating procedure during his post as military assistant to then-Secretary of Defense William Perry, in 1994. He sat beside Perry during the arduous implementation and assessment of the Defense Acquisition Reform Initiative, and he took every opportunity to apply lessons from that initiative on the *Benfold*. For example, in purchasing food for the ship, Abrashoff switched from high-cost naval provisions to cheaper, better-quality name-brand food. With the money he saved, Abrashoff sent 5 of the *Benfold's* 13 cooks to culinary school—and as a result made the ship a favorite lunchtime destination for crews across the San Diego waterfront.

Abrashoff's leadership formula produces benefits that are both financial and operational. In fiscal year 1998, the *Benfold* returned $600,000 of its $2.4 million maintenance budget and $800,000 of its $3 million repair budget. Abrashoff notes that because any surplus goes back to the navy's top line, "there's no rational reason for saving that money—except that we've created an environment in which people want to do well." The navy's bean counters slashed the ship's maintenance budget this year by exactly $600,000—yet Abrashoff expects the ship to return 10% of its reduced allotment.

At the same time, the *Benfold's* performance has set new standards. For the past two years, the ship's "readiness indicators" have featured the lowest count of "mission degrading" equipment failures and the highest gunnery score in the Pacific fleet. The crew also completed the navy's predeployment training cycle in record time. That process normally requires 22 days in port and 30 days under way. The *Benfold's* crew required 5 days in port and 14 days under way to complete the cycle—and to earn coveted shore leave.

Another critical performance measure is a ship's retention rate. The *Benfold's* rate is off the charts. On average, only 54% of sailors remain in the navy after their second tour of duty. Under Abrashoff's command, 100% of the *Benfold's* career sailors signed on for an additional tour. Given that recruiting and training costs come to a minimum of $100,000 per sailor, Abrashoff estimates that the *Benfold's* retention rate saved the navy $1.6 million in personnel-related costs in 1998.

Yet the most compelling sign of Abrashoff's success may be the smooth interaction that now exists among the ship's company. The *Benfold's* experienced department heads, its divisional officers (most of them fresh out of the naval academy or ROTC), and its enlisted sailors all show a deep appreciation of the ship's relaxed discipline, its creativity, and its pride in performance. Commander Abrashoff walked Fast Company through six principles that have made the USS *Benfold* a working example of grassroots leadership.

DON'T JUST TAKE COMMAND—COMMUNICATE PURPOSE.

The *Benfold* is a warship. Our bottom line is combat readiness—not just in terms of equipment but also in every facet of training and organization. But the military is an organization of young people. Many of them go into the military to get away from bad situations at home. Many have been involved with drugs or gangs. Although they know what they don't want, they don't quite know what they do want. Getting them to contribute in a meaningful way to each life-or-death mission isn't just a matter of training and discipline. It's a matter of knowing who they are and where they're coming from—and linking that knowledge to our purpose.

Within two days of when new crew members arrive, I sit down with them face-to-face. I try to learn something about each of them: Why did they join the navy? What's their family situation like? What are their goals while they're in the navy—and beyond? How can I help them chart a course through life? Ultimately, I consider it my job to improve my little 300-person piece of society. And that's as much a part of the bottom line as operational readiness is.

LEADERS LISTEN WITHOUT PREJUDICE.

Most people in this organization are in "transmit mode"—meaning that they don't "receive" very well. But it's amazing what you discover when you listen to them. When I first took charge of the *Benfold*, I was having trouble learning the names of everyone in the crew, so I decided to interview five people a day. Along with Master Chief Bob Scheeler, the senior enlisted guy on the ship, I met with each person individually and asked three simple questions: What do you like most about the *Benfold*? What do you like least? What would you change if you could? Most of these sailors had never been in a CO's cabin before. But once they saw that the invitation was sincere, they gave me suggestions for change that made life easier for the whole crew and also increased our combat-readiness ratings.

From those conversations, I drew up a list of every practice on the ship and divided those practices into non-value-added chores and mission-critical tasks. I tackled the most demoralizing things first—like chipping-and-painting. Because ships sit in salt water and rust, chipping-and-painting has always been a standard task for sailors. So every couple of months, my youngest sailors—the ones I most want to connect with—were spending entire days sanding down rust and repainting the ship. It was a huge waste of physical effort. A quick investigation revealed that everything—from the stanchions and metal plates to the nuts and bolts used topside— were made of ferrous material, which rusts. I had every nut and bolt replaced with stainless steel hardware. Then I found a commercial firm in town that uses a new process that involves baking metal, flame-spraying it with a rust inhibitor and with paint, and then powder-coating it with more paint. The entire process cost just $25,000, and that paint job is good for 30 years. The kids haven't picked up a paintbrush since. And they've had a lot more time to learn their jobs. As a result, we've seen a huge increase in every readiness indicator that I can think of.

I not only know the names of my crew members—I also know where they're from, as well as a little bit about their families; I know what they aim to do in life. I learned from the interviews that a lot of them wanted to go to college. But most of them had never gotten a chance to take the SAT. So I posted a sign-up sheet to see how many would take the test if I could arrange it. Forty-five sailors signed up. I then found an SAT administrator through our base in Bahrain and flew him out to the ship to give the test. That was a simple step for me to take, but it was a big deal for morale.

PRACTICE DISCIPLINE WITHOUT FORMALISM.

In many units—and in many businesses—a lot of time and effort are spent on supporting the guy on top. Anyone on my ship will tell you that I'm a low-maintenance CO. It's not about me; it's about my crew. Those initial interviews set the tone: In my chain of command, high performance is the boss. That means that people don't tell me what I want to hear; they tell me the truth about what's going on in the ship. It also means that they don't wait for an official inspection or run every action up and down the chain of command before they do things—they just do them.

Lieutenant Jason Michal, my engineering-department head, recently had to prepare for engineering certification. That's one of the most critical and stressful inspections on the ship, but I kept away until he asked me to come down to review his work. What I saw blew my mind. He had been tweaking procedures for months and had implemented about 40 changes in the operating system. Of course, he aced the inspection. When the people who do the work know that they—not the manual or policy—have the last word, you get real innovation in every area.

One of our duties during the 1997 Gulf crisis was to board every ship going to or coming from Iraq and to inspect it for contraband. This inspection was a laborious process that involved filling out a time-consuming four-page report each time a ship made a crossing. One of my petty officers created a database to store information about each ship and to generate reports automatically. I gave a copy of the database to another CO, who showed it to the admiral. Now that database method is policy throughout our battle group.

None of this means that we've sacrificed discipline or cohesion on the ship. When I walk down the passageway, people call attention on deck and hit the bulkhead. They respect the office but understand that I don't care about the fluff—I want the substance. And the substance is combat readiness. The substance is having people feel good about what they do. The substance is treating people with respect and dignity. We gain a lot of ground and save a lot of money by keeping our focus on substance rather than on extraneous stuff.

THE BEST CAPTAINS HAND OUT RESPONSIBILITY—NOT ORDERS.

Companies complain about turnover, but a ship's company isn't a static population. Not counting dropouts and other separations, about 35% of a ship's crew transfers out every year. That means that I must be constantly vigilant about cultivating new experts. After improving the food on this ship, my next priorities were to advance my people and to train my junior officers, who are called on repeatedly to make life-and-death decisions.

I not only have to train new folks; I also have to prepare higher-level people to step into leadership roles. If all you do is give orders, then all you'll get are order takers. We need real decision makers—people who don't just sleepwalk through the manual. That means that we have to allow space for learning. Removing many of the nonreadiness aspects of the job—from chipping-and-painting to cleaning—lets us spend more time on learning how to use all of the sophisticated technology in our combat-information center and on running through war scenarios on our computer system.

And because we're more interested in improving performance than we are in pomp, we can create learning experiences at every turn. When something goes wrong on a ship, the traditional attitude is "Hurry up and fix it, or we'll look bad." Well, if you don't care about getting promoted, you'll give a sailor time to learn how to do the job right—even if you run the risk of having the admiral stop by before the problem is fixed.

As a result, we have the most proficient training teams on the waterfront and a promotion rate that's over the top. In the last advancement cycle (that's the process that determines base pay, housing allowance, and sea pay), *Benfold* sailors got promoted at a rate that was twice as high as the navy average. I advanced 86 sailors in 1998. That amounts to a huge chunk of change and a lot of esteem for roughly one-third of my crew.

SUCCESSFUL CREWS PERFORM WITH DEVOTION.

At a conference for commanding officers that I attended recently, more than half of the officers there argued that paying attention to quality of life (QOL, as we call it) interferes with mission accomplishment. That's ridiculous. It doesn't make sense to treat these young folks as expendable. The navy came up 7,000 people short of its 52,000-person recruitment goal in 1998, and it expects to be 12,000 people short of its goal in 1999. In every branch of the military, one-third of all recruits never complete their first term of enlistment. We've got to provide reasons for people to join, to stay—and to perform. The leader's job is to provide an environment in which people are not only able to do well but want to do well.

I looked at what usually happens when new 18- or 19-year-old recruits check in: They fly in from boot camp on a Friday night. They feel intimidated and friendless. They stow their gear in their berths and immediately get lost in San Diego. To change all of that, we've created a welcoming plan: Now, when new recruits come on board, their bunks are assigned, their linen and blankets are there, and we match them with a hand-picked sponsor who shows them the ropes. They can even call home—on my nickel—to tell Mom and Dad that they've made it.

The biggest complaint when we're out to sea for weeks on end is military-issue entertainment. When we pulled into Dubai—one of the better liberty ports in the Persian Gulf—a sailor took me aside to tell me that the crew members were frustrated because their tour-bus drivers didn't speak English and wouldn't deviate from assigned routes. On the spot, I rented 15 10-passenger minivans. I told the crew to divide into groups, and I assigned a senior petty officer to serve as a monitor on each bus.

Now, that wasn't strictly legal, but it helped morale so much that it has become a popular procedure for ships throughout the Gulf. A more serious issue for crew members at sea involves time away from their families. Most ships report several family problems during every deployment, and most of those problems result from lack of communication. I created an AOL account for the ship and set up a system for sending messages daily through a commercial satellite. That way, sailors can check in with their families, take part in important decisions, and get a little peace of mind.

Back in port, the top frustration for the crew involves 24-hour shipboard duty between deployments. The standard practice is to divide the crew into four sections that stand duty in rotation—with each section serving a 24-hour shift every 4 days and getting only 1 weekend off each month. That's criminal! So I suggested an eight-section duty rotation, which would require a 24-hour shift every 8 days while providing 2 weekends off each month. In order to maximize flexibility, I cross-trained all of the sailors to perform every function of their duty section. The system has worked so well that many ships on the waterfront are now copying it.

Maintaining "quality of life" is simply a matter of paying attention to what causes dissatisfaction among the crew. You do what you can to remove those "dissatisfiers" while increasing the "satisfiers." Increasing satisfaction may be as simple as recognizing that everybody loves music and then setting up a great sound system or buying a karaoke machine. "Quality of life" is also a matter of creating an environment in which everyone is treated with respect and dignity. The *Benfold* is one of the first ships in the navy that was built from the keel up to accommodate women. It's no secret that the military has had problems with sexual harassment and with prejudice in general. Yet when we do equal-opportunity surveys for the *Benfold*, we get stunning results: Only 3% of minorities on board reported any type of racial prejudice, and only 3% of women reported any form of sexual harassment.

That's not because I give long lectures on prejudice or sexual harassment—it's because I talk about the effects of community and about the need to cultivate unity and teamwork with as much care as we give to maintaining our equipment.

TRUE CHANGE IS PERMANENT.

Ships in the navy tend to take on the personality of their commanding officers. But neither my crew nor I worry about what will happen now that I've moved on. We've set up a virtuous circle that lets people know that their contribution counts. This crew has produced phenomenal results, and now it's motivated to do even better. My attitude is, once you start perestroika, you can't really stop it. The people on this ship know that they are part owners of this organization. They know what results they get when they play an active role. And they now have the courage to raise their hands and to get heard. That's almost irreversible.

Polly LaBarre (plabarre@fastcompany.com) is a senior editor at *Fast Company*. You can visit the USS *Benfold* on the Web (http://www.benfold.navy.mil), and you can reach D. Michael Abrashoff by email (mabrashoff@aol.com).

During engagements in hot spots like the Persian Gulf, the navy hands out its toughest assignments to the USS *Benfold*. That's because the *Benfold* has the highest level of training, the best gunnery record, and the highest morale in the fleet. According to D. Michael Abrashoff, who until recently was the ship's commander, its stellar performance reflects a powerful way of leading a ship's company. Here are some of the principles behind his leadership agenda.

1. Interview your crew.

Benfold crew members learned that when they had something to say, Abrashoff would listen. From initial interviews with new recruits to meal evaluations, the commander constantly dug for new information about his people. Inspired by reports of a discrepancy between the navy's housing allowance and the cost of coastal real estate, Abrashoff conducted a "financial wellness" survey of the crew. He learned that it was credit-card debt, not housing, that was plaguing the ship's sailors. He arranged for financial counselors to provide needed advice.

2. Don't stop at SOP.

On most ships, standard operating procedure rules. On the *Benfold*, sailors know that "It's in the manual" doesn't hold water. "This captain is always asking, 'Why?'" says Jason Michal, engineering-department head, referring to Abrashoff. "He assumes that there's a better way." That attitude ripples down through the ranks.

3. Don't wait for an SOS to send a message.

Listening is one thing; showing that you've heard what someone has said is quite another. Abrashoff made a habit of broadcasting ideas over the ship's loudspeakers. Under his command, sailors would make a suggestion one week and see it instituted the next. One example: Crew members are required to practice operating small arms—pistols and rifles—but they often find it hard to secure range time while they're on base. So one sailor suggested instituting target practice at sea. Abrashoff agreed with the suggestion and implemented the idea immediately.

4. Cultivate QOL (quality of life).

The *Benfold* has transformed morale boosting into an art. First, Abrashoff instituted a monthly karaoke happy hour during deployments. Then the crew decided to provide entertainment in the Persian Gulf by projecting music videos onto the side of the ship. Finally, there was Elvis: K.C. Marshall, the ship's navigator and a true singing talent, managed to find a spangly white pantsuit in Dubai and then staged a Christmas Eve rendition of "Blue Christmas." The result: At a time when most navy ships are perilously under-staffed, the *Benfold* expects to be fully staffed for the next year, and it has attracted a flood of transfer requests from sailors throughout the fleet.

5. Grassroots leaders aren't looking for promotions.

Abrashoff says that because he wasn't looking for a promotion, he was free to ignore the career pressures that traditionally affect naval officers. Instead, he could focus on doing the job his way. "I don't care if I ever get promoted again," he says. "And that's enabled me to do the right things for my people." And yet, notes Abrashoff, this un-career-conscious approach helped him earn the best evaluation of his life as well as a promotion to a post at the Space and Naval Warfare Systems Command.

LEADING AMIDST CHANGE

In this section, we highlight articles that examine leaders' roles in recognizing the need for, design of, and implementation of organizational change. They emphasize the challenges of change and the reasons why people and organizations so often resist change efforts. The first two articles are thought pieces showcasing new ideas on leading change. The first highlights Debra Meyerson's book, *Tempered Radicals,* which shows how leaders can bring major change to their organizations through "small wins." The second thought piece introduces Karl Weick and his innovative work learning from high reliability organizations, including fire jumpers and aircraft carriers. The remaining pieces are fascinating profiles of how exemplary leaders have effectively transformed their organizations. These profiles include well-documented change stories, such as EDS, Motorola, and Xerox, as well as less well-known stories, such as Yellow Freight. Their stories bring to life the complexities of leading major change, as well as the strategies for making it happen.

Practical Radicals

YOU SAY YOU WANT A BUSINESS REVOLUTION? NOT SO FAST.

Name: Debra Meyerson
Occupation: Professor, Simmons Graduate School of Management; visiting professor, Stanford University; author of *Tempered Radicals*
Aspiration: "This is not a revolutionary style. But it is the stuff of change. It is the true content of leadership."

Ever since she arrived as a child from Mexico, Maricela Gallegos has heard the same question: Couldn't she Americanize her name? "Mary" would be so much easier to pronounce. "I say, No, my name is Maricela. All my brothers and sisters changed their names. They always said to me, 'Why do you go against the grain? Roll with the punches.' But I could never do that. I'd be shortchanging myself."

This has been one small act of rebellion for Gallegos, 48, a stance that asserts her authentic identity in an alien culture. There have been other acts since. A few years ago, Gallegos was working in the human-resources department of a Hewlett-Packard factory located in California. She grew compelled by questions of affirmative action and diversity, but her managers at the time didn't consider race and gender to be pressing problems. Instead, they agreed to let her work on programs for employees with disabilities.

"It was a foot in the door," she recalls. "I knew that gender and race were important issues. But I needed to work on something that the organization was willing to support." She organized a local network of workers with disabilities, then used their numbers to convince a small group of managers to declare a "disability-awareness day."

"They didn't realize what I was going to do," she says. What she did was bring in people from 30 nonprofit organizations to educate employees. She also borrowed 100 wheelchairs so that people at hp could feel what it was like to work in one. She got 100 sound-blocking devices so that people could experience deafness. She blindfolded employees and sent them on an obstacle course.

"That made all the difference," Gallegos says. "It transformed the work site." She organized the same event for four more years, then started organizing networks for women, people of color, and gay and lesbian employees. She won the confidence of senior managers, and, with their support, she produced workshops that dealt with racism, sexual harassment, and homophobia for thousands of employees. "These things were risky," says Vicki Martinez, who was a staffing representative at hp at the time. "But they paved the way for change."

There are Maricela Gallegoses everywhere—in the cubicle next door, perhaps, or in a remote regional sales office. You know the sort: They operate deep within big companies, well beneath the cultural radar, and are practically invisible to the top brass. They are part of their organization, yet somehow apart as well, professional irritants who are tolerated more than embraced. They survive and persist: Employing many different styles and strategies, typically waging small battles rather than epic wars, they work slowly to change the rules.

Debra Meyerson calls these individuals "tempered radicals." From her academic perches at Simmons Graduate School of Management and Stanford University, Meyerson, 43, has studied such people for more than a decade. Her forthcoming book, which is tentatively titled *Tempered Radicals* (Harvard Business School Press, April 2001), will document the phenomenon.

Meyerson defines tempered radicals as employees who operate on a fault line. They are committed to the organization that they work for. To some measure, moreover, they want to advance on their employer's terms; their company's success is theirs too. At the same time, though, they are at odds with their company. Marginalized by gender, race, or ideology, they identify with causes that defy the dominant culture. While they feel bound to their organization's goals, they also aim to stay true to their own personal ideals.

And so they pursue change, constantly challenging the status quo. It is often a personally torturous path. Because tempered radicals pursue goals that are rooted in their own identities, their efforts tend to be passionate. But because they also happen to sympathize with their organization, the changes that they introduce are mostly incremental. They are ambivalent, cautious catalysts, and they are content with small victories that, over time, lay the groundwork for something grander. "This is not a revolutionary style," Meyerson says of the tempered radical's approach. "But it is the stuff of change. It is the true content of leadership."

In these early days of the Internet Age, we have grown accustomed to the harsh language of revolution. Startups vow to "overthrow" big-company rivals. New CEOs promise to "reinvent" the companies that they've been charged with leading. And that transformation is supposed to arrive in a flash, because everything is supposed to happen fast.

But here's the reality: Revolution isn't all we'd cracked it up to be. Most real change doesn't occur instantaneously. To bring about change, people need to have a leadership style that's different from that of the starkly aggressive, abusive captain we once lionized. It requires people working patiently inside organizations, seeking only modest progress. It demands radicals, surely—but radicals of a more considered sort.

Tempered radicalism, then, represents a truer picture of change. It's not dramatic. It doesn't meet our craving for instant transformation. But it's how real leaders really operate.

THE MAKING OF A (TEMPERED) RADICAL

Debra Meyerson grew up in Southfield, Michigan, where her father was a builder and her mom was a housewife. The Meyerson home wasn't an intellectual or political cauldron; nothing in her upbringing, in fact, hinted at the feminist path that Meyerson would later pursue. If there was any symbol at all of what her life would become, it came in the form of the 470-class sailboat that she raced with her dad.

"We were always out in winds that were a bit too high to handle for our weight," Meyerson remembers. "And I routinely pushed a bit too far, so we'd end up capsizing, often with Dad out on the trapeze. He just wanted to push the edge and have fun; I mostly wanted to win. We had a blast."

Meyerson studied political science at MIT, then got her MBA at MIT's Sloan School of Management. Lacking any real career direction, she waitressed and skied for a year in Vail, Colorado. Then her consciousness was sparked when she taught skiing for Women's Way Adventures. Based in Squaw Valley, California, the travel/adventure company gave women the confidence to take risks, in part by letting them define their own adventure. "It planted the seed for me," Meyerson says. "I saw how people are constrained by their circumstances, how small interventions can change possibilities."

She worked for a consulting firm for about a year, hated it, and decided to return to school. She wanted to find a doctoral program in which she could study how social interactions between individuals and institutions occurred, and how social institutions could be made to be less oppressive. She had no thought of becoming an academic. "I was interested in being relevant, in making a difference." She landed at Stanford's Graduate School of Business.

And there, her incipient radicalism festered. Stanford, like most business schools, was a fairly conservative place. Its core mission involved creating young captains for capitalist industry. Its language, which was rooted in war, dominance, and "win-lose," didn't easily accommodate equity and social justice, much less the feminist ideals that Meyerson brought to the table. Her dissertation, a study of social workers in hospitals, met with studied indifference. "As a student, I began to feel that I was really deviant for caring about this stuff."

Meyerson and Maureen Scully, who was another PhD candidate in organizational behavior, would spend hours in their cozy shared office venting their frustrations. The two women wondered what had happened to the radicals of the 1960s and 1970s. Had they disappeared? Had they been co-opted?

Neither, really. They had become ... tempered.

Exhibit A was Joanne Martin, Meyerson's Stanford mentor and thesis adviser. In 1984, Martin, who is now 53, had become the first woman ever to gain tenure at the business school. She was successful. She was respected. And she had quietly used her institutional credibility to help advance the following agenda: to open the doors of academia and business to more women, minorities, and men whose mind-sets were very different from that of the average business-school student. "I talked with Deb and Maureen about how I balanced the demands of a business-school culture with my values and the needs of my family," Martin says. "I was trying to conform enough to be effective, but not so much as to be co-opted."

Martin was, in effect, a prototypical tempered radical. Meyerson and Scully soon encountered many more people like her. Having finished her PhD, Meyerson took a junior-faculty position at the University of Michigan, where she met Sharon E. Sutton, an African-American professor of architecture.

Sutton, now 59, seemed strikingly out of place: Before entering academia, she had been in private practice in New York. She had concluded that building design should better serve the needs of users—and so she had directed her efforts toward a more holistic design approach that depended on community participation.

When she arrived at Michigan in 1984, Sutton felt as if she was lost. "I thought I had gone to the edge of the earth," she recalls. Her offbeat ideas on teaching design weren't welcomed by the mainstream architecture department. At faculty meetings, she says, she was disparaged—not least by two fellow African-American professors.

She lay low, steering clear of departmental politics. Over time, though, her work attracted national attention. "I didn't care anymore whether I got tenure," Sutton recalls. She won tenure anyway, but remained "a prophet everywhere but in my own camp." Even so, she stayed put until 1998. Michigan gave her a national pulpit from which to make change. It also allowed her to have an influence on future generations of architects. "I compromised myself in exchange for the power of the institution," she says.

Meyerson was fascinated by the enduring ambivalence of Sutton and those like her. "How do you hold on to what it means to be an African-American woman, and at the same time fit into a predominantly white-male context?" Meyerson asks. "Not just fit in, but also succeed? These are people who want simultaneously to rock the boat and stay inside it. They want to stay inside because they are invested, to a greater or lesser extent, in the system."

Meyerson believes that such ambivalence, when managed in the right way, can strengthen leaders. Whereas compromise seeks a flavorless middle ground, ambivalence "involves pure expression of both sides of a dualism." Individuals, she and Scully wrote in a 1995 paper, "can remain ambivalent and [yet be] quite clear about their attachments and identities." They can operate as "outsiders within," granted access to opportunities for changing organizations, but remaining detached enough to recognize what needs changing.

THE POWER OF "SMALL WINS"

Meyerson began to broaden her research. Her notion of tempered radicalism was born of a feminist orientation and of observations of how women operated in male-dominated organizations. The theory neatly explained how many women effect change. She learned, though, that the characterization resonates with other marginalized groups too—with racial minorities, with gays and lesbians, and even with some white men.

These new everyday leaders come in all stripes. Roger Saillant, 57, is a white man who grew up in a string of foster homes. Since the rules changed with every new home, he says, he learned that "the only rules that matter are the ones that are right for you." So when he arrived as a chemist at Ford Motor Co. 30 years ago, he recalls, "I couldn't accept blindly the things that I was told."

Saillant went after his own agenda, which was rooted in his passion for the environment and his sympathy for the disadvantaged. Now, as VP and general manager of a division within Visteon Corp. (which spun off from Ford in June), a leading supplier of integrated automotive-technology systems, Saillant has acquired the credibility necessary to put his ideals into place. He is trying to expose his top executives to principles of environmental sustainability. For example, he's having people figure out how much material Visteon dumps into landfills each year. He hopes to forge associations with small companies that will help make Visteon greener.

"I don't think the system trusts me," Saillant says. "But my people love it." Indeed, says Micky Moulder, a Visteon manager who worked with Saillant in the late 1980s, "I came away from that time a much better person, a better leader. And I know that I influenced others. If you ask, How has Roger changed Visteon?, it's hard to say, exactly. But his footprints are everywhere. You can feel the change."

Meyerson grew captivated by the tensions faced by tempered radicals like Saillant—and also by the differences between what drove the ambivalence of white men like him and what motivated women and people of color. To learn more, she studied upwards of 100 leaders and change agents in two large business organizations.

What she found: First, there is no one template for tempered radicals. Such leaders exist along a continuum. Their degree of radicalism depends partly on their perceptions of their own organizational credibility, or on their sense of financial security. Almost always, though, their degree of temperedness is tied to a deeper motivation. Highly tempered radicals, Meyerson argues, "are driven by a real impulse for personal authenticity. They say, 'I just want to save my soul. I don't want to sell out.' Many of them deny being radicals, even tempered ones." Typically, their personal goals are aligned closely with those of their employer; they may be more invested than others in the company's success. "But they're still nudging at the system—and I say that those little nudges make a difference."

And it truly was nudging that Meyerson observed in her subjects. "These people aren't challenging the whole system," she says. "People have benefited from the system, and there's power in remaining inside it. So they just want to move it a little bit."

One man in her study, for example, refused to let work overwhelm his commitment to his family. He wanted to contribute to his company, and he wanted the company to succeed. But he also wanted to coach his kids' soccer teams—and that meant leaving the office before any of his colleagues. He made clear, as well, his desire not to be bothered by work calls between 6 PM and 8 PM, his treasured family time. "So people stopped calling then," Meyerson says. "And gradually, it became an organizational norm that no one wanted to be disturbed during those hours at home. This man was very much driven by his desire to maintain his values—but he unwittingly paved the way for this small company to change its practices."

Meyerson calls such events "small wins" and regards them as a central strategy for effective radicals. For one thing, the approach nicely reduces large problems to ones that are easier to manage. More importantly, small wins are inherently less risky. "What these people do is push back and negotiate resistance. They test the system, subtly challenging norms. They prod gently, because that's all the system can take."

Indeed, tempered radicals understand, either instinctively or through painful experience, what the organizational limits are. Kirk Tucker, 56, who heads planning and strategy for Harley-Davidson's big York, Pennsylvania motorcycle manufacturing plant, was reassigned midway through his engineering career when he pressed too hard and too early for organizational changes. He realizes now that "you have to recognize how far you can push. If you push it too far, you will become ineffective. When you're ineffective, you put yourself at risk. One mentor told me years ago, 'Have patience. It's going to take them a while to figure out that you're right.'"

At PricewaterhouseCoopers, partner Monique Connor, 35, finds satisfaction in the smallest of victories. She quit the security of the tax-consulting track to get her MBA and rejoin the firm in human resources, hoping to press for broad cultural change. But such change, she understands, arrives in increments. "Just changing the language of an organization can be a huge success. In a lot of the work that we do with partners, we'll invent scenarios for illustration and populate them with 'she's. That represents a real cultural shift here."

Negotiating those small wins, though, represents no small task; like any change, they require organizational capital and political savvy. Roger Saillant knows that, whatever else he does, he has to contribute to Visteon's bottom line. "Once I do that, they become increasingly forgiving with regard to some of the other things I want to pursue." When Jacqui MacDonald, 49, head of fair trade at the Body Shop, pushed for fair-trade reforms, she made sure that she accommodated the pricing and delivery demands that the Body Shop's purchasing managers were facing. "To be effective, you had to talk their language and help them solve their problems," she says.

At the other end of Meyerson's continuum are tempered radicals who explicitly pursue organizational change. Less tempered, often with less invested in the organization, "they're taking bigger personal risks, trying to rattle the system. They're still concerned about their own authenticity—but they want bigger changes. They turn that series of microinteractions into bigger opportunities."

Dixie Garr, 45, Cisco Systems's VP of customer-success engineering, continually creates opportunities for herself and others. She mostly says exactly what's on her mind, aiming to "shock people so that they think." While she's tempered enough to have survived five big corporate employers, she's also an unabashed system rattler.

Garr was the youngest of eight kids growing up in tiny Dubach, Louisiana. Neither of her parents finished junior high school, but they were radical thinkers around Dubach. "They helped me understand that I didn't have to buy into the things I heard around me," Garr says. She didn't. As a young engineer at Texas Instruments, for example, she told a manager that she wanted to become an executive at the company. "He laughed at me. I had only been there for two years. It was totally outside his way of thinking, especially coming from a black woman. But he later worked for me."

Finding TI to be less than inclusive of diversity, Garr was founding chair of the company's Minority Leadership Initiative, and she fought for the promotion of African-Americans. At Cisco, she battles for diversity of a different sort. With every second or third job opening under her control, she aims to hire someone about whom people will say, "'You hired him?' He'll be someone who brings a different perspective, a kook—and he'll turn out to be wonderful."

A tempered radical, Garr says, "must not compromise on the vision, but must be flexible on the approach. You have to broach ideas that go against the natural instinct of the organization—but you have to do that in a palatable way. Organizations have antibodies, just like people. It's important that you deliver change in such a way that the antibodies don't totally attack it before it's had a chance to grow."

THE LONELY WORK OF MAKING CHANGE

Meyerson proposes that in an effective change environment, radicals across the spectrum of temperedness ought to complement each other and work together to effect change. Yet more often, she says, radicals at different points on the continuum mistrust and alienate one another. Those at the more radical pole chide what they see as the timidity of those who are more tempered, while those at the tempered pole are put off by the aggressiveness of those who are more radical.

"And these are people who should be natural allies," Meyerson says. She recalls working for a year at Stanford's Institute for Research on Women and Gender. Finally, she thought: Here is an environment where I won't be seen as a radical, where I'll fit right in. Instead, she found, "I was seen as suspect because of my affiliation with the business school. I was viewed as one of them."

The phenomenon of mistrust is even odder given that radicals' degree of temperedness often fluctuates over the course of their work life, as their financial status or their role within their organization changes. Individuals who feared standing out early in their careers can be emboldened over time by advancement into positions of greater authority.

Or they can travel the other way. Michael V. Littlejohn, an African-American executive, had no problem voicing his opinions on the deficiencies in minority hiring and retention while a rising manager at Price Waterhouse. He admits, actually, that he probably pushed too hard or too visibly, creating resentment among his peers and superiors.

Littlejohn, 42, is currently general manager of IBM's Learning Services in the Americas, running a division of 1,500 employees. He remains true to his identity as a black man: His office is filled with African-American art; he hires several minority interns each year; and he heads his division's Black Executive Network.

But he also feels more visible now, and he feels more responsibility to appear to be acting in all employees' interests. In a way, he admits, he has become gradually more co-opted by the organization that he works for. "The higher you rise, the more people look at you and wonder, Are you the sort of executive we need? So the higher I've risen, the more risk-averse I've become. I'm not sure if that's maturity, or coming to terms with greater power. I realize that I'm walking on thinner eggshells now."

Ultimately, tempered radicals' failure to cooperate with each other across the continuum of radicalness only serves to accentuate the sense of isolation that most of them experience. Operating on the organizational fault line, afraid to affiliate too closely with any one group, such individuals can be, simply, lonely.

"It was very hard sometimes," Maricela Gallegos recalls of her time spent championing diversity at the plant level. "You feel very alone, trying to move hard and to convince people to embrace change. You have to look at making change over the long term, because day to day, you don't really see it. That was my struggle for 10 years. It was important for me to think about the company's future. But sometimes my efforts to bring about change hurt my career. You don't move as fast in your promotions, because you're offending the people who have a say in your career path."

Today, however, Gallegos is thriving. She has moved from the local plant to hp's Global Diversity office, where she helps create strategies for disability programs worldwide. She is also working with the company's Latin-American operations to tackle diversity issues. She serves on both state and presidential committees serving people with disabilities. She has reached a place, she says, where "it's okay to challenge."

Likewise, Roger Saillant is now operating near the top of Visteon. After making little progress for the first 15 years of his career, he was selected to launch a new plant located in Mexico—a role in which he excelled. Based on that success, he was quickly promoted two more levels. Kirk Tucker, having survived his exile from Harley-Davidson's headquarters, now has a senior-management job at the company's biggest plant. And Dixie Garr reports to a senior VP one level below the chief executive at Cisco, one of the most successful companies in America.

These tempered radicals, in other words, have not been killed off. They are irritants to their organizations in the way that pearls are irritants to oysters. There is something about these individuals that their organizations want to keep and nurture—even if the relationship is mutually painful. "I got here because this place has the capability of creating people like me," Saillant says. "Ford could have ground me to chalk, or at least diminished what I was trying to do. But it was curiously enabling."

The relationships between individuals and institutions are mutually enabling, actually. Tempered radicals stay where they are in the face of ongoing frustration because they appreciate the sheer power inherent in their big, if flawed, employers. "Why have I stayed here?" Saillant muses. "I could go out and become a top officer in a lot of different companies. And yet, if I make a change here, it will have a huge impact globally. Just in my division, there are 12,000 people in 11 countries. Why play in New Haven when you have a chance to play on Broadway?"

So it is for Debra Meyerson at Stanford. She has taught at the business school on and off since 1994, and now has made her home in California with her husband and three children. She still thinks of herself as an outsider at this elite but conservative academic institution—a status confirmed by her ongoing work at Simmons Graduate School of Management, in Boston, where she is a professor of management. Simmons is certainly an ideologically more welcoming place for her.

It's important for Meyerson, professionally and personally, to stay on the organizational margin. Yet she also recognizes that, on some level, Stanford has accepted her. It wants to have her and her intellectual radicalism around the joint. It recognizes, perhaps, the longevity that accrues to institutions with a greater diversity of ideas. Stanford is better for the conflicted experience. So, perhaps, is she.

Keith H. Hammonds (khammonds@fastcompany.com) is a *Fast Company* senior editor based in New York. Contact Debra Meyerson by email (debram@leland.stanford.edu).

TIPS FOR TEMPERED RADICALS

Professor Debra Meyerson has spent more than a decade studying how real grassroots leaders make a difference in their organizations. Her forthcoming book, tentatively titled *Tempered Radicals,* will document her findings and offer case studies of the hard work of radical change. Here is a short course on some of her insights.

1. **Seek small wins.** Bringing about deep-seated cultural change in a large organization is a massive proposition—and an enormous, long-term challenge. Better to break the problem up into smaller, more manageable pieces than to pretend that you can tackle it all at once. Leaders can experiment with these smaller efforts to unearth resources, allies, and potential sources of resistance.

   Smaller efforts also foster less fear and mistrust among peers and superiors. A string of small wins is usually more palatable to the organization than is an attempt at wholesale change.

2. **Act locally and authentically.** Change doesn't always come from an explicit effort to make change—and it rarely comes about at the urging of outside consultants or as a result of bloodless strategic plans. Tempered radicals often act solely from an urge to remain true to their own ideals; their local actions can unintentionally spark broader results.

   Take this modest example: An African-American employee refused a superior's request that she unbraid her hair for a client meeting. Her immediate boss congratulated her for her courage, and then congratulated the entire organization for expanding its image of professionalism. That small gesture, made out of personal belief, sent a large and powerful signal.

3. **Speak the language.** Often, people in organizations accept change more easily when it's expressed in terms that they can relate to both personally and professionally. A diversity effort, for example, may resonate louder for corporate managers if they grasp the business implications of the initiative. Before pitching a "fair trade" strategy that would require her company to pay higher prices to its suppliers, the Body Shop's Jacqui MacDonald made sure that she understood the cost implications for purchasing managers.

4. **Build affiliations.** Radicalism can be isolating. Effective leaders develop networks of people outside (and sometimes inside) their organizations who can provide information, resources, emotional support, and empathy. Michael V. Littlejohn at IBM maintains three such networks: his family, a circle of close friends in similar roles, and a group of fellow radicals in the company. "You can't survive unless you have that support system," he says.

BY KEITH H. HAMMONDS   FROM *FAST COMPANY* ISSUE 58, PAGE 124

Five Habits of Highly Reliable Organizations

THE WORST THING ABOUT RECENT BUSINESS SCANDALS IS THEIR LINGERING AFTEREFFECT: HOW CAN YOU MOVE FORWARD WHEN YOU DON'T KNOW WHO YOU CAN DEPEND ON? KARL E. WEICK SAYS THE ANSWER IS INSIDE HIGHLY RELIABLE ORGANIZATIONS. FOR THEM, UNCERTAINTY IS THE "GOOD STUFF."

It is a world after Enron. After the Global Crossing and K-Mart bankruptcies. After accusations of improprieties on Wall Street and irregularities at some of the nation's most storied professional-services firms.

It is a time when businesspeople ask, "Who can we rely on?"—and they are asking with good cause.

The answer comes from an unexpected source: Karl E. Weick, the smartest business thinker you've never heard of. A private, academic noncelebrity who labors at the University of Michigan at Ann Arbor, Weick is revered by such public celebrities as Jim Collins and Tom Peters. And his work—notably, the opaque but groundbreaking 1969 book, *The Social Psychology of Organizing*—is among the most cited in the sphere of organizational theory.

As an organizational psychologist, Weick has studied the inner workings of everything from firefighting crews to jazz combos. In *Managing the Unexpected: Assuring High Performance in an Age of Complexity* (Jossey-Bass, 2001), Weick and coauthor Kathleen Sutcliffe (also from the University of Michigan) assess what's called "high-reliability organizations"—operations such as aircraft-carrier and nuclear-power-plant crews. High-reliability organizations, or HROs, share two essential characteristics: They constantly confront the unexpected and operate with remarkable consistency and effectiveness.

In the wake of today's business turbulence and, more recently, just plain bad business, Weick's analysis of HROs offers important lessons. His message: The best way for any company—and its people—to respond to unpredictable challenges is by building an effective organization that expertly spots the unexpected when it crops up and then quickly adapts to meet the changed environment. In a series of interviews, Weick revealed the five habits of highly reliable organizations.

1. **Don't be tricked by your success.** HROs don't gloat over their successes. In fact, it's just the opposite: They are preoccupied with their failures.

They are incredibly sensitive to their own lapses and errors, which serve as windows into their system's vulnerability. They pick up on small deviations. And they react early and quickly to anything that doesn't fit with their expectations.

Navy aviators often talk about "leemers," a gut feeling that something isn't right. A pilot feels puzzled, agitated, or anxious. Even though he doesn't know exactly what's wrong, he knows that he needs to abort the mission. Typically, those leemers turn out to be good intuitions: Something, in fact, is wrong.

HROs create climates where people feel safe trusting their leemers. They question assumptions and report problems. They quickly review unexpected events, no matter how inconsequential. They encourage members to be wary of success, suspicious of quiet periods, and concerned about stability and lack of variety, both of which can lead to carelessness and errors.

2. **Defer to your experts on the front line.** There are so many deviations out there, so much dissonance. How do we know what's really worth paying attention to? The answer: Listen to your experts—the people on the front line.

People at the top may think that they have the big picture. More accurately, they have a picture, certainly not the picture, and certainly not bigger in the sense that it includes more data.

The picture that frontline workers see is different. It is drawn from their firsthand knowledge of the company's operations, strengths, and weaknesses. What is important about the frontline workers' view is that these people capture a fuller picture of what the organization faces and what it can actually do. In most cases, they see more chances for bold action than the executives at the top. So it's better for HROs to allow decisions to migrate to frontline expertise rather than to the top of preestablished hierarchies, where positions are often filled for reasons other than experience.

3. **Let the unexpected circumstances provide your solution.** I've written about the Mann Gulch fire that killed 13 smoke jumpers in 1949. In all, it was a tragic organizational failure. But what was amazing was the reaction of the foreman, Wagner Dodge, when the fire was nearly on top of his men. On the spot, he invented the escape fire—a small fire that would consume all of the brush around him and his team, leaving an area where the larger fire couldn't burn.

He acted in a way that was contrary to all of the things that firefighters have habitually done. That's part of being resilient. Put simply, it's about having a steady head.

When something out of the ordinary happens, your stress level rises. The safest prediction for what will happen next is that your perception will narrow—you will get tunnel vision—and you will miss a lot of stuff. You have to be able to resist that dramatic narrowing of cues—because within everything that is happening unexpectedly, you will find what you need for a remedy.

4. **Embrace complexity.** Business is complex, in large part because it is unknowable and unpredictable. In the face of all of this complexity, HROs are reluctant to accept simplification. They understand that it takes complexity to sense complexity.

We all instinctively try to simplify the data that we receive, but there are better and worse simplifications. Better simplifications arise from a deeper knowledge of the environment along with a deeper understanding of the organization and its capabilities. That knowledge and understanding develops when people attend to more things, entertain a greater variety of interpretations, differentiate their ideas, argue, listen to one another, work to reconcile differences, and commit to revisiting and updating whatever profound simplicities they settle on as guidelines for action.

A complex organization is made up of diverse people with diverse experience. Its complexity fosters adaptability.

5. **Anticipate—but also anticipate your limits.** We try to anticipate as much as we possibly can. But we can't anticipate everything. There's such a premium on planning, on budgeting, on making the numbers. In the face of all that, the notion of resilience has an affirming quality: You don't have to get it all right in advance.

Good strategy does not rely on anticipation alone. It's built on a smaller scale, updated more frequently, and driven by actions. You don't present it to your board of directors that way, but it's more useful guidance than the kind you can get from a grander notion of strategy. It's not, Think, then act. Instead, it's, Think by acting. By actually doing things, you'll find out what works and what doesn't.

That doesn't mean you should stop anticipating. But you should add in two subtleties. First, focus your attention on key mistakes that you do not want to make. Second, trust your anticipations, but be wary of their accuracy. You can't see the whole context that is developing. Your anticipation is probably a reasonable first approximation of what might be happening, but no matter how shrewd you are, it won't cover some key features.

Most important, you should build a capacity for resilience. Life events are indeterminate. We can't fix or know everything. The beauty and the frightening quality of hubris is that people believe they're in the know completely.

I hope that emergency-room doctors, nuclear-power-plant operators, and firefighters know what the hell they're doing. But I don't believe it for a second. How they struggle with that—and how you and I struggle with that—is, for me, the good stuff. That's the human condition.

Keith H. Hammonds (khammonds@fastcompany.com) is a *Fast Company* senior editor. Contact Karl E. Weick by email (karlw@umich.edu).

HOW MINDFUL IS YOUR COMPANY?

In *Managing the Unexpected,* Karl E. Weick and Kathleen Sutcliffe argue that high-reliability organizations exhibit "mindfulness." Basically, mindfulness indicates a combination of high alertness, flexibility, and adaptability. Take this quiz to rate your company's mindfulness. Give yourself the following number of points for each of the corresponding statements: 1 point for "Not at all," 2 points for "To some extent," and 3 points for "A great deal."

1. There is an organizationwide sense of susceptibility to the unexpected.
2. Everyone feels accountable for reliability.
3. Leaders pay as much attention to managing unexpected events as they do to achieving formal organizational goals.
4. People at all levels of our organization value quality.
5. We have spent time identifying how our activities could potentially harm our organization, employees, customers, other interested parties, and the environment at large.
6. We pay attention to when and why our employees, customers, or other interested parties might feel peeved at or disenfranchised by the organization.
7. There is widespread agreement among the firm's members on what shouldn't go wrong.
8. There is widespread agreement among the firm's members on what could go wrong.

A total score higher than 16 indicates an exemplarily mindful infrastructure in your firm. A score lower than 10 suggests a need for immediate improvement.

BY BILL BREEN AND CHERYL DAHLE   FROM *FAST COMPANY* ISSUE 30, PAGE 390

Resistance Fighter

WITHOUT A STRATEGY FOR WINNING PEOPLE OVER, CHANGE AGENTS CANNOT IMPLEMENT THEIR PROGRAMS FOR CHANGE.

Once you've designed it, the toughest part of any change effort is clearing the next hurdle: the inevitable opposition. You may have put together a can't-miss program; you may have lined up top-level sponsorship. Those things don't matter.

History shows that managers and frontline workers alike will resist your best-laid plan. A few will openly fight it. Many more will ignore or try to sabotage your plan. If you don't have a strategy for winning people over, you can forget about your change program.

Mark Maletz knows this firsthand. In his role as an independent consultant affiliated with McKinsey & Co. in Boston, he has helped launch more than 75 large-scale change initiatives at such companies as Xerox, American Airlines, and computer giant Siemens Nixdorf. Maletz, 40, transformed himself into a full-fledged change agent while developing large-scale, artificial-intelligence expert systems. His toughest challenge: convincing highly skilled people to let him mine their expertise so he could put it on a computer. Overcoming their resistance was an almost insurmountable task.

"The technology side was by far the easy part," Maletz recalls. "The change side—the human-dynamics side—was the complex and compelling part." In an interview, Maletz outlined the dynamics of dealing with people who fight change.

It's almost a given that in the corporate world, most people, most of the time, will resist change. Why?

People know that historically, there's very little upside for them—that change itself is rarely for the better. If you've been with a company for a few years, and you've seen these flavor-of-the-month change programs come and go, you quickly recognize a pattern: Management launches some kind of change effort to great fanfare. Managers talk up the benefits and explain why this program will be good for both the company and its employees. They make promises, but at the end of the day, they fail to deliver. Nothing really happens, and the whole effort seems like a waste of time. Well, it makes sense to resist things that are a pure waste of time.

That's one kind of resistance. But there's another scenario: A bunch of consultants analyze a corporate department consisting of 100 people, and they conclude that the company needs just 48 people to do the work. If you're in that department, one of two things will happen: Either you'll lose your job, or you'll stay—and end up working even harder.

So there's typically a history within lots of organizations that says, "Change, in the past, has not been good. And there's no reason to believe that this time, it's going to be better."

So you can count on people being hostile.

You should expect some hostility, but it's rarely the in-your-face kind. Usually, resistance is passive-aggressive, meaning it's far more underground: People hear you out, saying nothing that's overtly negative, but they don't buy the change program. As soon as they're alone with their peers, they'll say something like, "This thing is going to pass, so let's just keep our heads down." And historically, they're often right. The impact of a lot of change never reaches too deep into the organization—and when it does, it's usually bad.

Other people will say they're on board, but then they'll try to kill your effort. Not too long ago, I worked on a change program at a high-tech company, and one of the senior guys sat in meetings with the CEO and claimed to be totally on board. But then he'd go back to his organization and order people not to meet with the change team. He'd say things like, "Make sure that your calendar pushes meetings with these guys out as far as possible. And cancel each meeting at least once before it takes place."

How do you handle a guy who's trying to stab you in the back like that?

In that case, we found out about it and confronted him. He blew up and told us that the program was a complete waste of time and that he'd never give it any play. And he was terminated within a month. The message was, "You can come out and say, 'This is a complete waste of time,' and we'll engage you. But you can't agree that you're on board and then try to sabotage the effort."

Okay, you can expect to take some hits. What should you do then? Hit back?

Absolutely not. You don't even push people—you pull them. You go out into the middle of the organization and the front lines, you find informal opinion leaders who have very broad networks, and you recruit them to be part of the change process.

We did this at Siemens Nixdorf. One of the people we went after was a very sharp, very young software developer. He had zero formal authority, but people throughout this 1,200-person software unit would come to him for technical help and advice. So if you get someone like him to ally with the change effort, you also get access to many more people within the organization.

If these people are real grassroots leaders, they won't hesitate to give you a few jabs if they see some problems with the change program. How do you win them over?

You don't. If you spend 40 minutes trying to get one of these guys to buy into the change program, the message you're really conveying is, "I'm not interested in listening to you. I just want to sell you."

Instead, you invest your personal time—you begin to build a relationship and invite the person to engage with you. You don't want to make a pitch, you want to have a conversation. The symbolic contract is, "I'm offering you a real voice in the process, and in turn, I'd like you to become a voice for the process. If you have a problem with some part of the program, I'll make a change if I think you have a valid point—or I'll tell you why that's not going to be the case." The important thing is to make it clear that not only will you listen to criticism, but that you'll be prepared to respond in some way.

So if you disagree with them, you've got to tell them, even if it's going to hurt you in the short term.

The smart strategy is to always be up front. Think about reengineering. For a while, people tried to claim that reengineering was not about downsizing. And yet we saw hundreds of reengineering efforts that were, in fact, all about downsizing. I've never understood why management refused to acknowledge up front that people were going to lose jobs—as if the employees wouldn't figure that out until it was too late. But in fact, they always figure it out. And then you've got people who are cynical and don't trust you.

Can people's resistance to change ever be a good thing?

You bet it can. In fact, change agents should not automatically resist resistance—they should learn from it.

I was involved in a change effort to make a high-tech, major industrial concern more entrepreneurial, and someone stood up and said that we'd totally missed the fact that there was no way to find critical resources for entrepreneurial ventures in this organization. And he was right. So we asked him to create an internal clearing-house that would identify key employees' functional specialties, so when we needed people's expertise, we'd quickly know how to find them. Not only did we learn from this guy's criticism, but we embraced it.

It's one thing to promise people that they'll have a real voice in the change process, but how do you deliver on that promise?

From the very first day, you make the process transparent. I learned that lesson about 15 years ago, when I was working on a change project at a money-center bank located in New York City.

We had a dedicated conference room for the change team. And I started noticing that people would go out of their way to walk by the room. Then it occurred to me that, at some level, whatever information that you send out to keep people apprised of the change effort is slightly suspect. Even in the best cases, people will wonder whether you're just spinning fiction. But they sense that what's happening in the room is real.

So the change-team members decided that anyone in the organization could come in and spend half a day with us. We would treat them just as if they were permanent members of the team. The only requirement we had was that any half-day visitor would have to be up to speed on the project. We weren't going to stop work and give them a tutorial on the change process. This set a tone that made a big difference in employees' participation level and trust in the process.

What happens when they walk into that conference room and show you that some tactical part of the change program just won't work?

If you're going to make the process transparent, you've got to be willing to admit when you're wrong, or when someone else has a better idea. Leaders and change agents should obviously avoid going public every time they screw up. But picking your spots and occasionally admitting that you're wrong sends an incredibly powerful message that you're serious about engaging in a healthy debate. And it surprises me how few senior executives are willing to do that. They think that acknowledging even one mistake will make them appear as ineffective leaders, when in fact the reverse is true.

Is there a way to determine whether people have really accepted your change effort—or are fighting it behind your back?

This is where your project-management skills come into play: Focus on what people are doing, as opposed to what they say they're doing. If people say they're with the program, ask them for explicit commitments. You should, in the spirit of transparency, make those commitments visible and ensure that people are delivering on them.

I worked with an insurance company that was trying to create a workplace that encouraged healthy conflict. Now that kind of behavioral stuff is a really hard thing to measure. But we got the company to design a series of interventions that would allow people to experiment with conflict in different ways. By setting up some intermediate milestones, we could track whether people were really making progress.

How can you distinguish between the knee-jerk resistance that comes with any transformation effort, versus a wall of resistance that's ultimately insurmountable?

You need to be absolutely clear about where you stand with the senior-level people who are backing up your effort. I'll often have change teams develop sponsorship maps, which track whether key stakeholders continue to provide them with the level of cover that they need to make the effort succeed. If that protection starts to crack, you need to do a reality check and reassess things. Losing your sponsorship is a pretty strong signal that you should figure out why, regroup, and live to fight another day.

I've Always Been a Human Modem

IT'S UP TO MOTOROLA'S JANIECE WEBB, ONE OF THE COMPANY'S HIGHEST-IMPACT CHANGE AGENTS, TO MAKE MOTOROLA A LEADER IN THE WIRELESS INTERNET—THE NEXT GREAT GLOBAL MARKET. TO PULL IT OFF, SHE—AND MOTOROLA—MUST MAKE NETWORKING PERSONAL.

Janiece Webb, 47
Senior VP, Personal-Networks Group, Motorola Inc.
Schaumburg, Illinois

Janiece C. Webb was barely 18 years old when she started making her mark at Motorola Inc. Her job testing semiconductors on the graveyard shift at the company's Phoenix plant was mind-numbing work. But Webb's questioning nature and her willingness to speak up meant that something out of the ordinary was bound to happen. "I would just ask, 'Why are we doing this?'" she remembers. "'Why do we sit around for 8, 10, sometimes 12 hours when the machines on the line break down and wait for the mechanics to fix them? There must be a better way.'"

The shift supervisor figured that he knew how to handle his curious employee: "He'd say, 'You're being paid to straighten leads. Shut up and color.'" But even as a young production-line worker, Webb showed a knack for getting people to buy into her ideas. She would appeal to their self-interest and would suggest changes in a way that didn't come across as threatening. "I asked my supervisor if he could give me 10 minutes any time of the day or night when I wasn't on shift, so I could talk to him about doubling production," she says. "That got his attention."

With her supervisor's blessing, Webb put together a troubleshooting manual with tips on how to operate machinery to avoid jams and how to make simple repairs. Then she rallied her team to see how far they could push their new efficiency. "I said, 'Let's set a goal.'" Her blue eyes flash like the big diamond earrings she's wearing. "'We can kick first and second shifts' butts.'"

It says a lot about Janiece Webb, now 47, that she can still get worked up about a challenge that she conquered 28 years ago. Today, as senior vice president in charge of the company's wireless-Internet business, she holds a key job at Motorola. But the relentless spirit of that spunky assembly-line worker is never far from the surface of a now-polished corporate executive. Webb has traveled this far because she knows how to build bridges: between her past and her present, between high-flying strategic vision and in-the-trenches business reality, between the old-school Motorola and the tumultuous opportunities of a wireless Web. "I've always been a human modem," she says. "I've created peace between the marketers and the engineers, between the hard-core techies and the salespeople."

Her relationships inside Motorola start with her own team. The 900 people in the personal-networks group are in some ways a microcosm of the entrenched interests and turf consciousness that pervaded Motorola in the past. With Webb's help, the company is trying to shed those destructive habits. Some members of the group are there because they are known and trusted by other parts of Motorola, whose cooperation is essential if Webb's wireless-Internet crusade is to succeed. Other members are young, energetic, irreverent, bright—the next generation of Janiece Webbs. A few others came to Motorola from the computer industry, and Webb is using them to infect the rest of the team with a bias toward building relationships with software developers—something new for Motorola.

"This job is testing me like no other," she says. "It's like trying to train speed swimmers to do synchronized swimming. The resources at Motorola are powerful, and people here are saying, 'I'm an expert, I know my game, don't mess with it.' But I'm saying the rules have changed. It's not enough anymore to be the fastest guy in the pool. We're being judged on how much we're in sync."

For all of Webb's savvy and drive, though, there's no question that she's in for one heck of a test. Motorola, an icon of innovation, quality, and growth in the 1980s, crashed to earth in the 1990s, unable to adjust its deeply ingrained culture to a world transformed by the Internet. With $33.1 billion in revenue last year, Motorola is still a giant. But it is not nearly as nimble as it needs to be. Despite being the world's second-largest cell-phone maker (after Nokia) in a hot market for wireless communications, Motorola is still a laggard when it comes to growth and profitability—not to mention style and design.

Under CEO Christopher B. Galvin, Motorola has been working mightily to regain its former glory. The company has cut costs and has learned from its stumbles. But if Motorola is going to become a high-growth company again, then it has to claim a leadership position in the wireless-Internet business. That puts responsibility squarely on the cashmere-covered shoulders of Janiece Webb. And it won't be enough to sell piece parts like Web-enabled cell-phones, which will quickly become commodities. To make a difference, Webb and her team have to design, build, and sell complete wireless-Internet systems that go end to end—from transmission equipment to software to handsets—and that can be woven into the next generation of wireless systems already being put in place by such companies as Deutsche Telekom AG, NTT DoCoMo, and Vodafone Group PLC.

"Janice is the kind of leader that Motorola needs times 10," says Noel Tichy, 54, a business professor at the University of Michigan and an adviser to change-minded CEOs such as Ford's Jacques Nasser and GE's Jack Welch. "She's got the guts to be a change agent in an organization that traditionally has not rewarded change."

OVERCOMING BARRIERS, BREAKING DOWN BOUNDARIES

Looking back, Janiece Webb's life has the symmetry of a fairy tale: A poor white girl from a Latino neighborhood on the outskirts of Tucson leaves home, takes a job on the factory floor at Motorola, and climbs through the ranks. She's a natural leader, and Motorola steers her through a series of tough assignments. In spite of the male culture that surrounds her, she thrives. She travels the world, accumulates a wealth of business sophistication, and makes more money than she ever dreamed she would.

But like all fairy tales, this one has its dark moments too. Webb's father died in a car accident when she was 2 years old, and her mother remarried a copper miner. Both of her parents were alcoholic, and money was scarce. One of Webb's earliest memories is the feeling of hot dust between her toes as she stood in the barren lot in front of her house, barefoot as usual. When she decided to join the Girl Scouts, her parents told her that she was on her own in that pursuit. So she found an old uniform at a secondhand-clothing store and earned the money to buy it herself. Week after week, she endured the stigma that set her apart at troop meetings. "My uniform was old and ugly, and all the other girls had fresh little uniforms. My parents did not teach me how to participate in life," she says. "I think they were intimidated by it."

She left home at 16, and, two years later, she followed a boyfriend to Phoenix, 200 miles to the north. She got a job testing semiconductors on the assembly line at Motorola. Her boyfriend's father encouraged her to consider college, and, with Motorola's help, she started attending classes at the University of Arizona during the day and working the graveyard shift at the plant.

At Motorola, it didn't take long for Webb to get noticed. She rose quickly through a series of jobs in Motorola's semiconductor group, moving first to Florida, then bouncing back and forth between Chicago and Arizona. She married another Motorola employee. The career shuttle wreaked havoc on her studies. It took her 12 years to complete a bachelor's degree in business administration. Somewhere along the way, Webb's paycheck and responsibilities surpassed those of her husband. She was 20 when they were married—"too young," she now says—and her advancement put extra strain on the relationship. In 1985, after 12 years, Webb and her husband divorced.

At Motorola, meanwhile, Webb was growing accustomed to breaking through the glass ceilings that had limited the advancement of other women managers. At 27, she penetrated a bastion of maleness, taking over responsibility for the missile-target-detection device that Motorola made for the U.S. Navy. When she got up to make her first presentation, the admiral in charge of weapons programs thought that she was a clerk checking the microphones. "Okay, honey, I think we've got it fixed," he said. "Let's bring up the next speaker." He was seated in the front row of an auditorium that held 300 men—mostly naval officers, along with a contingent of senior executives from the major defense contractors. Webb was the only woman. "Excuse me, admiral," she said. "My name is Janiece Jordan from Motorola, and I'm here to report on the status of the MK 45 target-detection-device engineering program."

The admiral was thunderstruck. He swiveled around in his chair to face the audience. "Good God!" he shouted. "What the hell is the world coming to that Motorola would send a broad to work on my ordnance?" The room exploded in laughter. When the noise died down, Webb was ready. "Sir, if you find that I'm not competent, I will resign," she said. "But I'd like you to turn around and give me a chance." Webb held that job for eight years.

In her next assignment, Webb had to prove herself all over again. Robert L. Growney, 57, now Motorola's president and chief operating officer, has a reputation for being the toughest boss in a company that's filled with them. Growney's direct reports had never included women before Webb was assigned to his staff in 1989 as director of Motorola's international-paging business. "The first year we were together, he was saying, 'What has Motorola done to me?'" Webb recalls with a laugh. Even today, Growney and Webb are an odd couple. In August, at a Motorola analysts' meeting, they stood together: Growney, with his silver hair, iron jaw, and glen-plaid double-breasted suit, talking with a conspiratorial smile to Webb, who, with her bright-blond hair, her stylish black-knit outfit, and glittering diamonds in her ears and at her wrists, would stand out anywhere—and who stands out even more at conservative Motorola.

But the partnership has worked. Webb managed a global portfolio of pager companies, using Motorola's clout as a leading investor to tighten their operations and to generate more than $1 billion in revenue for Motorola over eight years. Growney became Webb's mentor, tapping her for key jobs, including one running Motorola's cell-phone business in the United States—a demanding and highly visible post. The stakes are even higher for Webb now, with Motorola's future hinging on her success. "The wireless Internet looks as if it could be a boundary-less kind of business," says Growney. "Janiece is able to work in an unbounded setting like that. Not everyone can. She's able to find an interesting balance between being a visionary and reducing an idea to ways that it can make money for the corporation."

WRITING THE RULES OF ENGAGEMENT

When Webb took over the personal-networks group in 1999, a key Motorola partnership with IBM was breaking down. The two companies had been looking for ways to collaborate on powerful new systems that would feed Web content over wireless networks, drawing on Motorola's understanding of telecommunications and on IBM's expertise in computers. But the partnership was going nowhere, largely because each company's engineers believed that they had better technology. Mark F. Bregman, 43, former general manager of pervasive computing at IBM, was ready to scuttle the partnership. "We're wasting our time flying back and forth every few months to hold these meetings," he told Webb.

One reason Webb is so good at building relationships is that she's willing to look at the world from the point of view of counterparts like Bregman. Over her career, in dozens of alliances and in hundreds of initiatives within Motorola, Webb has refined her ability to locate the key results that a partner needs in order to succeed, and then to tie those results to her own needs. "It's not a coy negotiation," she says. "You can't afford to be coy anymore. People are looking you in the eye and asking themselves, Is she real?"

Bregman's call meant that it was time "to restate the rules of engagement," Webb says. "That means starting with what you must have in order to make the partnership a success." For Bregman, it was essential that the system incorporate WebSphere, IBM's platform for global e-business. Without that, Bregman couldn't justify the effort or the expense of joining forces with Motorola to break into the market for wireless-Internet systems. "Fine," Webb said. "That's your core, and we'll make sure we don't enter your space."

She explained that Motorola needed control of the communications elements—the gateways that people would use to connect to the wireless Web. "When it comes to the telecom piece, that is part of who we are. We won't give that up."

It took about 10 minutes for Webb and Bregman to arrive at a basic understanding of how they could work together. But there were still issues. The deadlock that had IBM and Motorola stalled was a debate over which operating system to use as the foundation for the software they would build to run over the wireless Internet. Webb's team at Motorola favored Microsoft NT; Bregman's team at IBM was committed to Unix. Webb saw a way to make the relationship even stronger. "I've come to the conclusion that we may need to build on Unix," she told Bregman. "If that's the case, I'll make my team adopt it—or I'll get a new team."

Commitment that deep is rare, and it turned Bregman into a powerful ally. "Janiece is not just looking for what it takes to make her business and Motorola successful," he says. "Hers is a more mature view of partnerships than what you typically find at a lot of American companies or even European companies."

Those same skills enabled Webb to navigate a delicate pass with Philippe Kahn, one of the most colorful personalities (and one of the healthiest egos) in Silicon Valley. In 1998, Motorola acquired Starfish Software Inc., the maker of electronic address books and calendars that Kahn founded and ran as CEO; in the process, Kahn became one of the largest individual shareholders in Motorola. Kahn was intrigued by the potential of wireless technology and turned his entrepreneurial talents to developing some far-out applications for wireless networks. When Webb took over the personal-networks group, she became Kahn's liaison at Motorola.

One day, Kahn went into Webb's office with a prototype that he had built for a wireless digital camera that snapped onto a cell-phone and that transmitted pictures the instant they were taken. Webb was captivated. The wireless digital camera that Kahn was proffering was just the kind of killer app that Webb needed in order to establish Motorola as a player in the wireless-Web market. "It's unbelievably cool," she told Kahn. "But we have stuff at Motorola Labs that can sort of do that." Kahn argued against moving the project inside Motorola, where he was afraid it would stagnate. "The people you need to work on a visionary venture like this are probably not the kind of guys who work inside a large company like Motorola," he told Webb. "You need a complete end-to-end solution that's commercial, not just a science project."

They went back and forth for a couple of weeks. "The discussions were painful and rough," Kahn says. "Initially, she didn't accept anything. I could tell Janiece was looking, talking to a lot of people in the company and asking them, 'What do you know about this stuff?'" But the technology inside Motorola wasn't as far along as

Kahn's, and Webb desperately wanted a wireless digital camera that she could push into the market rapidly.

Kahn got what he wanted: the freedom to pursue his project with his own team of engineers, backed by an investment of $20 million from Motorola. But Webb's initial resistance was more than just an exercise. The sparring sessions gave Kahn deeper respect for Webb's judgment, and they provided Webb with the due diligence that she needed to throw all of her energy into championing a risky new product. Now she's racing to introduce the wireless digital camera by early next year. "Once Janiece got it, she turned into an enthusiastic, feisty bulldog," Kahn says. "It became her vision, her mission, and the next step in wireless technology: instant visual communication."

The true test of Webb's skill in building strong, resilient relationships will occur within Motorola itself. Competition and infighting among business units has gotten so bad in the past that some analysts blamed Motorola's financial woes on its lack of cohesiveness. The new corporate slogan, "One Motorola," gets a lot of lip service. But it's up to Webb to prove whether the company can really pull together and deliver an integrated wireless-Web system or whether that slogan is just rhetoric. "I'm trying to make the personal-networks group ebb and flow into other parts of Motorola like an amoeba, so that I don't know where their people end and mine start," she says. "It's not instinctual in a high-testosterone culture. But I've never valued my worth in terms of how big my kingdom is. I've valued it based on the impact that I'm having."

THE FUTURE IS NOW

The conference room of the Westin O'Hare is filling up fast with Wall Street analysts and institutional investors. More than 300 financial types file in and take their seats, along with Motorola's board of directors and 100 or so senior managers. They're here to listen to the company's top executives provide an annual briefing on Motorola's results and prospects.

Janiece Webb is the only woman to make a presentation, in a group of executives that includes Galvin, Growney, Webb's immediate boss Merle Gilmore, and a half-dozen others. By now, she's used to being the only woman in such rarefied settings. Still, it's a big deal—for the company and for her. The day before, she received an urgent call from Gilmore, who told her that she would be briefing the analysts on Motorola's wireless-Web strategy. She worked until 9 PM on the presentation, which had to be carefully scripted since the analysts scrutinize every statement made by executives.

If she's nervous now, it hardly shows. She's measured and calm when she takes the stage, and her presentation goes without a hitch. Compared with facing down that admiral, standing in front of analysts isn't all that intimidating. When the presentations are over, and the executives take questions from the floor, one of the investors, a woman, stands up. "I'd like to congratulate you that Janiece should not only be seen this year but heard," she says. Lo and behold, Motorola's changing. And Janiece Webb is right where you would expect to find her—in the middle of it.

Paul C. Judge (pjudge@fastcompany.com) is a *Fast Company* senior editor. Contact Janiece Webb by email (janiece.Webb@motorola.com).

WHAT'S FAST

In a remarkable 28-year career at Motorola Inc.—a journey from an assembly-line post to a top executive position at the core of the company's Internet strategy—Janiece Webb has made her mark by making change. Here are some of the lessons that she's learned along the way.

Nobody wins unless everybody wins. Change requires partners, both inside and outside the company. But it's unrealistic to expect partners to work on your behalf unless you've demonstrated how your work benefits them. "The person you're dealing with has to know that you have integrity," Webb says, "and that you care a lot about them and their issues."

Results start with relationships. Webb is a master at relationships: brokering them, managing them, surviving them, and striking them in such a way that the benefits of such relationships are evident to all sides. "I got stood in the corner my first day of school, when I was six years old, for trying to sit between two kids who didn't like each other," she jokes. "It messed up the teacher's seating arrangement."

Nice guys (and gals) finish first. Changing how a company competes, and how its people work, generates lots of stress and anxiety. The way to help people face those necessary pressures, Webb believes, is to avoid adding to them. Webb is "not afraid to break glass," says leadership guru Noel Tichy. "But she's got a nice style, so she doesn't do it in a personally challenging way."

BY KEITH H. HAMMONDS   FROM *FAST COMPANY* JULY 2001

The Not-So-Quick Fix

WHEN ANNE M. MULCAHY TOOK OVER AS PRESIDENT OF XEROX, THE COPIER GIANT WAS IN SHAMBLES. HER MISSION? FIGURE OUT HOW TO INSTITUTE SOME BIG CHANGES—WITHOUT WRECKING THE COMPANY IN THE PROCESS.

How do you right a massive, sinking corporate ship? What do you do when the red ink runs to hundreds of millions of dollars, when your costs are out of control, when key executives are sprinting for the lifeboats, and when your aggressive accounting comes under regulatory scrutiny? How do you act when your cash reserves drop low enough to spark talk of bankruptcy?

You change everything fast—but not too fast.

When Anne M. Mulcahy was appointed president and COO of Xerox Corp. on May 11, 2000, she leaped into a whirling, violent organizational vortex. Richard Thoman, hired by Xerox chairman Paul Allaire from IBM a year before to take charge of the iconic copier maker, had just been fired after presiding over a $9 billion loss in the company's market value. And the Xerox board had subsequently reinstalled Allaire as CEO.

More to the point, Xerox's core businesses were in shambles. The company had completely misjudged the potential of compact desktop-computer printers from rivals like Hewlett-Packard to grab market share. Sales were evaporating—and Thoman's botched reorganization of his sales team had created confusion and discord.

Mulcahy was a popular Xerox veteran who most recently had led the company's $6 billion general markets operations, following a variety of sales jobs and a stint as senior vice president responsible for communications, government relations, and human resources. Over the course of her 25-year career with the company, she had earned plenty of internal credibility. She and Allaire set to fixing the ailing company. But over the next nine months, things only got worse. Xerox's loss for 2000 totaled $384 million, and by January 2001, its cash had dropped to perilously low levels. Its stock had also sunk to $5, from a high of $64. Almost unbelievably for this legendary company, analysts began speculating about bankruptcy.

Now, about a year after Mulcahy's appointment, the bankruptcy talk has stopped. Xerox has slashed expenses, exited businesses, sold off assets, and cut thousands of jobs. Mulcahy and Allaire predict that the company will be profitable again in the second half of the year; its stock price has rebounded to around $10.

In June, Mulcahy spoke with Fast Company about her harrowing first year as Xerox's president and COO and about the task of changing a big company fast—but not too fast.

Your predecessor, Rick Thoman, was criticized for trying to change Xerox too fast. At a time when everyone seems to aspire to speed, that's a fascinating criticism. As a leader, how do you judge an organization's capacity for speed? How fast can Xerox change?

You can move a company too fast—but you can create a bigger problem by moving it too slowly. Finding the right "clock speed" for change is all about judgment, about knowing what you can accomplish and who you need to accomplish it. And it's about really understanding the implications of what you're implementing.

I look at Xerox and think that we've changed more in the past 12 months than in all the 25 years I've been here. We've taken on the most dramatic change I can imagine. We've announced a $1 billion cost restructuring. We've already reduced our cost base by $600 million, eliminated 7,000 jobs, and are outsourcing some of our manufacturing. There's nothing we haven't touched in this company in the past 12 months to position it for a better future.

Doing all that has required judgment and leadership. You have to know: Do you have a team in place that can pull off that amount of change? Do they understand the company's culture well enough to use it to facilitate change? Implementing change successfully is about understanding how to get 88,000 people going in the same direction—which is what you need to get change that sticks. It's much more about judgment and experience than it is about sheer pace.

If the perceived urgency is greater, you can move an organization faster, right? If a company can go 50 MPH when business is good, maybe it can go 65 MPH when there's a crisis.

Crisis definitely helps you push change. That's why it's so important to be relatively aggressive in a short period of time. That's why we had to be ahead of the curve in all aspects of this turnaround plan—so we didn't lose the momentum that comes when people believe that the company and their jobs are at risk.

So, in terms of organizational change, two years ago, we couldn't have done what we've done in the past year. But crisis only creates context: Leaders still have to make effective change themselves. I recently had to announce the closure of the small office-home office business. It's a 1,500 people business, and it's a business I ran for two years—so I know the people, and I had no good news for them: We had to lay off 300 of them.

But, I was amazed at the reaction we got. While it was painful for employees, they clearly understood the rationale for the decision, and as tough as it was, they knew that it was right. They understood that we know the business and that we were handling things as sensitively as possible. And I think that makes a difference.

People understood that we had worked every option and that the decision wasn't just a fly-by-night one. Now we have people signed up to help make change happen, instead of having a real fight on our hands.

History and relationships help when you have to deliver tough decisions. It helped that I knew every part of the company, and every general manager around the world, when it came to winning the alignment that's required to do tough things.

Good relationships tell you what's possible, what's culturally permissible.

Absolutely. You have to listen. You don't back off from tough things, but you have to know where to stop and take a time out to make sure that you're not doing stupid things. You have to allow for diverse opinions and then make some balanced judgments about what you can do.

Leading change is also about reducing the risk in your implementation plan. Part of Xerox's problem in the past was that we didn't have the execution plans to reduce the company's risk given the amount of change we were facing. It's a lesson I learned as I watched some of the things that haven't worked for the company.

I've really tried to be diligent about the precision of our execution plans, which are hard work to do well. We're now in the process of totally restructuring our manufacturing operations. We're outsourcing our office manufacturing and resizing our remaining operations in dramatic ways. We're reducing square footage by 80% and maintaining only the things we do really well.

In advance, we spent six months doing a deep, competitive assessment with a critical view of where we could retain expertise, competency, and competitiveness. We had to admit where we were disadvantaged, and where we could find partners who had capabilities that we could never hope to replicate. We had to have consensus on what we didn't do well.

There was enormous pressure to do all this as quickly as possible. But I believe that when it comes to the critical parts of your value chain, you have to be damned careful. We will not do it before we have the best possible solution. We have announced that we will do something, but not what—and we're taking our time getting there.

The flip side of urgency is that you operate in a fishbowl, with every twitch of your face subject to interpretation.

I'm not terribly astute in terms of delivering messages that are contrary to what I feel in my gut or what I'm passionate about. There are times when you can't share as much as you want to; you have to hold back and be stoic—and that's hard. It's stressful having to play a role for your employees when you know certain things that they don't.

It's been a difficult time for Xerox publicly. It's been painful to watch the company go through the difficulties it has and to receive the negative press it has, sometimes unfairly. Xerox is a big brand name, and there's been a lot of coverage of the story's negative aspects, rather than coverage of any light at the end of the tunnel.

It's a challenge for us to manage the news. Our 88,000 employees can read about a bankruptcy crisis within hours of its being printed. Whether there's any legitimacy or not, you've suddenly got a big problem. You need to address those things quickly, so you don't lose people's hearts and minds.

How did you handle those reports of bankruptcy?

People need to hear things personally to gain confidence in the company and its management. During the first few months of my job, I lived on planes. I spoke to thousands and thousands of employees. During one three-week period, Paul Allaire and I reached nearly 60,000 of our 88,000 employees, either live, by phone bridges, or in massive town meetings.

In the early days, we made sure that we were highly visible and in constant communication. It was pretty wearing, but if people understand your leadership style and you earn credibility, you get permission to take a lot of actions. People say, "I'm okay with that because I saw her, I heard her. I'm confident it can work because of her leadership." When you're in a situation like ours, that confidence dramatically affects your ability to pull off change.

Do you still have permission? For how much longer?

My goal is to never lose it. I want to have an environment that allows us to keep pushing the company, to be better and more competitive.

But it's not practical to keep up the level of intensity we've had for the past year. The turning point for us is the return to profitability. We'll continue with cost restructuring, and we'll finish disposing assets. And we'll continue to engage employees in "turnaround talk," keeping them abreast of progress and enlisting their support throughout the balance of this year. After that, "the turnaround" may not be the mantra for moving forward. But I think that we'll be positioned to create a new Xerox with new rules and an operating style that will allow a much greater level of intensity than in the past.

If you stop using the word "turnaround," you'll have to find a new mantra.

[Laughing] Yeah, I look forward to that.

Keith H. Hammonds (khammonds@fastcompany.com) is a *Fast Company* senior editor.

BY BILL BREEN   FROM *FAST COMPANY* ISSUE 51, PAGE 106

How EDS Got Its Groove Back

BEFORE DICK BROWN TOOK THE REINS AT EDS, PEOPLE WROTE THE COMPANY OFF AS SLOW, STODGY, EVEN UNCOOL. BY FOCUSING ON THE SOFT STUFF—THE COMPANY'S CULTURE—HE'S TURNED EDS INTO THE LEADING EXAMPLE OF AN OLD-ECONOMY COMPANY THAT GETS IT.

The phone that didn't ring—that was the clue that told Dick Brown something was wrong. He summoned a technician to his office who explained the problem: To avoid incoming calls, the previous CEO had had his phone lines cut. The leadership of EDS, the company that invented the information technology-services industry, had had itself disconnected.

More out-of-touch signs soon surfaced. Brown wanted to know how many people were employed at EDS. It took six phone calls—once his lines were restored—to find out. He asked to see the previous month's financials. The numbers weren't available. The company closed its books on a quarterly basis. He asked for the previous month's sales results. Same answer. Sales were totaled at the end of the quarter. "Unbelievable," says Brown. "We're a $19 billion company, and we were closing quarterly."

The kicker came when Brown tried to send an email to EDS's 140,000 employees. It couldn't be done. The company, he learned, was tangled up in 16 different email systems: AOL, Exchange, Hotmail, Notes—some EDSers even used their clients' systems. EDS was responsible for keeping more than 2.5 billion lines of code running at 9,000 corporations and government agencies worldwide, but its CEO couldn't send an email to his own people. "Totally unacceptable," Brown says, shaking his head at the memory.

When he took the reins at EDS in January 1999, Brown joined a company that was floundering in a world it had created. EDS had pioneered the IT-services industry—the fastest growing industry in the world. But when it split off from General Motors in 1996, EDS was too slow for the fast-forward IT marketplace. Faster, nimbler startups—Razorfish, Scient, Viant—ate away at EDS's market share. IBM launched its own IT-services division, Global Services, and promptly steamrolled EDS on the way to grabbing the lead. At a time when the market for computer services was estimated to be at half a trillion dollars—and growing rapidly—EDS's growth slowed, and its market cap declined.

The company's sins were numerous: It missed the onset of the Internet wave. It missed the start of the client-server wave. It missed the beginning of the run-up to

Y2K. Even worse, it wasn't seen as a cool company. The digerati dismissed EDS as stodgy, arrogant, and chained to old technology.

"When Scott McNealy of Sun Microsystems first had us do a piece of a contract for him, he wouldn't let us publicize the deal, because he thought we were too old economy," recalls John Wilkerson, who shotguns indirect sales channels at EDS. "Sun was cool. We were the knuckle draggers."

That was then. This is now: At the end of July, EDS announced a 17% increase in its quarterly profits, a 7.5% rise in revenue, and an $80 billion backlog of signed contracts. The quarter caps a remarkable turnaround for EDS, a transformation that began last October when the company outmaneuvered IBM to win a whopping $6.9 billion contract from the U.S. Navy. EDS signed an additional $32.6 billion worth of new business in 2000, up 31% for the year. This year, as the Scients and Viants fell to earth, EDS's E Solutions unit grew by 35% in the first quarter. At a time when the tech sector is awash in pink slips, EDS has hired 6,000 people since January. It has signed very public and very profitable partnerships with most of tech's corporate leaders: Cisco, Dell, EMC, Microsoft. And as for Sun? In July, it unveiled a partnership with EDS that is expected to bring both companies an additional $3 billion in revenue over five years.

The EDS turnaround offers an instructive story for the post-dotcom era. It's an object lesson in how an old-line company with real assets, real size, and real profits can reinvent itself for the digital economy, fully absorb the Internet, and turn into an old-economy company that really gets it. But as powerful as those turnaround lessons are, they aren't even the best part of the story.

One hundred days after Brown arrived at EDS from Britain's Cable & Wireless, where he had been CEO for two years, he took a half-dozen of his top executives to the New York Stock Exchange. As they looked out over the trading floor, Brown vowed that they would restore EDS to its full financial health. The company would boost its operating margin by 30%. It would climb back to double-digit earnings per share. And its revenue growth would meet or exceed the market's overall growth rate. Brown committed the company to some hard numbers. Then he set about changing the company by focusing on the soft stuff: EDS's culture and its people.

"Most business leaders are afraid to talk about culture," says Brown. "They're far more comfortable with numbers. While I am very numbers focused, you can't change a business with numbers. Numbers are the end result. You change a business by changing the behavior of its people."

This, then, is the story of how EDS, a global company that is larger than some cities, built a massive change effort on one of the fuzziest, most elusive terms in business: culture.

LEADERS GET THE BEHAVIOR THEY TOLERATE

When Ross Perot launched EDS in Dallas, Texas in 1962, he also created the radical notion that other organizations would hire a company to handle all of their computer operations. Back then, the word "outsource" hadn't even entered the business lexicon. To sell the fledgling concept, Perot built the ultimate can-do culture, comprised mostly of the sons and daughters of Midwestern farmers and returning Vietnam veterans. "Ross told us to hire the people who have to win," recalls EDS vice chairman Jeff Heller, who flew attack helicopters in Vietnam before joining the company in 1968. "And when we couldn't find any more of those folks, he said to go after the people who hate to lose."

EDS came to rule the industry that it created, and it grew exponentially after GM acquired it in 1984. Under GM's wing, EDS established ground-level operations in 42 countries and bulked up to become a $14 billion giant before it split off from the carmaker in 1996. In retrospect, the GM-sponsored success turned out to be EDS's most crippling competitive handicap.

A hefty annuity from GM, which amounted to 30% of EDS's 1996 revenue, first lulled EDS into complacency and then fostered an unwillingness to change within the company—while the world was changing all around it. Individual operating units had no incentive for cooperating with each other to win business. The company's top leaders had grown aloof and cut off from people at the front lines. "We'd have meetings, meetings, meetings, but nothing would ever get decided," says Heller. "It would all end up in warm spit."

In December 1998, EDS's board of directors recruited Dick Brown from British telecom Cable & Wireless, making him the first outsider to lead EDS in the company's 36-year history. He arrived with an unambiguous message: "A company's culture is really the behavior of its people. And leaders get the behavior they tolerate."

Brown quickly signaled that he would not put up with the old culture of information hoarding and rampant individualism. In one of his first meetings, Brown asked 30 top managers to email him the three most important things that they could do to improve the company and the three most important things that he could do. He made his request on a Monday and asked the managers to email him their action items by the end of the week—at the latest. "I was interested in what they'd send, but I was more interested in when they'd send it," Brown says. "This was a litmus test on urgency."

Ninety percent of the managers waited until Friday afternoon to reply to Brown. "It never crossed their minds that they could email me within the hour," Brown says. "They just did it at the last minute. And that's the message that they sent to their people: Do it at the last minute. In the end, almost all of them loaded up on what I needed to do. They were pretty light on what they needed to do."

Today, most of those managers are gone from EDS.

THE PHONE CALL YOU NEVER MISS

Brown moved swiftly to change old beliefs and behaviors at EDS, unleashing a set of practices—dubbed "operating mechanisms"—that were designed to create a company-wide culture based on instant feedback and direct, unfiltered communication. One of these practices is the "monthly performance call." At the beginning of each month, 125 of the company's top worldwide executives punch into a conference call that begins promptly at 7 AM central daylight time. Participation is not optional. "If you miss the call, you get taken to the woodshed," says Heller.

The ostensible purpose of the call is to review in detail the past month's revenue and profit targets. As chief financial officer, Jim Daley reads through the figures for each unit. Everyone knows who hit their numbers, who exceeded them, and who whiffed. But something else is at work here. When executives realize that they will miss their numbers—and no one hits all of their targets all of the time—they must act before that call. "We don't try to embarrass people with those calls; we try to help them," says Brown. "At the same time, facts are facts, and it's critical to measure each executive and each organization against their commitments. I use the word 'commitments' deliberately. It's easier to miss a budget than a commitment, because a budget is just an accumulation of numbers. A commitment is your personal pledge to get the job done. And that's how we strive to behave as a team."

BLOW UP THE COMPANY

Soon after joining EDS, Brown visited Continental Airlines at its Houston headquarters. EDS handles all of the airline's legacy systems: accounting, payroll, maintenance, and, most critically, its reservation system, making Continental one of EDS's largest clients. It was in danger of becoming an ex-client.

"Systems were crashing, deliveries were failing, projects were late," says Janet Wejman, Continental's senior VP and chief information officer. "When projects were finally delivered, the quality was unacceptable. I asked for meetings with the management to explain our problems, but all I got was, 'You don't know what you're talking about. We'll handle it.'"

Wejman was taken aback when Brown came calling. Not only had she never met EDS's previous CEO, she didn't even know his name. She told Brown: "Things can't go on like this." Brown assured her that there would be changes—and he delivered within two weeks: A new account team was brought in. The new account executive conceded that there were problems and promised to work with Continental to solve them. The new relationship, Wejman says, "isn't always nirvana. But EDS does a better job than anyone in the world."

Still, the difficulties with the Continental account pointed to deeper systemic problems within EDS. Cultural change wasn't coming fast enough. Almost everyone paid lip service to the call to collaborate, but not enough people acted on it.

The real problem, Brown and his leadership team realized, lay within the structure of EDS. The company had splintered into 48 separate units, each with its own management and its own P&L. Since the operating units refused to communicate or cooperate, EDS lacked a single overarching, market-facing strategy. The company was rolling out duplicate offerings, duplicate capabilities, and diametrically opposed strategies.

"Once we were doing a strategy session on e-business, and a guy from the energy unit announced that he had 20 people working on a transaction system for oil- and gas-pipeline settlements," recalls Bob Segert, managing director of corporate strategy and planning. "Someone from finance jumped up and interrupted him, saying, 'You're wasting your time. We already have a system for that.' They were both working out of the same building, but neither knew what the other was doing."

Brown and his team had a solution: Blow up the company. Build something new.

LEADING THE BREAKAWAY

The mechanism was "Project Breakaway," a team of seven leaders from different units, each with a different industry expertise. Brown gave them an assignment and a six-week deadline: Draft a blueprint for an organizational structure that is centered around the client—a structure that increases productivity, promotes accountability, and drives a collaborative culture across the entire enterprise. The goal: to break away from the old ways of doing business.

Getting there wasn't easy. "As soon as Dick left the room, the fighting started," says Segert, who won the dubious honor of facilitating the discussions. "I set up a straw model for what a new organization might look like, and they just tore it apart. One of the executives—who is no longer here—stood up and challenged the entire process. But I was thinking, 'Great, the discussion has started.' We had just formed, and we were already starting to storm."

They debated for 16 hours a day, seven days a week—right through the July 4 holiday. After six weeks, they had hammered out a new model: The 48 units were slashed to four lines of business, all of them focused directly on the client. Each client had its own "client executive"—a top performer who would be responsible for troubleshooting problems with the client. To get the job done, the client executive could draw from all four lines of business.

The "Group of Seven," as they came to be known, unveiled the new model at an August off-site for EDS's top executives. "There was a lot of skepticism," recalls Segert. "But then one of the leaders grabbed a microphone and said, 'I feel like I'm at a new EDS. This thing might have flaws, but I'm excited to think about how far we can go with this new model.' And that turned the tide. And thank God it did, because if the senior leaders weren't walking the talk of collaboration—if they weren't living the business model—the effort would have collapsed."

7-ELEVEN SEES RED

Despite the massive reorg, there was still one practical problem: customers. EDS's once-a-year customer-satisfaction surveys offered little in the way of urgency or transparency. When Brown asked, "How are we doing on the Continental account?" no one had a good answer.

The solution: the "Service Excellence Dashboard," a Web-based tool that measures and tracks service quality in every EDS business at all times. The Dashboard displays a color-coded rating system—green, yellow, and red—for critical customer-service benchmarks, including value, timeliness, and delivery.

But the Dashboard is more than a display of cold, hard facts. It's also another force for transparency and cooperation. The status of 90% of EDS's accounts is displayed on the desktops of the company's worldwide leaders. If you're responsible for Continental, and your client executive has put up a "code yellow" for the account, your peers will know about it. The Dashboard also fuels collaboration, because many of those executives will quickly contact you with offers to help. Such was the case with EDS's 7-Eleven account.

EDS supports the network, hardware, and applications for 7-Eleven's retail-information systems, which link up all 5,200 of the franchise's stores. In August 2000, the system flatlined. Servers crashed. Applications failed to work correctly. Stores tried to place product orders but couldn't dial into the host system. When they did manage to dial in, the system sometimes couldn't connect with 7-Eleven's suppliers. "If we can't process our orders, we can't get product into the stores," says Jimmy Pitts, 7-Eleven's point man for coordinating with EDS. "And if we don't have product in the stores, we don't have sales."

7-Eleven CEO Jim Keyes put in a direct call to Frank DeGise, EDS's client executive for the franchise. Shortly thereafter, DeGise put up a red light for the entire account. Within 24 hours, EDS had mobilized.

Don Uzzi, EDS's executive sponsor for the 7-Eleven account, quickly assembled a SWAT team of senior leaders. The team brought in the company's top network guru and handpicked an A team of systems administrators. More significantly, it partnered with 7-Eleven's top IT troubleshooters and formed a joint-company project—"Going for the Green"—to fix the network. Working together, the two companies did an architecture review that revealed design flaws in the network's structure. It took 60 days to reconfigure the network and streamline the hardware. After an additional month of testing, all systems were go. The 7-Eleven account flashed green.

"At the old EDS," says DeGise, "the culture was, 'Fix the problem yourself. And while you're fixing it, make sure you're signing new business.'" The new EDS is sharing information internally—and the next EDS will extend that reach to its clients. By the end of the year, all of the color codes, metrics, and comments from the client executive and other leaders from within EDS will be pushed to the client's desktop.

"We're taking the original design intent behind the Dashboard—which is to create new relationships that are based on trust and collaboration—and we're bringing it right to the client," says Charley Kiser, who leads the Dashboard team. "Clients will see the good, the bad, and the ugly. They will truly be part of the team."

WHEN EAGLES FLOCK

Walk into the fifth-floor reception area at EDS headquarters in Plano, Texas, and you can't miss it: a great bronze sculpture of a screaming eagle, its wings unfurled and its talons flashing. It's a legacy of the Perot era, a symbol of the qualities that Perot valued. The eagle is courageous. It is predatory. But eagles don't flock.

There are signs that the old culture still reigns at EDS. Despite the downsizing, there are still multiple layers of hierarchy. Despite the reorg, there are still instances where salespeople from different business practices call on the same client. Despite efforts to increase the cool factor, blue suits still prevail at corporate headquarters.

There is also abundant evidence that the company that was wired to compete has learned to collaborate. Consider how Brad Rucker and Robb Rasmussen work together. Both are leaders in the E Solutions business, both are EDS veterans, and both are leading the company's push into the digital economy.

At the old EDS, Rucker and Rasmussen would have been competitors, fighting toe to toe to win new business. They are still competitors, but now their energy is directed against EDS's competition. "People are motivated by how they get paid," says Rucker. "I'm compensated based on how my organization performs against its financial goals. I'm also compensated according to how we do at E Solutions. If Robb is having a problem, I need to help him solve it."

"And let's be honest," interrupts Rasmussen, eager to make a point. "This year he's the one who is carrying me."

"And last year, he carried me," Rucker continues. "But the point is, we've made everything open and transparent. I know what percentage of hours he's billing, and he knows my percentage. If Robb has people who are on the bench and aren't billing, I have an incentive to help him get those people off of the bench. I trust that man with my career, and I know he feels the same way about me. That's a different peer relationship than I've ever had at this company."

As the two men talked, they offered real-time, real human evidence that EDS has changed. After two years of effort, the culture—that soft-and-fuzzy factor—is working for the company. No one can predict whether the change will last. But for now, it's clear: The eagles are flying together.

Bill Breen (bbreen@fastcompany.com) is a *Fast Company* senior editor. Contact Dick Brown by email (dickbrownmailbox@eds.com).

DICK BROWN ON CHANGE

How do you change an old, proud, but lagging company into a nimble, high-performing—even cool—competitor? Here are six of EDS chairman and CEO Dick Brown's catalysts for change.

The Straight Stuff, Straight From the Top: Every other week, Brown sends an email message to all 128,000 EDSers, telling them where EDS is going, how it will get there, and what challenges lie ahead. Each email is also an explicit call for dialogue, since anyone at EDS can write him back.

Go Off-Site to Get Close-Up: Two or three times a year, Brown convenes the company's senior executives for a three-day meeting. Leaders learn how to team by teaming.

Nowhere to Run to, Nowhere to Hide: Once a month, the top 125 worldwide leaders participate in an hour-long conference call, in which the CFO goes through the previous month's numbers for each executive. The call serves to make every EDSer's performance transparent.

Money Doesn't Talk, It Screams: Brown has introduced a pay-for-performance system that ranks every employee. Top performers are rewarded; poor performers are given the opportunity to get better.

Color-Coded Clients: Go, Caution, Crisis The company's "Service Excellence Dashboard" is a Web-enabled tool that lets clients rate EDS. It forces speed and collaboration.

Here's Your Coachable Moment!: Brown is a big believer in delivering real-time feedback, which he calls "coachable moments." The phrase has entered EDS's lexicon: "May I give you a coachable moment?" The goal is to make coaching a part of everyday behavior.

REINVENTING THE BRAND

Soon after Dick Brown joined EDS, he realized that he and his team had to do more than reinvent the company—they had to remake the brand. Dotcom mania was at a frenzy, but EDS was out of it. It was seen as an old-economy company in a new-economy industry.

To head EDS's global-marketing efforts, Brown brought in Don Uzzi, whose record included a marketing turnaround at Gatorade and a dismissal from Sunbeam by "Chainsaw" Al Dunlop. Brown wanted Uzzi to make EDS a household name. And there was a second, equally critical goal: to market EDS to EDSers. A cool brand could make people feel good again about working at the company.

After Uzzi arrived, he quickly decided to launch a new campaign at the biggest media event of all: the Super Bowl. It was a huge risk. The Super Bowl is for truly major advertisers, and EDS was nearly invisible in the ad world. Moreover, EDS would have to spend millions of dollars buying airtime—before it could come up with the actual campaign.

Uzzi asked Fallon Worldwide, EDS's ad agency, to design a campaign that would let EDS poke fun at itself and that would show how the company solves complex issues for its clients. Fallon pitched three ideas; Uzzi settled on "Cat Herders." It would be shot in the style of a John Ford western—big sky, big country, stirring musical score—but it would feature rugged cowboys herding 10,000 house cats. "I thought that 'Cat Herders' would work because it was truly epic," says Uzzi. "When it comes up on the screen, it just stops you. And the metaphor captured perfectly what we do: We ride herd on complexity. We make technology go where clients want it to go."

Three weeks before the Super Bowl, Uzzi previewed the commercial at an off-site for EDS's top executives. Most gave it a standing ovation. But there were doubters. "I thought it was terrible," says EDS vice chairman Jeff Heller. "I asked Don if we could pull the ad and get our money back. Boy, was I wrong."

Indeed he was. "Cat Herders" won many of the biggest online polls for best Super Bowl commercial. Clients called from all over the world, asking for tapes to show at meetings. *TV Guide* published a listing of when the spot would run again. More important, Uzzi got email from all over EDS. The consensus: "Cat Herders" had put the luster back on the EDS logo.

Fresh Start 2002: On the Road Again

AFTER SUFFERING THROUGH THE WORST YEARS IN ITS HISTORY, YELLOW FREIGHT SYSTEM HIRED BILL ZOLLARS TO DRIVE AN OLD-ECONOMY COMPANY IN A NEW DIRECTION. NOW, ALMOST SIX YEARS LATER, YELLOW IS FASTER AND MORE RELIABLE AND CATERS TO CUSTOMERS LIKE NEVER BEFORE.

The first time the headhunter called about the top job at Yellow Freight System, Bill Zollars said that he wasn't interested. He was perfectly happy as a senior vice president at another big transportation company, Ryder, where he had helped build the integrated-logistics unit into a $1.5 billion business. But the recruiter kept urging Zollars to reconsider: Here's a chance to build a new company out of one that's been around for more than 70 years.

It was Summer 1996, and Yellow was trying to set out on the road to recovery. The previous year had been the worst in the company's history: It saw $30 million in losses and the second round of layoffs in two years. In 1994, the Teamsters had gone on strike for 24 days, which cost the company dearly.

Zollars, who had left Kodak after 24 years for the chance to run Ryder's logistics unit, was intrigued. He met with Maury Myers, the new CEO of Yellow Corp., the holding company that included Yellow Freight and two regional carriers. Yellow Freight generated $2.5 billion in annual revenue, or about 80% of Yellow Corp.'s total sales. The survival strategy, Myers told Zollars, wasn't to reestablish the Yellow brand as a long-haul carrier, but to transform the company into something completely different: a carrier that offered multiple services and that was built around unprecedented customer service.

It was an opportunity that Zollars couldn't resist. He signed on with Yellow to help a troubled company start over. And today, nearly six years later, Yellow is a different company. It still transports primarily big, heavy freight—minimum 100 pounds—called "less-than-truckload" (since a single shipment doesn't fill an entire trailer, workers load multiple ones on the same vehicle). But how and when those parts and products reach their destination is another story. Gone is the one-dimensional long-haul approach and the complacency ingrained from years of regulation. No more telling customers, "Sorry, we can't do that." The new mantra is literally, "Yes we can." In an attempt to offer what Zollars calls "one-stop shopping," Yellow has added a variety of services, including regional and expedited shipping, to satisfy a broader range of transportation needs.

The old Yellow gave customers a rough estimate of when a shipment would arrive. It might show up then. It might not. The new Yellow is faster, more precise, and, the economic meltdown notwithstanding, more profitable. The four years before 2001 were the most successful in the company's history, with the annual revenue for 2000 reaching a record $3.6 billion. Even as the overall tonnage and revenue fell off in 2001, the newest services continued to grow—a sign that Yellow is headed in the right direction, says Zollars.

That financial success has deep strategic roots. Long known for its bright orange trucks, the company is now considered to be a technology leader in its industry. Yellow's systems monitor 13,000 trucks nationwide and around 70,000 national and international shipping orders each day. The once-rigid delivery schedule is flexible. Customers decide when their freight will be delivered: in a week, three days, or several hours. They specify morning or afternoon delivery or, if they prefer, the exact hour. Yellow offers a money-back guarantee on expedited deliveries.

"We've gone from being a company that thought it was in the trucking business to being one that realizes it's in the service business," says Zollars matter-of-factly. That's a pretty simple way to describe a pretty big transformation.

FIRST, SAY WHAT'S ON YOUR MIND

Before he began shaking things up at Yellow, Bill Zollars decided that he had to explain himself and his ideas to the staff. He also decided that he had to do it quickly, frequently, and in person. But there was a problem: Only a fraction of the 25,000 employees at the time worked at the company headquarters in Overland Park, Kansas, outside of Kansas City. Most worked at terminals that were located in several hundred cities. So in early 1997, after a few months on the job, Zollars hit the road. For the next year and a half, he regularly visited terminals around the country, where he conducted a series of town-hall meetings. There were no fancy slides or videos. Just Zollars, an affable former college-football player from Minnesota, standing on a loading dock or in a sales office, talking to the people responsible for carrying out his plans. "There were days when I gave the same speech 10 times at 10 different locations," he says. "I'd start at 6:30 AM with the drivers, then I'd talk to the dock workers, the people in the office, and the sales staff. At night, I'd meet with customers. I wanted as many employees and customers as possible to hear it from me face-to-face."

Zollars didn't meet every employee, but he did reach thousands. His presence made a strong impression. "People thought, 'He's the president of the company, but here he is talking to us,'" says Mike Brown, vice president of strategic market planning and marketing communications. "It's something this company hadn't experienced before. It was a breath of fresh air." The goal went beyond putting a face on the new leadership. Zollars, who returned to many terminals more than once, wanted people to know that his vision for a new Yellow wasn't just this year's fad—it was a long-term shift. "Repetition is important, especially when you're trying to change the way a company thinks about itself," he says. "You're trying to create new behaviors."

Again and again, he reminded employees of the company's new focus: customers. He knew that this represented a different way of thinking about the business. Early on, during a visit to one of two customer call centers, Zollars listened to calls to get a flavor of the process. Although he was impressed with the instant transfer of information to the terminals, he noticed a problem: When customers contacted Yellow, its representatives didn't ask them when they wanted their freight. Instead, the reps told customers when Yellow could deliver it. The schedule was convenient for Yellow but not necessarily for its customers. "I remember one caller who said, 'I'd like to get this stuff from Chicago to Atlanta in two days,'" says Zollars, "and we said, 'We can get it there in three days.' The customer thanked us and hung up. We didn't think there was anything wrong with that. The attitude was, If you don't like what we do, too bad."

For a long time, he says, Yellow adhered to an "operational obsession." Employees monitored how much freight moved through the network daily, how full the trailers were, and other internal metrics. Yellow was a model of efficiency. But it had no idea whether its customers were satisfied. At the town-hall meetings, Zollars would ask employees to guess the defect rate: how often shipments were picked up or delivered late, billed wrong, or damaged. Usually, they'd say it was 10% or 20%. Try 40%, he'd tell them. "I'd never seen a defect rate in any industry that bad," he says. "The response was classic denial. People thought, 'We're as good as anyone else in the industry.'"

In many ways, when Zollars arrived, Yellow still behaved as though deregulation hadn't occurred in 1980—as though everybody's rates and service were the same. Meanwhile, the competition was reducing its long-haul transit times, and smaller, more nimble outfits were grabbing up regional shipments. "We were a defensive company—a follower, not a leader," says James Welch, who became president and COO of Yellow Freight in 2000 after Zollars replaced Myers at Yellow Corp. "We were yearning for leadership. This company was ready to change."

NEXT, LISTEN TO WHAT CUSTOMERS WANT

If Yellow was going to satisfy its more than 300,000 customers as never before, it needed to hear from them. That was Mike Brown's job. In late 1997, with the help of an outside firm, Yellow surveyed 10,000 randomly selected customers. Since then, the company has been surveying 600 different customers a month. Those 15-minute conversations are vital. "It used to be that one anecdote or the opinion of one customer would carry the day," says Brown. "Now we have the opinions of tens of thousands of consumers."

For a company that relied on internal criteria, letting people from outside the company—its customers—evaluate performance wasn't easy. Especially when Yellow learned that its assumptions about customers were wrong. "We'd had the attitude that speed and price were the most important things," says Greg Reid, senior vice president and chief communications officer. "But according to our research, what matters most is that you pick up when you say you're going to, deliver when you say you're going to, and don't damage the freight."

The customers made a compelling case for dramatically improving reliability: Those who said that they would use Yellow again and recommend it to others had gotten good service. Those who hadn't were less loyal. It was a fairly obvious lesson for a traditional service provider, says Reid, but it was a critical one for a company that was trying to become customer-centric. "What happens when consumers anywhere get bad service? They don't go back," says Reid. "Why should we expect our business to be any different?"

Nothing epitomizes the company's new commitment to customers better than Yellow's Exact Express. Launched in 1998, it represents a breakthrough for Yellow: its first expedited, time-definite, guaranteed service. Everyone involved, from the customer rep to the driver, is committed to doing what it takes to satisfy the customers' needs—even if that means using an outside air-cargo partner to meet a deadline. So far, says Valerie Bonebrake, senior vice president of new services, which includes Exact Express, the deliveries have arrived when they were supposed to 98% of the time.

Exact Express is Yellow's most expensive and most profitable service. It's also growing at the fastest clip, with double-digit increases every year. Because of the service's guaranteed on-time delivery and its speed, Yellow is moving the sort of "hot" freight that it didn't get before: an overnight shipment of 40,000 flashlights from Los Angeles to Washington, DC for an outdoor event that took place during the 2001 presidential inauguration; marketing material that related to an acquisition, which had to reach 349 banks on the same Monday morning; 10,000 pounds of air freshener that was rushed to ground zero of the World Trade Center attack. Although customers call on Exact Express in emergencies, says Bonebrake, the goal is for them to make it a routine part of their just-in-time supply chain. Yellow no longer measures itself against the competition alone, says Zollars. It strives to be as fastidious about service as Nordstrom, Starbucks, and FedEx.

Exact Express is helping Yellow win back customers such as Timothy Slofkin, the traffic and purchasing manager for Interprint, a printing company in Clearwater, Florida. About six years ago, he stopped using Yellow because its shipping schedule was simply too inflexible, too limited. "Yellow was never willing to work with me," he says. A few years later, one of Yellow's sales reps told Slofkin about the company's online-ordering-and-tracking capability. Slofkin was skeptical, and since he didn't have a computer, he didn't have much use for the Web. But Yellow persisted, persuading Interprint to equip its shipping department with a computer and then training Slofkin on how to use MyYellow.com. Now he's one of 51,000 users registered on the site, and he's hooked. He routinely places orders online, tracks his shipments while they're en route, and reviews past shipments.

AND DON'T FORGET ABOUT THE POWER OF TECHNOLOGY

One of the main reasons that Yellow has been able to expand and improve service is its state-of-the-art technology. Since 1994, the company has spent about $80 million a year on its highly integrated information systems. The investment has led to significant changes in virtually every stage of the business. It has affected how orders get processed and relayed from the call centers to the terminals, how the dispatchers assign drivers for pickups and deliveries, and how the dock workers load and unload trailers.

Yellow's early years were rather low-tech by comparison. In the 1920s, the Harrell brothers, A.J. and Cleve, who once hauled freight by horse- and mule-drawn wagons, operated a small but growing fleet of yellow Model T taxicabs (according to company lore, the original yellow cab) and buses in Oklahoma City. In 1924, the Harrells incorporated the Yellow Cab Transit Co. Two years later, they acquired a couple of trucks to handle the freight that they had been hauling on their buses, mainly oil-rig parts bound for Tulsa. Back then, there was no way to track shipments or to guarantee that freight would arrive at a certain time. It got there when it got there. How long it took often depended on the condition of the two-lane highway that day.

Nowadays, even though Yellow essentially does the same thing that it did then, the operation is considerably more involved. What was a small regional company for many years has become a global enterprise with more than 14 million shipments a year, 377 terminals across the country, and partners around the world. And yet the technical demands are often overlooked. When Lynn Caddell left America West Airlines to become president of Yellow Technologies, a Yellow Corp. subsidiary with 350 employees, a colleague remarked on how boring trucking seemed compared with the airline industry. Caddell didn't see it that way. "We're moving a product from one place to another, but there's a lot more complexity to it," she says. "Each of my 'passengers' is a different size and weight and needs a different amount of space. And they don't simply go from airport to airport. They go to hundreds of zip codes and addresses. Many of them need to arrive at their final destination at a specific time. Coordinating all of that is a huge challenge."

When customers call 1-800-MY-YELLOW, the system automatically opens a customer profile that corresponds to the caller's number. The representative instantly knows where the customer's company is located; what type of loading dock it has; the size, weight, and contents of previous shipments; previous shipping destinations; and who has signed for deliveries. If a customer calls back at a later point with the identical shipping order, say, several thousand pounds of freight from Memphis to Seattle, the process takes about 15 seconds. In other words, less time than it takes to order a pizza.

Each dock worker is equipped with a wireless mobile data terminal, or MDT, designed to speed up the loading and unloading process. Before a tractor trailer arrives, the worker can see what's on board, as well as which doors on the dock correspond to those destinations. If he is taking longer to unload the pallets than the system estimates that it should take given the amount of freight, an alert is sent to his MDT. The dock supervisor also has access to the incoming and outgoing freight at his computer station. If he notices that a truck is running behind, he can dispatch a second employee and a forklift to speed things along. The old system was inflexible: one employee per trailer.

The technology enables Yellow to give the employees who are closest to the customers the information they need to solve problems quickly. And the leadership style allows those employees to make decisions themselves, rather than wait for a supervisor's response. That's how Yellow's facility in Chicago is able to operate as effectively as it does, says Bob Zimmerman, its director of operations. With 367 doors and two terminals that are a quarter-mile apart, it's the largest distribution center in the network. The staff fills 500 trailers a day, loading and unloading thousands of shipments. Many trucks are in and out in half the time that it used to take. "We call it the 'zoom process,'" says Zimmerman.

A sense of urgency has replaced the long-haul mentality. Yellow used to hold a trailer on the platform for hours, he says, eager to fill every inch of available space, even if it meant that the truck fell far behind schedule. These days, in order to meet the shorter transit times, the terminals have regularly scheduled departures, just like the airlines. But the trailers aren't leaving the terminals half full, says Zimmerman, because about 90% of Yellow's freight is predictable.

Yellow's Regional Advantage represents another crack at the lucrative regional market for the company. The deliveries are shorter, including two-day shipments within 550 and 1,100 miles. And the demand is growing, unlike that for long-haul deliveries, which have been on the decline. The difference for Yellow this time is the technology, says Zimmerman. Dispatchers and dock workers can identify regional shipments in the system and keep them on schedule. About 70% of Yellow's shipments take three days or less, a significant decrease compared to several years ago. But the trucks aren't traveling any faster. The engines are equipped with governors that limit the top speed to 62 MPH. The fleet runs faster because Yellow is managing its network smarter: fewer stops, fewer freight transfers, and fewer damaged shipments. "Every time the freight is handled," says Zimmerman, "it's slowing down, and the risk of damaging it increases."

The central dispatch office in Overland Park serves as Yellow's air-traffic control tower. Dispatchers have what John Braklow, senior manager for service improvement, calls "a 40,000-foot view" of the day's shipping activity on a map of the United States. They identify service failures in the making and work with the terminals to devise solutions. The system, which updates every 10 minutes, allows the dispatchers to see each shipment in the system, color-coded according to whether it's on schedule, or each driver in the system, color-coded according to his availability. The red shipments are the ones that are in danger of arriving late. "One of the guys calls it the 'Visine system,'" says Braklow, "because you're supposed to get the red out."

THE ROAD AHEAD

These are tough times for the ground-freight industry. As James Welch, the current head of Yellow Freight, says, "We truck the economy." So when the economy hit the brakes and manufacturing came to a stop in 2001, there was less freight for Yellow to move. The company's stock price dropped, it missed its earnings estimates, and it had two rounds of layoffs that totaled 591 nonunion employees. About 800 drivers were issued furloughs as well. Immediately after the September 11 terrorist attacks, there was speculation that ground-freight carriers might see more business as companies avoided using air cargo. But it didn't happen.

Despite the setbacks, Zollars remains upbeat about the road ahead for several reasons. First, Yellow's defect rate is down from 40% to 5%, and its on-time performance (excluding weather delays) is in the high nineties. The number of customers surveyed who said that they would recommend Yellow has doubled since 1997. And in an industry that is notorious for slim margins, the company continues to create promising sources of revenue, including Transportation.com, a logistics service for small- and medium-sized businesses. Zollars predicts that, like the airline and telecommunications industries after deregulation, a handful of big ground-freight companies will ultimately survive. One of them will be Yellow. "We were a one-trick pony before, and now we're able to provide a full suite of transportation services," he says. "This is the time to be even more aggressive. We should be grabbing more market share and thinking strategically."

Yellow, which used to advertise primarily in trade journals, is going to great lengths these days to make its brand more visible. The company has produced its first-ever television ads; the "Yes we can" spot features Ray Simon, a truck driver in St. Cloud, Minnesota, who won the 2001 National Truck Driving Championships, making him the event's only three-time champion. Yellow also sponsors a racing team in NASCAR's Busch Series. Beyond network exposure that Reid estimates is worth about $5 million in equivalent advertising, Team Yellow Racing has proven popular with customers and employees alike. For a ground transportation company with about 20,000 union members, says Reid, "This is a big deal."

Apparently, so is wearing orange. Employees don't just wear shirts featuring the Yellow logo to the office or the terminal. Some of them wear more orange than the students at Syracuse University and Clemson University combined. (Why, you ask, does a company named "Yellow" choose orange as its official color? When A.J. Harrell asked DuPont for the color that would be most visible—and presumably safest—on the road, Harrell was given "swamp-holly orange.") Without a doubt, vice president Mike Brown is the Cal Ripken Jr. of Yellow fashion. Brown has worn orange socks to work nearly every day—"99% of the time," he says—since October 22, 1997. That was the day that he and Reid, another orange-sock devotee, made a presentation on the company's new customer-centric brand to senior management at Arrowhead Stadium. The highlight was a video called *How to Kill a Business,* which featured movie clips that showed the worst service imaginable. That was the old Yellow.

After going through a serious metamorphosis, the new Yellow began hosting an annual conference in Las Vegas called "Transformation." Each year, 1,000 employees and 500 customers attend workshops on change. The underlying message is that the changes at Yellow are far from over. "Now that people have gotten used to how we do things, I'll tell them, 'Well, it'll be different five years from now,'" says Zollars. "And some of them will say, 'I thought we were done.' But I don't think that you're ever done. You have to keep reinventing the company, because the market keeps changing. If you don't, you end up coasting."

Chuck Salter (csalter@fastcompany.com) is a *Fast Company* senior writer. Learn more about Yellow on the Web (http://www.yellowcorp.com).

ROADMAP FOR REINVENTION

Yellow has become a different company since 1996. It is driven by CEO Bill Zollars and a frontline revolution that emphasizes the customer. The following principles are its road map for reinvention.

Share the new vision every day. Early on, Zollars spent 18 months visiting employees and explaining why and how Yellow had to focus on its customers. Zollars believed that because this was a new way of thinking, employees needed to hear it more than once. They also needed to hear it directly from him so that they could gauge his conviction. "If the people doing the work don't believe what's coming from the leadership," he says, "it doesn't get implemented. Period."

Avoid behavior that undermines the mission. When a new leader joins an organization, actions tend to get magnified, for better or for worse. "For every negative thing you demonstrate to people, it takes 50 positive things to overcome it," Zollars says.

Get out of the office. During his first year at Yellow, Zollars spent most of his time in the field. "It's the only place where you find out what's really going on with customers and operations without any filters," he says. "At headquarters, you don't hear any of the bad stuff."

Don't be afraid to tell the truth. Zollars uses an employee newsletter, *YFS Week,* to give the staff an honest assessment of its performance and the industry on a regular basis. "We don't just talk about victories. We talk about losing business, about claims problems. We want to give a clear picture of where we were."

THE LEADER AS LEARNER (ESPECIALLY FROM FAILURE)

This section brings to light the reality that leadership involves risk. As leaders seek to be transformational in their organizations, there is a real risk for failure. The challenge thus becomes learning to grow and develop from experience, even when that experience involves failure. The first piece showcases Peter Senge's decade of work on the leader's role in creating a real learning organization. It is followed by an interview with Judy Rosenblum, who offers a ten-point curriculum for effective learning. The remaining two pieces are profiles of leaders who learn not only in real time, but also from their own failures.

Learning for a Change

TEN YEARS AGO, PETER SENGE INTRODUCED THE IDEA OF THE "LEARNING ORGANIZATION." NOW HE SAYS THAT FOR BIG COMPANIES TO CHANGE, WE NEED TO STOP THINKING LIKE MECHANICS AND TO START ACTING LIKE GARDENERS.

It's been almost 10 years since Peter Senge, 51, published "The Fifth Discipline: The Art & Practice of the Learning Organization" (Doubleday/Currency, 1990). The book was more than a business best-seller; it was a breakthrough. It propelled Senge into the front ranks of management thinkers, it created a language of change that people in all kinds of companies could embrace, and it offered a vision of workplaces that were humane and of companies that were built around learning. Along the way, the book sold more than 650,000 copies, spawned a sequel—"The Discipline Fieldbook: Strategies and Tools for Building a Learning Organization" (Doubleday/Currency, 1994)—and gave birth to a worldwide movement.

But that movement hit a few speed bumps. People who adopted the themes and practices of "The Fifth Discipline" sometimes found themselves frustrated by the challenge of bringing about effective change—and sometimes found themselves out of work for trying. Now Senge and his colleagues have published "The Dance of Change: The Challenges to Sustaining Momentum in Learning Organizations" (Doubleday/Currency, March 1999). According to Senge, who is a senior lecturer at the Massachusetts Institute of Technology and a member of the Society for Organizational Learning (SoL)—a global consortium of companies and researchers who are examining learning and change—the new book presents "what we've learned about learning." The book begins with two key lessons: First, initiating and sustaining change is more daunting than the optimistic presentation that was offered in "The Fifth Discipline" had suggested. And second, the task of making change happen requires businesspeople to change the way they think about organizations: "We need to think less like managers and more like biologists," Senge argues.

To learn more about the evolving landscape of organizational learning, Fast Company interviewed Peter Senge in his office on the campus of MIT, in Cambridge, Massachusetts.

What's your assessment of the performance of large-scale change efforts over the past decade?

Most leadership strategies are doomed to failure from the outset. As people have been noting for years, the majority of strategic initiatives that are driven from the top are marginally effective—at best. Corporate reorganizations are even more common than new strategies, but how many reorganizations actually produce companies that are dramatically more effective than they were before? Throw in mergers and acquisitions: Look at all of those that have failed. The traditional model of change—change that is led from the top—has a less-than-impressive track record.

And that's just the public track record. My own experience at MIT and at SoL has mostly been with big companies. How much change have they actually accomplished? If I stand back a considerable distance and ask, "What's the score?" I have to conclude that inertia is winning by a large margin. Of course, there have been enough exceptions to that conclusion to indicate that change is possible. I can identify 20 to 30 examples of significant sustained change efforts in the SoL community. On the other side of the ledger, there are many organizations that haven't gotten to first base when it comes to real change, and many others that have given up trying.

When I look at efforts to create change in big companies over the past 10 years, I have to say that there's enough evidence of success to say that change is possible—and enough evidence of failure to say that it isn't likely. Both of those lessons are important.

Why haven't there been more successful change efforts?

If it were simply a matter of more resources, people would have figured out how to get more resources. If it were a matter of more time, more money, more consultants, or just more effort, we probably would have been able to fill those needs by now. Or if the problem were intelligence—and you could simply assert that most bosses are pretty dumb, or that most CEOs are just not very bright—then presumably the intelligent ones would succeed, their companies would rise to the top, and that would solve the problem. The marketplace would reward the bright ones who could change, and it would punish the dumb ones who couldn't.

But it doesn't seem as if any of those things are happening—which suggests that it's not a matter of resources or intelligence. In fact, I can tell you from firsthand experience that a lot of very competent executives fail at producing and sustaining momentum around change. That suggests to me that something more universal is at work here.

So what is the deeper explanation for the failure of corporate change efforts?

At the deepest level, I think that we're witnessing the shift from one age to another. The most universal challenge that we face is the transition from seeing our human institutions as machines to seeing them as embodiments of nature. I've been thinking about this shift for 25 years or more: We need to realize that we're a part of nature, rather than separate from nature.

Think about any environmental problem that we face, from global climate and resource issues to population crises. Or look at the problems that seem to afflict people in organizations: Why are contemporary institutions so inhumane? And somewhere in the middle, between environmental issues and personal issues, there are institutional issues: Why do we view our organizations as rigid hierarchies rather than as communities of practice?

Whether you're talking at the macro, the personal, or the institutional level, the questions all point in the same direction: The real character of an age is evident in how it conditions us to think, and how it conditions us to think determines how it conditions us to act. The thinking and acting of the past 200 years—nurtured in Europe, accelerated in the United States, diffused throughout the world today—is a machine mind-set. That mind-set directly affects how we see organizations—and, therefore, how we think about creating change in those organizations.

What implications does a machine mind-set have for companies that seek to undergo change?

In the Machine Age, the company itself became a machine—a machine for making money. That's a key point in Arie de Geus's book, "The Living Company" (Harvard Business School Press, 1997). Ironically, the word "company" couldn't be more at odds with the idea of a machine. "Company" has roots that go back long before the Industrial Age. In fact, it has the same root as the word "companion": It means "the sharing of bread."

Somehow, during the course of the Industrial Revolution, this very humane sense of "company" changed, and the company became more and more machinelike. For the most part, seeing the company as a machine has worked. There are people who design this machine: They put it together and get it up and working. They are founders. There are people who operate or control the machine: We call them managers. The machine also has owners, and when it operates correctly, it produces income for those owners. It's all about control: A good machine is one that its operators can control—in the service of its owners' objectives.

The company-as-a-machine model fits how people think about and operate conventional companies. And, of course, it fits how people think about changing conventional companies: You have a broken company, and you need to change it, to fix it. You hire a mechanic, who trades out old parts that are broken and brings in new parts that are going to fix the machine. That's why we need "change agents" and leaders who can "drive change."

But go back and consider all of the evidence that says that most change efforts aren't very successful. Here is our first plausible explanation: Companies are actually living organisms, not machines. That might explain why it's so difficult for us to succeed in our efforts to produce change. Perhaps treating companies like machines keeps them from changing, or makes changing them much more difficult. We keep bringing in mechanics—when what we need are gardeners. We keep trying to drive change—when what we need to do is cultivate change. Surprisingly, this mechanical mind-set can afflict those who seek "humane" changes through "learning organizations" just as much as it can afflict those who drive more traditional changes, such as mergers and reorganizations.

Where, specifically, does the mechanical approach go wrong in effecting change?

The easiest way to see this is to look at our interpersonal relationships. In our ordinary experiences with other people, we know that approaching each other in a machinelike way gets us into trouble. We know that the process of changing a relationship is a lot more complicated than the process of changing a flat tire on your car. It requires a willingness to change. It requires a sense of openness, a sense of reciprocity, even a kind of vulnerability. You must be willing to be influenced by another person. You don't have to be willing to be influenced by your damn car! A relationship with a machine is fundamentally a different kind of relationship: It is perfectly appropriate to feel that if it doesn't work, you should fix it. But we get into real trouble whenever we try to "fix" people.

We know how to create and nurture close friendships or family relationships. But when we enter the realm of the organization, we're not sure which domain to invoke. Should we evoke the domain of the machine? After all, much of our daily life is about interacting with computers, tape recorders, automobiles, and ATMs. Or should we evoke the domain of living systems—because a lot of our daily life is about interacting with family, friends, and colleagues?

There are those who come down firmly on the people side: They tend to be HR professionals and line managers—people who understand that relationships, teamwork, and trust are essential to effective operations. But high-level executives are frequently separated from the day-to-day stuff of the enterprise: They look at the organization from the perspective of numbers, financial statements, and prospective deals. Their number-one variable is the company stock price. That outlook distances them substantially from the living, human aspects of the enterprise. You end up with organizational schizophrenia. Some people operate the company as if it were a machine, and some treat it as part of the messy, living world.

What happens when you see a company as a part of nature?

It shifts profoundly how you think about leadership and change. If you use a machine lens, you get leaders who are trying to drive change through formal change programs. If you use a living-systems lens, you get leaders who approach change as if they were growing something, rather than just "changing" something. Even on a large scale, nature doesn't change things mechanically: You don't just pull out the old and replace it with the new. Something new grows, and it eventually supplants the old.

You see the same thing at the level of behaviors: If new behaviors are more effective than old behaviors, then the new behaviors win out. That insight gives us a doorway into a different way to think about how enterprises might change: What if we thought of organizational change as the interplay among the various forces that are involved in growing something new?

Looking at nature, we see that nothing that grows starts large; it always starts small. No one is "in charge," making the growth occur. Instead, growth occurs as a result of the interplay of diverse forces. And these forces fall into two broad categories: self-reinforcing processes, which generate growth, and limiting processes, which can impede growth or stop it altogether. The pattern of growth that occurs unfolds from the interplay of these two types of forces.

Looking at organizations, we find that one of the first things that changes is how we define the term "structure." "The Fifth Discipline" proposed a definition borrowed from system dynamics—which looks at structure in terms of feedback interactions within a system. Our new definition of that term is "a pattern of interdependency that we enact."

Again, think about the relationships within a family, rather than those within a company: People come to relate to each other in predictable ways, which form a pattern that then defines the structure of relationships—norms, expectations, taken-for-granted habits of communicating. Those patterns aren't fixed; they can change. And, more to the point, those patterns aren't given. Ultimately, the structures that come into play in our families are the result of the choices that we've made all along the way. We "enact" our families.

All of this applies directly to our ideas about leadership and, in particular, to the cult of the CEO-as-hero. In fact, that cult is one pattern that makes it easier for us to maintain change-averse institutions. When we enact the pattern of the CEO as hero, we infantalize the organization: That kind of behavior keeps everyone else in the company at a stage of development in which they can't accept their own possibilities for creating change. Moreover, it keeps executives from doing things that would genuinely contribute to creating significant change. The cult of the hero-leader only creates a need for more hero-leaders.

How does challenging the idea of the hero-leader promote change?

Deep change comes only through real personal growth—through learning and unlearning. This is the kind of generative work that most executives are precluded from doing by the mechanical mind-set and by the cult of the hero-leader: The hero-leader is the one with "the answers." Most of the other people in the organization can't make deep changes, because they're operating out of compliance, rather than out of commitment. Commitment comes about only when people determine that you are asking them to do something that they really care about. For that reason, if you create compliance-oriented change, you'll get change—but you'll preclude the deeper processes that lead to commitment, and you'll prevent the emergence of self-generated change.

Again, you end up creating a kind of addiction: People change as long as they're being commanded to change—or as long as they can be forced to change. But, as a result, they become still more dependent on change that's driven from the top.

If the idea of the hero-leader takes us in the wrong direction, what's the right direction?

The first problem with all of the stuff that's out there about leadership is that we haven't got a clue about what we're talking about. We use the word "leader" to mean "executive": The leader is the person at the top. That definition says that leadership is synonymous with a position. And if leadership is synonymous with a position, then it doesn't matter what a leader does. All that matters is where the leader sits. If you define a "leader" as an "executive," then you absolutely deny everyone else in an organization the opportunity to be a leader.

But when we studied leaders inside the companies that are involved in the SoL consortium, that's not what we saw. We had several companies that were able to sustain significant momentum over many years, and there were no executives involved at all. In case after case, the most compelling lesson we learned was that if you want real, significant, sustainable change, you need talented, committed local line leaders. Find the people who are at the heart of the value-generating process—who design, produce, and sell products; who provide services; who talk to customers. Those value-generating activities are the province of the line manager, and if the line manager is not innovating, then innovation is not going to occur.

The next thing we noticed was that, in some organizations, the first round of change activities somehow led to second-order efforts. The original group would spawn a second group, and gradually new practices would spread throughout the organization. How did that happen? We identified people who were "seed carriers." They were internal networkers who knew how to get people talking to one another and how to build informal communities. In effect, they were creating communities of practice. These networkers represent a second type of leadership. Of course, we also found executives who were providing leadership by doing activities that were more mature and more profound than simply offering themselves as heroes. These were executives who focus on acting as a coach or as a mentor.

Out of these observations, we developed our own definition of "leadership." To me, the simplest definition of that word is "the ability to produce change": "We used to operate that way; now we operate this way." Then, using what we saw inside companies, we identified three leadership communities: local line leaders, internal networkers or community builders, and executive leaders. For significant change to take place, you need to create an interplay among those three communities. One community can't be substituted for another. Each community represents part of a necessary set.

What's the best way to begin creating change?

I have never seen a successful organizational-learning program rolled out from the top. Not a single one. Conversely, every change process that I've seen that was sustained and that spread has started small. Usually these programs start with just one team. That team can be any team, including an executive team. At Shell, the critical generative work was done in a top team. Then, in a matter of a year or so, it spread to the top 150 managers, who percolated ideas among themselves—and they, in turn, formed new clusters of teams. At Ford, two teams started working almost in parallel. In case after case, the change effort begins small, and as it takes hold, networks form that carry change into wider groups.

Just as nothing in nature starts big, so the way to start creating change is with a pilot group—a growth seed. As you think about a pilot group, there are certain choices that you have to make in order to make the group work. The first choice goes back to the issue of compliance versus commitment: Will the change effort be driven by authority or by learning? To make that decision is to choose a central path. Then there are reinforcing elements: new guiding ideas; innovations in the infrastructure; theories, methods, and tools.

After a pilot group forms, what are the next steps?

Thinking about nature as the model again leads you to ask, "What are the self-reinforcing processes whereby the seed begins to realize its potential to grow? And what are the limiting processes that come into play as the seed interacts with the soil?"

There are a number of self-reinforcing factors that help a pilot program to take root. People develop a personal stake in it. People see that their colleagues take it seriously, and they want to be part of a network of committed people. There's also a pragmatic factor: It works. There are real business results—so it's worthwhile to become engaged. But the most fundamental reinforcer of a pilot program is hearing people say that they've found a better way of working. Most people would rather work with a group of people who trust one another. Most people would rather walk out of a meeting with the belief that they've just solved an important problem. Most people would rather have fun at work. It may be obvious, but what we've observed again and again is that personal enthusiasm is the initial energizer of any change process. And that enthusiasm feeds on itself. People don't necessarily want to "have a vision" at work or to "conduct dialogue." They want to be part of a team that's fun to work with and that produces results they are proud of.

But even if the pilot has potential to grow, there is no guarantee that growth will occur. All pilot groups encounter "challenges to initiating"—initial limiting processes that can keep growth from ever really starting. For example, it doesn't matter how promising a team is if its members don't have time to commit to the change effort, if they can't reorganize their schedules to accommodate weekly meetings, if they don't have time during which they can get together to reflect. Learning takes time. Invariably, you will get that time back—and then some—because most teams today waste lots of time, and therefore better learning capabilities will make them much more productive than they were before. But first you have to be able to make an investment of time.

Another example of an important potential limiting factor: A change effort has to have some relevance to people. It has to have some connection to them. It has to matter. Why should an engineer need to learn how to conduct a dialogue? Why should she care about that skill? The answer may be that the organization trips over certain technical issues that aren't really technical issues; rather, they're problems with internal conversations that lead to fights instead of creative resolutions. The point isn't to learn how to conduct a dialogue. The point is to invest some time and to get some help to change how people work together.

In your new book, you identify the 10 challenges of change. Why focus on challenges?

The short answer: to produce effective leadership. In a natural system, the way to sustain growth is by paying attention to the interplay between reinforcing processes and limiting processes—and by paying special attention to the limiting processes. The limiting processes represent 90% to 98% of the real leverage in sustaining deep change. These 10 challenges are the limiting processes that we've seen again and again. They include processes that operate from the outset of a pilot—such as time and relevance—and they include processes that come into play once a pilot begins to succeed. After an initial success, things tend to get harder, not easier. So, if we want to have effective leadership, if we want to have humane communities that can sustain significant change, we need to learn how to focus on these types of challenges

Are these the only 10 challenges? This is just the first cut; undoubtedly there are others. But if the discourse about change starts to focus on challenges and on strategies for dealing with those challenges, we may be able to build a body of knowledge that will allow for effective leadership and sustainable change.

Back to the first question: A decade after "The Fifth Discipline" appeared, do you think that big companies can change?

Ultimately, organizational learning is about growing something new. Where does new growth take place? Often it happens in the midst of the old. Indeed, often the new grows out of the old. How will the old react? The only realistic expectation is that the traditional system of management, as [W. Edwards] Deming used to label it, will work harder and harder to maintain itself. But growing something new doesn't have to be a battle against the old. It doesn't need to be a fight between believers and nonbelievers. In any case, our Industrial Age management, our Industrial Age organization, and our Industrial Age way of living will not continue. The Industrial Age is not sustainable. It's not sustainable in ecological terms, and it's not sustainable in human terms.

It will change. The only question is how. Once we get out of our machine mind-set, we may discover new aptitudes for growth and change. Until then, change won't come easily.

Alan M. Webber (awebber@fastcompany.com) is a founding editor of *Fast Company*. You can visit Peter Senge on the Web (http://www.sol-ne.org). Time line compiled by Art Kleiner (art@well.com).

CHRONOLOGY OF LEARNING ORGANIZATION CONCEPTS

1938: In his book "Experience and Education," John Dewey publicizes the concept of experiential learning as an ongoing cycle of activity.

1940s: The Macy Conferences—featuring Margaret Mead, Gregory Bateson, and Lawrence Kubie—bring "systems thinking" to the awareness of a cross-disciplinary group of intellectuals.

1940s: Scottish psychologist Kenneth Craik coins the term "mental models," which later makes its way to MIT through Marvin Minsky and Seymour Papert.

1946: Kurt Lewin, founding theorist of National Training Laboratories, proposes idea of a "creative tension" between personal vision and a sense of reality.

1956: Edgar Schein's research on brainwashing in Korea paves the way for an understanding of "process consultation."

1960: "The Human Side of Enterprise," by Douglas McGregor, is published.

1961: Jay Forrester publishes "Industrial Dynamics." This book, the first major application of system dynamics to corporations, describes the turbulence within a typical appliance value chain.

1970: Chris Argyris and Donald Schon begin work on "action science," the study of how espoused values clash with the values that underlie real actions.

1972: "The Limits to Growth: A Report for the Club of Rome's Project on the Predicament of Mankind," by Donella Meadows and Dennis Meadows, is published. The book draws on Forrester's theories about system dynamics.

1971 to 1979: Erhard Seminars Training (EST) demonstrate the kind of powerful attitude shifts that can occur during a seminar that lasts several days.

1979: Consultant Charlie Kiefer, Forrester student Peter Senge, and researcher-artist Robert Fritz design the "Leadership and Mastery" seminar, which becomes the focal point of their new consulting firm, Innovation Associates.

1984 to 1985: Pierre Wack, scenario planner at Royal Dutch/Shell, spends a sabbatical at Harvard Business School and writes two articles about scenario planning as a learning activity.

1982: Senge, Arie de Geus, Hanover Insurance CEO Bill O'Brien, Analog Devices CEO Ray Stata, and other executive leaders form a learning-organization study group, which meets regularly at MIT.

1987: Peter Schwartz, Stewart Brand, Napier Collyns, Jay Ogilvy, and Lawrence Wilkinson form the Global Business Network, with a charter to foster organizational learning through scenario planning.

1989: Oxford University management scholar Bill Isaacs, an associate of quantum physicist David Bohm, introduces Senge to the concept of dialogue as a process for building team capability.

1989: "The Age of Unreason," by Charles Handy, is published.

(continued)

CHRONOLOGY (*CONTINUED*)

1989: The Center for Organizational Learning is formed at MIT, with Senge as director and with Ed Schein, Chris Argyris, Arie de Geus, Ray Stata, and Bill O'Brien as key advisers. The staff of the "learning center," as it's called, includes Bill Isaacs, Daniel Kim (whose research involves linking the learning organization work to the quality movement), and research director George Roth.

1990: "The Fifth Discipline" is published. The book draws on many influences: system dynamics, "personal mastery" (based on Fritz's work and the concept of creative tension), mental models (based on Wack's and Argyris's work), shared vision (based on work done at Innovation Associates), and team learning (based on David Bohm's concepts).

1990: Daniel Kim founds the "Systems Thinker," a newsletter devoted to "fifth discipline" issues. The following year, the newsletter's parent organization, Pegasus Communications, launches an annual conference series called Systems Thinking in Action.

1993: Harvard University professor David Garvin publishes an article on organizational learning in the Harvard Business Review, arguing that only learning that can be measured will be useful to managers.

1994: "The Fifth Discipline Fieldbook" is published. Authors of the book, which Senge edited, include Charlotte Roberts, Rick Ross, and Bryan Smith (president of Innovation Associates of Canada), and Art Kleiner (who serves as editorial director). The "Fieldbook" becomes a new management-book genre.

1994: The use of "learning histories" as a method of assessment begins at the Center for Organizational Learning.

1994: The first major Organizational Learning Center projects reach completion. Many of them have produced remarkable results. But a few have resulted in disappointing career prospects for some of the line leaders who were involved in them.

1995: Working with Dee Hock, the Organizational Learning Center begins a two-year process of building an ambitious international consortium called the Society for Organizational Learning, with Peter Senge as chairman.

1996: "The Age of Heretics," by Art Kleiner, and Synchronicity: "The Inner Path of Leadership," by Joseph Jaworski, are published.

1997: "The Living Company," by Arie de Geus, is published.

1999: "The Dance of Change" is published.

THE TEN CHALLENGES OF CHANGE

In "The Dance of Change: The Challenges to Sustaining Momentum in Learning Organizations," Peter Senge and his colleagues identify 10 challenges of change. Grouped into three categories—challenges of initiating change, challenges of sustaining momentum, and challenges of systemwide redesign and rethinking—these 10 items amount to what the authors call "the conditions of the environment that regulate growth."

Challenges of Initiating Change

"We don't have time for this stuff!" People who are involved in a pilot group to initiate a change effort need enough control over their schedules to give their work the time that it needs.

"We have no help!" Members of a pilot group need enough support, coaching, and resources to be able to learn and to do their work effectively.

"This stuff isn't relevant." There need to be people who can make the case for change—who can connect the development of new skills to the real work of the business.

"They're not walking the talk!" A critical test for any change effort: the correlation between espoused values and actual behavior.

Challenges of Sustaining Momentum

"This stuff is ..." Personal fear and anxiety—concerns about vulnerability and inadequacy—lead members of a pilot group to question a change effort.

"This stuff isn't working!" Change efforts run into measurement problems: Early results don't meet expectations, or traditional metrics don't calibrate to a pilot group's efforts.

"They're acting like a cult!" A pilot group falls prey to arrogance, dividing the company into "believers" and "nonbelievers."

Challenges of Systemwide Redesign and Rethinking

"They ... never let us do this stuff." The pilot group wants more autonomy; "the powers that be" don't want to lose control.

"We keep reinventing the wheel." Instead of building on previous successes, each group finds that it has to start from scratch.

"Where are we going?" The larger strategy and purpose of a change effort may be obscured by day-to-day activity. Big question: Can the organization achieve a new definition of success?

Will Companies Ever Learn?

JUDY ROSENBLUM HAS DEALT WITH ALL OF THE OBSTACLES THAT KEEP COMPANIES FROM GETTING SMARTER. HERE IS HER 10-POINT CURRICULUM FOR GETTING SMART ABOUT LEARNING.

"Introducing learning into a large, diverse, global organization is a struggle," says Judy Rosenblum. "But when you look at customers and how they're changing, at the competitive environment and how it's changing, it's clear that learning is critical to any business."

Rosenblum should know. For 5 years, from 1995 until June of this year, she was vice president and chief learning officer at the Coca-Cola Co., where she was responsible for devising and executing Coke's learning strategy. She joined Coke after spending 14 years at Coopers & Lybrand, including a 3-year stint as the firm's vice chairwoman for learning and education. So what is her advice for people who seek to create learning organizations in their companies?

"I don't believe that there's any one way to do that in a company," Rosenblum says. "It depends on the culture of the company and on what its leaders will stand for." That said, Rosenblum learned a lot from her experience at Coke. "Learning has got to be connected directly to the business," she says. "The idea is to stay away from a standard 'learning program.' Instead, learning needs to be embedded in processes, projects, and experiences. If you put your energy into people who are ready and willing to join you, and if those people add value to the business, others will come."

At Coke, Rosenblum created an entity, called the Coca-Cola Learning Consortium, that acted as a catalyst for learning. The consortium was composed of two parts: directors of learning strategy, who acted as a liaison between learning efforts and business units; and four small consulting operations, which were organized around learning skills, knowledge management, competency development, and global training support. "One thing that we accomplished," Rosenblum says, "was to teach leaders that learning is a strategic choice; it doesn't just happen. Learning is a capability. It requires skills. It requires processes. And it requires leaders who value it."

Earlier this year, a change in focus at Coke, coupled with her own desire to work at an organization where learning is the primary focus, led Rosenblum to leave Coke and to join Duke Corporate Education Inc., a company launched by Duke University and the Fuqua School of Business this past July. Now 48, Rosenblum lives in Chapel Hill, North Carolina, where she serves as executive vice president and director of corporate advisory services at the new company.

What has Rosenblum learned about learning? In an interview with Fast Company, she outlined the 10 lessons that any would-be learning organization needs to learn.

LEARNING IS NOT A GIVEN.

That's the first principle, because it represents the nub of the learning issue for any company or organization. The fact is, this statement is both true and not true. Learning is a given. It happens, just as change happens. The real question is, Do you drive learning, do you create change—or do you just let it happen? What is not a given is whether you will adopt learning as a part of your organization's way of doing business. It's not a given that you'll be able to create your future by virtue of learning.

People are learning things all the time. But can you harness that process and make it work for your organization? Before that can happen, learning has to become a strategic choice: Someone in your organization has to decide that learning is strategic, that it's connected to the business. Someone has to decide that the company is going to make learning not just an individual experience but also a collective experience. When that happens, learning isn't just something that occurs naturally—it's something that the company uses to drive the future of the business.

You can see learning becoming a way of doing business in companies that have very short product life cycles—companies like Intel. And you can see that in companies with very strong leaders—companies like General Electric. One of the best examples of an organization that embraced learning as a way to drive change is the Army. Leaders there decided to take a hard look at the system that they had created and to embrace learning as a strategic activity. One of the tools that came out of that decision was after-action reviews, in which the Army takes time after a war game or a simulation to reflect on what happened: "What did we learn?"

Why is it so hard for other organizations to make learning strategic? You'd think that it would be relatively simple for a leader to get up and say, "We will learn, and we will use learning to create our future." But put that aspiration in the context of a very large, decentralized, performance-based business. Think about all of the people and markets that would be affected by that kind of announcement. Think about how hard it would be to get lots of different people in lots of different places to accept learning as a shared aspiration. And even if people have bought into the initial premise, think about how hard it is to take the next step—to get them to devote energy to building the skills that are necessary to learn.

MOST ORGANIZATIONS HAVE REAL STRUCTURES THAT LIMIT LEARNING.

There's a tremendous urgency in business today. Everyone is connected to the financial markets, and quarterly results matter more than ever before. That sense of urgency creates a bias for action. And that, in turn, prevents organizations from taking the time to learn. You have this phenomenal asset—your organization's collective experience—but this bias for action keeps you from focusing on it.

After all, taking the time to think would mean stopping what you're doing. And you're not rewarded for stopping what you're doing. You're rewarded for doing more. The way that most organizations work is very simple: You think about what you already know, and, using what you already know, you take action. From that action, you get results. And in most organizations, that's where it stops. Either the action worked, or it didn't. If it worked, you do more of it. If it didn't, you try something else. In a learning environment, you ask people to go further: After you get results, you take the time to ask, "Why did we get those results? And how can we use those results to grow what we know?" It's that last loop that people in most organizations feel that they don't have time for.

There are other structural obstacles to learning. In most organizations, "learning" still equals "training." More and more companies have people called "chief learning officers." But, say what you will, what those people really focus on is old-style training. Another obstacle is compensation: Most companies reward people on the basis of individual performance—so why should anyone focus on collective learning? If you're serious about learning, you have to confront those structural obstacles.

LEARNING INVOLVES BOTH A LEADERSHIP DECISION AND A WAY OF LEADING.

The way that we think about leadership, what we expect from leaders, and what leaders demand of themselves—these things can stop learning in its tracks. The fact is, not all leaders see learning as a way to lead. There are still a lot of leaders who think that their job is to control their organization. And control and learning don't usually mix very well. At the same time, there are plenty of organizations in which followers impose this old style of leadership on themselves. New-style leaders will go to their people and say, "Here's a direction that I'm interested in exploring, but I need your best thinking about it." Too often, the response from people is "You're supposed to tell us! You mean that you don't know?" Again, it's hard for an organization to be committed to learning when its people expect to be told what to do.

This is a real dilemma: If you go all the way toward a command-and-control style of leadership, then learning simply can't occur. At the same time, learning can't occur without some kind of direction. So lots of leaders are caught between "control" and "direction."

CORRIDORS ARE ESSENTIAL FOR PRODUCTIVE LEARNING.

Where do you see a solution to the leadership dilemma? You see it in companies that are explicit about their values—companies that hold constructive conversations about their mission, their core strategies, the core competencies of their people. Those fundamentals provide what I call "corridors"—spaces within which people can move. People know that they can learn and work within those corridors, so managers spend a lot less time trying to chase down people who are outside the "appropriate" space.

Think of it this way: Imagine a building with no hallways. If you're in that building, it's very difficult to find out where you're going, or what direction you're moving in. You find yourself wandering around more, and you have to check with more people more often just to see if you're headed in the right direction. You have to stop and look at different signposts to know where you are. To me, that describes a company that can't articulate clearly to its people what it stands for. So a company needs to provide corridors: "Here's our purpose, here are our values, here's how we do things, here are the core strategies that we're focusing on, and here's what people need to do to succeed here." People who work in a company without those corridors end up wandering around. They spend time on what they think are constructive activities, but they never really know whether they're focusing on the right things—things that are essential to the future of the business.

Having those kinds of corridors in a company is good both for leaders and for followers. Corridors give people informal guidance—a sense of whether they're in the right space, going in the right direction. People don't have to ask for directions all the time. They don't have to check to see whether what they're working on is relevant or not. They don't get nailed for doing things that aren't "on strategy." They have freedom to act—and their leaders don't have to exert very much command-and-control authority. Providing corridors gives both sides the freedom to act and to learn. In my experience, a learning environment is neither completely open nor completely boundary-less. But it does have corridors—spaces that are well defined, clearly marked, and designed to lead people in the right direction. That way, followers won't get lost, and leaders won't have to micromanage them.

COMPANIES NEED TO CLARIFY WHETHER LEARNING IS A "PEOPLE THING" OR A "BUSINESS THING."

It can be both—but only if you're clear about the outcomes that you want. I used to go into companies and say, "I think that what you want to do with your learning initiative is good and noble—but tell me why you want to do it. What outcome are you after?" As it turns out, that's not a question that most people are prepared to answer. They simply see learning as good and noble. Often, they don't even believe that there has to be an outcome, except maybe the creation of a learning environment.

If I push them harder, if I say to them, "The only way you're going to create what you really want is by visualizing the outcome that you're trying to achieve," what I usually hear back is "We want to retain our key people." Now, think about that for a minute. The presumed outcome of creating a learning organization is a set of connections that can help move a company in the direction that it needs to go. In other words, the point is to use learning as a strategic tool. That's very different from using learning as a tool to help you retain your key people.

Unless you're clear about the outcome that you're trying to achieve, you're going to be disappointed. There's no question that learning can be part of a retention strategy. One important reason why good people leave companies is that they don't feel that they're growing or developing. A learning program can help solve this problem: It can give people a community that they belong to and feel great loyalty to. But a learning program doesn't give you a complete retention strategy. It doesn't take into account all of the other levers that help you retain key people: their career path, where they move in an organization, how fast they move, how well they're compensated. And it doesn't take into account the real heart of learning: the creation of processes that help people not only to understand their experience but also to create a new vision for their business. If your company's goal is to use learning as a core retention strategy, that seems like overkill.

If you want to retain people, there are lots of things that you can do—and learning is definitely one of them. If you want to win in the future, then learning has to be an element of your retention strategy. But regardless of which path you take, the important thing is to articulate why you want to take it. In particular, be clear about the potential dichotomy between learning as a people thing and learning as a business thing. If you don't want to be disappointed at the end, ask the hard questions at the beginning—and do the hard work to answer those questions.

THERE IS A LINK BETWEEN THE "PEOPLE" AND "BUSINESS" APPROACHES TO LEARNING.

If you want to get a twofer from your approach to learning, focus on the capabilities that your organization needs in order to meet its objectives. Let's say that you identify "customer understanding" as a fundamental capability that your company must have in order to succeed: "I want customer understanding in my business, I don't understand why I don't have it today, and it's one of the key things that's causing me not to get the results that I want. We don't understand our customers well enough."

One thing that you can do in that situation is to use learning to think through what gaining a better understanding of your customers would mean. How would it affect people development, for example? You can use learning to come up with processes for customer understanding, for building a knowledge base around each customer, and for designing ways to share that knowledge in order to propel the business forward. If you take that approach to learning, you get the "people development" win, and you get the "business strategy" win. You're building the skills of your people, and your people feel directly connected to the central elements of your strategy.

Now, here's the dilemma: A lot has been said and written about capabilities—but most companies don't really understand how to plan for them. And capability is a factor that still doesn't have an equal place in the business-planning process: It's not at the table along with finance and marketing. This goes beyond the old problem of the HR department not having equal standing in a company. This isn't just about human resources. Capability is an issue that affects almost every function in a company. But when you sit through business-planning meetings, there's an enormous amount of time and energy devoted to strategy, vision, finance, and marketing—and almost no time devoted to the issue of capability. And, in the end, it's capabilities that carry the day.

LEARNING IS ITSELF A CAPABILITY.

When you hear about companies that have embraced learning, what you often hear about are the events, the practices, the activities that those companies have developed—such as General Electric's "Workout" sessions. What I've learned over the past five years is that learning is not about events. It's not about concepts. It's not even about a way of thinking. Learning is a capability. It needs to be embedded in an organization, and it needs to be viewed as a system. You need to take a holistic approach to learning if you want it to become a part of your business.

If you think about learning as a capability, you can quickly see the factors that go together to make learning a corporate priority. First, people need skills. For learning to be relevant, learning skills need to have equal weight with sales skills. Second, a company needs to focus on its processes. And those processes—particularly the business-planning process—need to be designed and led from a learning perspective. The business-planning process should be the central learning process of any company—although it seldom is. It's hard for learning to have any credibility in a company whose business-planning process is a "hope you survive" exercise. Third, a company needs to identify its critical knowledge assets and to manage those assets as a portfolio. Fourth, the environment that a company builds should foster learning and the exchange of knowledge. That can happen only in a company whose leaders make it clear that they value learning. And finally, measurement systems need to be designed around learning—not only around what the organization is learning but also around how people contribute to learning. When you combine those elements, you get a total approach to learning.

THE KEY TO DEVELOPING A CULTURE OF LEARNING IS ANSWERING THE QUESTION "WHY?"

There is gold in answering the simple question "Why don't we have what we want today?" Companies spend lots of time articulating goals and describing a vision. If they spent as much time trying to understand why they don't have what they want, a great deal of learning would occur that might increase the probability of meeting those goals and achieving that vision. Think about it: If vision is so important, and if we're such bright people, why is it that just articulating a vision doesn't make it happen?

Now, it's not hard to understand why many companies don't like to ask the question "Why?" Faced with the press of time, people assume that they already know the answer to that question—so why waste more time on it? In cases where the question concerns less-than-favorable results, asking why can be perceived as a search for the guilty party: It gets tagged as dwelling on negativism, or rehashing old history. Most companies prefer to bury their mistakes, or they just deny those mistakes and move on. But real learning remains hidden if you don't clearly define success up front. And you don't learn if, at key milestones, you don't ask the question "Have we achieved success, and if not, why not?"

MOST TRADITIONAL ORGANIZATIONS NEITHER UNDERSTAND NOR ACCEPT THE TIME AND EFFORT THAT IT TAKES TO BUILD A LEARNING CAPABILITY.

Companies that are still operating in the old economy simply haven't confronted the new reality: They haven't had to deal with short product life cycles. For them, it's a lot easier to say that learning is just a human-resources thing—that it's a passive experience, just another part of what they offer as training. Their attitude is "We'll do it when there's time." In other words, for these companies, learning is event-driven. They teach their people new skills when and only when they want their people to learn those skills. I call this the "just-do-it approach to learning." The alternative is to take an active approach: "We have to lead it, we have to embed it in our processes, we have to build capabilities into the way we do business. Learning isn't about doing it—it's about being it."

For most big, old-economy companies, that distinction hasn't sunk in yet. The big issue for learning is whether it will become part of leadership over the next 10 years—or whether it will be put aside as something that fell short because it didn't generate business results.

LEARNING CAN FALL VICTIM TO OVERSTATED EXPECTATIONS.

Done right and done well, learning does offer short-term wins. But overall, learning is a marathon, not a sprint. Leaders are still held to short-term performance measures, and if learning doesn't generate business results in the time that's allotted to it, then leaders will be tempted to abandon it. And that would be a great loss.

The question that we've all got to answer is "If learning is so intuitively appealing to so many people, why is it so hard for companies to adopt it?" High expectations play a large role. But so does having an installed base that defines "how things get done around here." So do entrenched mind-sets. So do the traits of certain leaders.

One hope for the future lies with the Web. The Web can help to embed a different type of learning model into the kinds of offerings that are out there. And the Web can facilitate feedback loops. In some respects, we're still stuck with a classroom model of learning: There's a teacher at the front of the room who has all of the answers, and there are students who need to have information poured into their heads. The Web moves learning toward performance support, coaching, feedback, and reflection on the difference between the desired performance and the actual outcome. The Web can embed a learning loop into how we teach people.

Another problem with the way that traditional learning happens is that we give knowledge to the wrong group of people, or we give people the wrong knowledge, or there's just too much knowledge. The problem is that we don't know which kind of learning a given community is naturally attracted to. If you focus on each community, then you can make learning a part of the agenda for that community.

So the Web and the technology of the new economy are huge enablers that can reshape how learning takes place. But the Web won't solve the leadership side of the problem. Ultimately, someone has to declare that learning is central to the way an organization operates. Someone has to say, "This is how we do things around here." Otherwise, learning gets minimized—and it never becomes a given inside the organization.

Alan M. Webber (awebber@fastcompany.com) is a founding editor at *Fast Company*. Contact Judy Rosenblum by email (Rosenblumjar@aol.com).

BY ANNA MUOIO   FROM *FAST COMPANY* ISSUE 33, PAGE 290

Where There's Smoke It Helps to Have a Smoke Jumper

IF YOU SPEND TOO MUCH OF YOUR TIME "PUTTING OUT FIRES," THEN TAKE SOME ADVICE FROM MASTER SMOKE JUMPER WAYNE WILLIAMS. HE'LL TEACH YOU HOW TO THINK CLEARLY, TO ACT DECISIVELY, TO WORK PRECISELY—AND TO SOLVE PROBLEMS BEFORE THEY BURN OUT OF CONTROL.

There's a common lament among businesspeople in all kinds of companies: "How am I supposed to get any work done I spend all of my time putting out fires." The "fire" in question might be a dissatisfied customer who demands lots of attention, or it might be an unexpected financial setback that, if left unaddressed, could become a strategic crisis. We'd certainly be more productive if more of our days were free of the kinds of crises that seem to erupt at a moment's notice. But in a fast-moving, always-changing, increasingly unpredictable economy, it is a required skill for business leaders to be able to jump into the middle of a tough situation with little or no information, to size things up, and to have the wits to take action—fast.

That's what smoke jumper Wayne Williams does for a living. Williams, 43, is part of the elite, highly trained wildland fire-fighting division of the U.S. Forest Service, and he has been fighting fires—literally—for 23 years. Forming what are known as "initial attack teams," smoke jumpers are like the Green Berets of the fire-fighting world. They get deployed anywhere, at any time, with remarkable speed. Within one hour, a smoke-jumping crew can arrive at a fire from as far away as 150 miles.

There is an undeniable aura surrounding smoke jumpers. They are a tight-knit team of men and women who fight fires in the middle of the wilderness, armed with only a few tools, tremendous courage, and their wits. They have been immortalized in books, mythologized on the silver screen, and featured in more than 80 documentaries. Norman Maclean, the award-winning author of "A River Runs Through It," explored the perilous world of smoke jumpers in his book "Young Men and Fire" (University of Chicago Press, 1992), which revisits the 1949 tragedy at Mann Gulch, in Montana's Helena National Forest, where 13 smoke jumpers lost their lives. In 1998, 20th Century Fox released "Firestorm," an action drama (and, according to Williams, an "inaccurate embarrassment") that portrays one smoke jumper in a glamorous light—a fearless hero who kills the bad guy and saves the damsel in distress.

In the real world, dealing with forest fires involves clear thinking, precise teamwork, smart strategies, lots of backbreaking work—and very little glamour. "There are two things that matter most when containing a wildfire: the speed at which you get to a fire, and the actions of the team that gets there first," explains Williams. Since most wildland fires burn in remote areas, the smoke jumpers' commute to work is usually a quick, harrowing parachute jump from an airplane. Once on the ground (wearing packs that can weigh more than 100 pounds), smoke jumpers hike over steep, wild terrain to the scene of the fire and do whatever is humanly possible to contain it—whether that takes a few hours or several days. The need for smoke jumping is growing like—well, like wildfire. In 1999, there were 86,202 reported wildfires in the United States, and they burned a total of 5,468,469 acres of land.

Fighting fires is not a job for the weak of body—or the weak of mind. Indeed, what you first notice about Williams are his hands. Thickly callused and as solid as boards, they move with surprising grace as he explains the unpredictable nature of fire—which, he agrees, is a perfect metaphor for the unpredictable nature of the problems that erupt in the new world of work. "Trying to understand a fire is like trying to understand someone with multiple personalities," says Williams. "Each fire has its own character, its own idiosyncrasies—and it changes. A fire can be quiet, minding its own business, and then, all of a sudden, it will get up and run. If you're not paying attention to every bit of information and every changing detail that the fire is throwing at you, it will catch you."

Fast Company recently caught up with Williams at the Forest Service's Smokejumper Center, in Missoula, Montana. With no fires raging, Williams had some time to share his lessons on the art of understanding fires and on what it takes to put them out.

FIGURE OUT WHAT YOU THINK—AND THEN THINK AGAIN

You can't fight a fire effectively until you've figured it out. You need to understand the kind of fire that you're up against, the conditions under which you'll be fighting it, and the events that are likely to unfold as the fire is being fought. Figuring out a fire requires two minds, or two memories. Before we leave base, we're briefed on the conditions that we're supposed to find on the ground. We may know the fire's spread rate, what fuel type we're dealing with, the incoming weather, and so on. That captures what we know about the fire at a certain moment in time—but not what's going to happen once we arrive.

From the airplane, we get a bird's-eye view of the fire. That big-picture information is essential both for understanding the problem and for formulating an initial strategy: where we're going to jump; where we'll drop our cargo; whether there are any natural fire breaks, such as rivers or open meadows; where we'll establish a safety zone and an escape route. This is the information that I store in one mind, or one memory.

But the first thing that I do once I get on the ground, after setting up the crew, is to walk around the entire fire and to start gathering information. This is when my other mind, or memory, clicks in. I set aside what I've been told—or what I think is going on—and simply do two things: I watch the fire, and I "feel" what's happening. A fire has complex behavior. It's a separate entity that doesn't unfold all at once but keeps throwing bits of information at you. The trick is to be open enough to see—and feel—those pieces of data, to figure out the type of fire "personality" that you're dealing with. Every change brings new details, and in my world, those details could have life-threatening consequences.

With a fire, conditions change constantly. If you're not aware of what's going on, the fire will catch you off guard. Sometimes it's the rookie smoke jumpers who are the most open to read such changes. They can't fall back on the comfort zone of experience, or on an archive of knowledge that might cut them off from what's really happening. But I never let myself become so focused on the fire that I lose sight of what's happening in a big-picture sense. Instead, I shift back and forth between my two "memories." And I stay alert—because, when you're working in the wilderness, you might be sweating your socks off one day, and (especially if it's late in the season) you might be freezing the next day. It may not always be the fire that catches you off guard.

SPEED MATTERS—BUT SLOWER CAN BE BETTER

One of the basic tenets of wildland fire fighting is speed: You need to reach a fire as quickly as possible, so that you can attack it while it's still small. In the case of small fires, the decisions that we make are fairly straightforward. We operate under a "10 AM policy": That is, we try to control the fire by the morning after it is discovered. On the flip side, if a fire is really up and roaring, it will make our decision for us. Typically, the best strategy is to play a waiting game. We wait until a fire runs into a different fuel type, until the weather changes, or until some other opportunity rolls in that lets us resume fighting the fire.

The most difficult decisions that we have to make come when we're faced with a medium-size fire. We're never sure which way it's going to swing. In an instant, it could lie down and die—or take off and run. In those situations, it's easy to get tunnel vision and to fall into what we call the "overhead trap," in which you become obsessed with doing well, no matter what. You get this fever to catch every fire, and you don't recognize that it may be time to retreat for a while. I used to be like that. There's no question that I want to catch every fire that I jump, but I know that I can't do that in every situation. And the last thing that I want is to have someone's death on my conscience—just because I couldn't accept the fact that some fires present challenges that are beyond my crew's ability.

A few years ago, we were fighting one of those medium-size fires. It was burning on both sides of a mountain. From the air, I had developed what I thought was a pretty sound strategy: First, we would attack the fire at its most inactive side, and then we'd work our way around it with our control line. But when I started walking around the fire, I realized that something was terribly wrong. It was 9 PM, and the air was way too hot for that time of night. All of a sudden, I realized that we were in the middle of an inversion layer: Hot air was getting trapped in the middle of the canyon's slope. An inversion jacks the heat way up and drives the humidity down— two ingredients that could make a fire's behavior very dangerous.

I always carry a camera with me when I fight a fire, and the thing that really tipped me off that night was taking pictures of an alligator juniper that was burning out of control. The alligator juniper is a pretty untorchable tree, but that one was as bright as a Christmas tree. When I looked through my viewfinder, I realized that my light monitor was registering too much light, given that it was the middle of the night. At that moment, I knew that we were in trouble. I immediately told members of my crew to stop what they were doing and to start hiking up the hill to our safety zone, a large rock outcropping. Ultimately, it's never one thing that goes wrong when you fight a fire. Instead, there's a bunch of stuff that piles up and suddenly overwhelms you. And in this situation, too many small things were starting to pile up. After we reached our safety zone, I began to question my decision to leave the fire. I wondered if I was just being lazy. But 10 minutes later, the fire blew up, and the canyon that we had just left became a sea of flames.

NEVER UNDERESTIMATE THE DANGERS OF THE UNFAMILIAR

Every fire involves danger, but the greatest danger of all comes when you encounter the unfamiliar—when you're fighting fires in a region where you've never been before, or working under conditions that you've never experienced before. Those are the kinds of situations that require the greatest amount of focus and discipline.

In 1993, we had one of the quietest fire seasons in Montana history. The next year, we had one of the busiest fire seasons ever. Putting out a fire now and then is one thing; dealing with dozens of fires at once is a different game altogether. Usually, a fire season has a predictable progression from beginning to end. The fires in Alaska and New Mexico typically start the show. When they fade away, fires in Montana, Oregon, Idaho, and northern California begin to burn. For the finale, southern California and the eastern United States start to burn. But in 1994, every state was "onstage" at the same time—and every firefighter was out performing. What's more, we had all types of fires going at once. Typically, we get either a lot of small fires, which require initial fire-fighting attacks, or a bunch of ragers, which require sustained fire-fighting activity. This time, we had brand-new small fires starting every day, yet the big, long-burning fires were still trucking. In August of that year, there were 10,000 firefighters and operations people battling blazes in Region One alone. (Region One covers more than 25 million acres in Idaho, Montana, Washington, North Dakota, and South Dakota.) Air tankers dropped more than 4 million gallons of retardant. Our base in Missoula shipped about 3.8 million pounds of equipment to various fire camps around the country.

That type of crisis creates two potentially dangerous situations. First, you have a shortage of people and supplies. Second, everyone is stretched to the max; everyone is working to the point of exhaustion. You can't underestimate the problems that those factors can cause. In fact, those conditions are what contributed that year to one of the biggest tragedies in fire history—a fire that took place in South Canyon, Colorado. That fire, with temperatures as high as 2,000 degrees, turned into a 200-foot wall of flame that raced up a steep slope at 40 MPH; it killed 14 firefighters. I knew a lot of the people who were working on that fire, and I was a member of one of the first rescue teams to head into the canyon. It was a disturbing tragedy, and it confirmed an invaluable lesson: The type of fire that you're fighting matters just as much as where you're fighting it.

Location makes a huge difference—and it affects the kind of strategy that you can devise.

Traditionally, Colorado is not a state that has a lot of fire activity. I've been fighting fires since 1977, and I had never fought a fire in Colorado. In 1994, I fought three there. Colorado has fuel situations that are similar to those found in southern California, a place where we're always putting out fires. In both states, there's a brushy kind of fuel, but the fuel in Colorado looks really different. The brush in southern California looks as if it will burn: It's dry and creepy. But in Colorado, the fuel is a plush, green oak, and you probably couldn't get it to burn even if you tried. But the South Canyon fire was so hot that it had burned underneath the brush. So, when the fire came ripping out of the canyon—with the proper winds and levels of humidity—that brush became trouble. This time, it was ready to burn. In a lot of ways, the conditions surrounding the South Canyon fire were typical. But for various reasons, that unfamiliar terrain tricked people and caught them off guard, making them do things that they wouldn't have done if they'd been in a different place.

EVERY CREW NEEDS A SKEPTIC

The worst thing that you can do is to have too many nice guys working on a fire. We work in small, tight teams that have a formal structure—foremen, squad leaders, and so on. But the beauty of being a jumper is that we're all really in charge. As the foreman, I involve everyone in the decisions that I make. When you're asking people to work themselves to the bone and, in a lot of cases, to risk their lives, it's absurd to exclude them from the decision-making process. I love it when someone on my team questions one of my decisions and says, "This is bullshit." In fact, I invite it. People deserve the right to do that.

Once, when we were fighting a fire in the middle of New Mexico's Gila National Forest, we saw a huge plume of smoke a short distance below us. I had decided that the best strategy was to continue cutting a control line downhill. But two of the jumpers on my team told me that they were uncomfortable with that decision. They felt that the fire down the hill could catch us if we stayed where we were. Not only was I familiar with this terrain, having fought fires in this area for years, but I also remembered spotting a big rimrock wall from the airplane as we approached the fire. I realized that the fire we were seeing was behind that wall and that there was no way it could reach us.

I could have told those guys not to worry—that their sorry asses were safe with me and that they should get back to work. But they were experienced smoke jumpers, and they had legitimate concerns. So I listened to them and decided to call in a helicopter to check it out. (There was already a helicopter working in the area.) The pilot flew by, radioed in, and confirmed that the fire was behind the cliffs. It may seem like that was a lot of work for nothing. But that's what it took to put those two men at ease. Just because I was the leader on that job didn't mean that I knew more than everybody else. And simply saying "I'm right" is never the best way to convince people that they should follow you.

Whenever I'm unsure about whether my crew can deal with the problem at hand, I gather everyone together and talk about it. We talk about strategies, we talk about comfort levels, we talk about risks. Of course, a fire may burn a few more acres in the meantime—but in the overall scheme of things, that's nothing. There have been plenty of times when the crew has given me a better way to think about a problem. You have to keep in mind that you're never going to have all of the answers. It would be foolish to think that you could have all of the answers.

YOU CAN FIGHT FIRE WITH FIRE

Sometimes the only way to diminish the force of a fire is to attack it head-on with another fire. That strategy, known as a backfire, can be dangerous business. But on one occasion, when we were fighting a "combination fire" in New Mexico, using backfire was our last resort. It was in the middle of the night, and we were building a control line to protect a "helispot" where we could land helicopters to bring in more crew members. We were way ahead of this huge, 1,000-acre fire—but it was hauling ass toward us. Our overhead personnel wanted us to wait and to let the fire burn as far as our control line. I knew that if we allowed that to happen, not only would we be in bad shape, but we'd also be blocked off from our only escape route. And that fire was not about to let a simple control line stop it.

So we began "burning out"—which means that we lit small fires a short distance away from our control line, getting closer and closer to the head of the main fire. The small fires burned out all of the fuel in between and, in the process, created a larger control line. But eventually, the main fire was right on our heels, breathing hard and sucking all of the air toward it. That's when we lit a backfire, which the raging combination fire drew toward itself automatically. When the two fires collided, the effect was awesome. Not only did the collision shoot a column of smoke thousands of feet into the night air, but it also threw fireballs over our line, causing several spot fires that we had to contain. We knew that our backfire wasn't going to put this fire out—but it did diffuse the power of the rager. In fact, this combination fire was one of those fires that end up burning all summer long; only a major change in the weather was able to put it out. Sometimes, no matter how hard you try, you can't control a fire.

Anna Muoio (amuoio@fastcompany.com) is a *Fast Company* associate editor and a recovering pyromaniac. Contact Wayne Williams (wwilliam/r1@fs.fed.us) by email.

TEN RULES FOR PUTTING OUT FIRES

In 1957, a Forest Service task force developed the "10 Standard Fire Orders"—a set of fire-fighting principles that remain an essential part of a smoke jumper's training regimen. It's not hard to see the relevance of those principles (summarized below) to "fighting fires" in the new world of work.

1. Fight fire aggressively, but provide for safety first.
2. Initiate actions according to current and expected fire behavior.
3. Recognize current weather conditions and obtain forecasts.
4. Ensure that instructions are given and that they are understood.
5. Obtain current information on the status of fires.
6. Remain in communication with crew members, your supervisor, and adjoining forces.
7. Determine safety zones and escape routes.
8. Establish lookouts in potentially hazardous situations.
9. Retain control at all times.
10. Stay alert, keep calm, think clearly, and act decisively.

"WATCH OUT" SITUATIONS

Soon after the creation of the "10 Standard Fire Orders," Forest Service training specialists identified "18 Watch Out Situations"—conditions that create dangers for smoke jumpers. Here, adapted from that list, are some of those situations.

1. The fire is not scouted or sized up.
2. Safety zones and escape routes have not been identified.
3. Firefighters are uninformed about strategy, tactics, and hazards.
4. Instructions and assignments are unclear.
5. There is no communication link between crew members and their supervisors.
6. Firefighters cannot see the main fire and are not in contact with anyone who can see it.
7. Rough terrain or dangerous fuel makes it difficult for firefighters to escape to safety zones.
8. A firefighter feels like taking a nap near the fire line.

How to Bounce Back from Setbacks

THE ROAD TO SUCCESS IS RARELY A STRAIGHT LINE. HERE ARE THREE PROFILES IN RESILIENCE: PEOPLE AND COMPANIES THAT SUCCEEDED BY CONQUERING FAILURE.

Mike Espy is no stranger to success—even when it has meant overcoming long odds. As a teenager in rural Mississippi, he was one of two student-body presidents of the first racially integrated class in his high school. He served for six years in Congress— the state's first black member since Reconstruction. Under Bill Clinton, he was named U.S. Secretary of Agriculture, becoming both a Washington celebrity and a committed government reformer.

And then disaster struck. In 1994, reports surfaced that Espy, now 47, had flown on corporate jets owned by companies that his department regulated and had accepted gifts, such as tickets to sports events, from those companies. Next came word that Espy's then girlfriend had accepted a scholarship from Tyson Foods, another company that the Agriculture Department regulated. These disclosures did more than raise eyebrows. They prompted the White House—and an independent counsel—to question Espy's ability to do his job.

Espy resigned from the Clinton cabinet humbled and depressed. He figured that the independent counsel's investigation would last six months—tops. "I wanted to move on with my life," he says. In the end, the investigation lasted four years, produced a 39-count indictment, and generated the sort of public scrutiny and private humiliation that only a Washington scandal can create. And it forced Mike Espy to confront a question that would determine the trajectory of the rest of his professional life: How do I bounce back from this devastating setback?

The road to long-term success is seldom a straight line, for companies or for individual leaders. New products get launched with great fanfare—and then disappear from sight. Companies make big bets on a strategy—only to discover that the playing field has shifted once again. All-too-human executives use poor judgment or permit just one ethical lapse—and find their reputations tarnished forever. There is no success without the occasional failure. Yet the mythology we've created about business rarely allows us to recognize that obvious fact. Successful leaders, we've come to believe, never make a bad call. They never reach a dumb decision. They never, under pressure, choose to do something that they later regret.

"In America, failure is considered a disruption in progress," says Scott A. Sandage, a history professor at Carnegie Mellon University who teaches a course on success and failure. "Even as the understanding of economic challenges increases, there's an intensification of shame around failure."

Andrew Shatte, 38, vice president of research and product development at Adaptiv Learning Systems—a firm that teaches executives how to be more resilient—agrees: "It's easy to become flustered by setbacks, because most of us believe that our companies and careers should keep advancing. Successful people learn how to gain control of situations that are out of their control, retool themselves, and rebound quickly from disaster."

Here are in-depth profiles of people and companies that have managed to bounce back from setbacks. Warning: The experiences are not pretty, the emotions are deep, and the victories are sometimes less than decisive. But these stories are candid and authentic, the lessons powerful and useful. So read on, be grateful that you've probably never faced setbacks quite this severe—and consider yourself better prepared to face whatever difficult circumstances you might encounter in the future.

MIKE ESPY: THE (LONG) ROAD BACK

One of Mike Espy's trademarks is that he writes a note to himself every day to set out his goals. Once he resigned from his U.S. Cabinet post, his goals were no longer set for him. He suddenly had to determine his own future, and his list making became more extensive. He was shocked by the vitriol in Washington and by his own poor judgment. "I considered myself legally and ethically innocent," he declares as he sits in his Jackson, Mississippi law office. "I didn't give favors to any companies. I focused on policy, not on politics. And I thought the administration would support me. But I took too much for granted. My judgment was faulty in many ways."

Facing the folks back home was nerve-racking. Espy still winces a little as he recalls a homecoming game at his daughter's high school. At the time, she was a sophomore and a member of the homecoming court. He dreaded having to escort her across the school's football field so that she could join her court. "I wanted to take myself off the radar screen," says Espy. But while lying low was a strategy for short-term survival, it wasn't a strategy for change. "I had no job or income prospects," he says. "I couldn't be a lobbyist. I couldn't be an attorney. I was disgraced. It was the worst year of my life." The daily notes to himself became a list of obligations: how to pay the mortgage, how to provide child support.

Meanwhile, as weeks turned into months, Espy realized that the road back would be much longer than he'd ever imagined. "I didn't have control of the process surrounding me, so I had to take control of my life," he says. He found a mentor in Tony Coelho, the onetime congressional leader who'd had his share of setbacks. Coelho met with Espy in the winter of 1995 for what would be a memorable lunch. Coelho drew a pie chart and divided it into six slices. "You start with a vision of what you will look like when you're at your ultimate state, and you fill in the pieces with what it will take to get you there," Espy recalls Coelho saying. One half of Espy's pie represented different aspects of himself that he had to rehabilitate. First slice: finances. Coelho suggested scheduling enough speaking engagements to bring in a good income. Second slice: mental outlook. To take Espy's mind off his troubles, Coelho suggested that he teach at a local college. Third slice: reputation. Getting involved in a well-known charity would improve Espy's image and his esteem. He joined Feed the Children as a consultant (he became a board member in 1999) and worked with the antihunger organization's international offices to use donations more efficiently.

Espy tried to resurface in the public eye, but he discovered that he couldn't. He scouted for legal jobs in Washington, DC but received no offers. He returned to Jackson and took a job at a 20-person law firm. There was no pomp, no army of staff. "I kept my door shut a lot, my head down, and my focus on myself," he recalls. "But I had to generate income for the firm. They wouldn't let me wallow in self-pity." Then, in 1997, he was officially indicted.

Espy's reaction was to get tougher—and to be tougher on himself, rather than blaming others. When he learned that Independent Counsel Donald Smaltz did 100 push-ups a day, he worked toward doing 200 a day. He also perfected his tae kwon do technique (he has a black belt). After learning that the independent counsel had given everyone on his staff a watch with Espy's name engraved on it as a holiday gift, Espy decided to take the high road, instead of firing back. He struggled with his attitude so he wouldn't sound bitter. And in his public statements, he was careful not to blame his predicament on race or politics alone.

Espy also decided to take the long road to vindication, rather than the easy road to a quick settlement. He refused three plea offers. "I could have gotten out early on a misdemeanor charge and run up only $100,000 in legal bills," he says with his arms folded, eyes cast down. "But how do you put a price on your good name?" In 1998, after testimony from a parade of witnesses—including fellow cabinet officers, former friends, and an artist who gave Espy a painting for his office—Espy was exonerated. Nine counts were dismissed, and a jury acquitted Espy of the remaining 30 counts. A *Washington Post* article detailing the road to his acquittal is framed on a wall at his law firm. Tucked inside the frame is one of the watches with Espy's name on it that Smaltz gave to his staff.

But the acquittal didn't allow Espy simply to return to the career path he'd been on before the scandal. Bouncing back from a setback often means taking a different road. Although Mississippi residents said in a poll that they'd welcome him as lieutenant governor, Espy is more than a little gun-shy about returning to public life. He's now with Mississippi's largest law firm, working hard to perfect his litigation techniques. He may never return to a career in politics, but he has escaped from the scandal that threatened to destroy him. "It's not about the test," he says. "It's about how you pass the test."

MICHAEL DOWD: DON'T WALK AWAY FROM A FIGHT

Peeking out from the teetering piles of paperwork on Michael Dowd's desk are pink slips—the good kind, the ones that receptionists use for phone messages. One is from a mother who has called Dowd about representing her son in a landmark abuse case against the Archdiocese of New York. One is from writer Peter Maas, whom Dowd represented in connection with Maas's book about mafia hitman Sammy "the Bull" Gravano. But Dowd ignores the slips, as well as his ringing phone, to consult with a lawyer who has walked in with a question. Then Dowd glances at the breathtaking vista of lower Manhattan. He is at the peak of his game. His caseload represents some of the most high-profile lawsuits in New York this past year. It's hard to imagine that Dowd didn't—couldn't—practice law for four years.

In the 1980s, Michael Dowd, now 58, made a name for himself defending women who had attacked or killed their abusive spouses. Dowd pioneered legal defenses that won his clients seemingly impossible acquittals. Courtroom sketches from one watershed case hang above his desk. But while his work set precedents, it didn't pay the bills. So when Dowd was offered a partnership in a side business collecting on overdue parking tickets, he took it. He ended up getting much more than he had bargained for.

In 1982, the political lords of Queens came knocking, asking for 5% of the fines that the business collected from parking violators. Dowd felt trapped. He didn't think saying no was an option. Not only would he lose the business, he thought, but he might endanger his life as well. So he started paying. But less than two years later, torn up about the arrangement, he decided to stop. "I felt tremendously guilty about my failure to have courage," he says. "I should have said no from day one and borne whatever loss I would have suffered and whatever hardship I would have endured."

Then, in early 1986, he took an even more dramatic step. He decided to blow the whistle on the kickback deals. He went to the U.S. Attorney's office, which at the time was headed by a crusading prosecutor named Rudolph Giuliani. The next morning, Dowd's name was in the papers, and camera crews surrounded his home. He had misjudged how he would appear in the public eye. Instead of being lauded as a whistle-blower, he was impugned as a criminal. "I was stunned by the accusation that I was a crook," he says.

Talk about a setback. A onetime lapse in judgment was haunting his livelihood and his professional status. Dowd couldn't convince people that his actions were right. But he wasn't going to walk away from a fight. He had to go on with his life. Two days after the media frenzy, he walked into the Queens courthouse to select a jury for his next trial. He knew the selection would be difficult because people might recognize him from the media reports. "In that situation, you're making choices, and it seemed worse to run or to hide," he says. "The absolute key is to maintain your self-respect and dignity. Without that, you're lost. And you're sending a message to other people that you're lost. It's a terrible message that people seize upon."

He picked a jury and successfully tried the case. After a lull in his caseload, he found new corporate clients, took on more battered-women's cases, and rebuilt his practice. Then, in 1990, he discovered that he was being investigated by the Grievance Committee for the Second and Eleventh Judicial Districts for his involvement in the parking-violations scandal. The committee charged Dowd with professional misconduct for the kickbacks and for not reporting immediately that the Queens borough president, who was also a lawyer, was involved in unethical conduct. Judges, prominent lawyers, and Giuliani testified on Dowd's behalf. But in August of that year, he was suspended for five years (ultimately, the suspension lasted only four years). "I didn't think it could happen," he says. "It was mind-numbing.

You're not capable of absorbing the enormity of it. It was catastrophic financially. I was already close to filing for bankruptcy. And it was painful, because I had no idea what I was going to do. I didn't know how to define myself."

The test for Dowd was how to survive the suspension. In struggling to define himself, he learned that he was more than just his job—a realization that too few people ever reach. "Changing your belief about the role of your job or the trajectory of your career can be liberating," says Andrew Shatte of Adaptiv Learning Systems, "if you see the benefit in doing other work, rather than the loss."

Dowd decided that even though he had to walk away from law, he wouldn't walk away from a cause. He wanted to continue as an advocate for battered women. During the suspension, then Governor Mario Cuomo appointed Dowd to New York State's Office of Domestic Violence. Dowd also spearheaded the Battered Women's Justice Center at Pace University School of Law (now the Pace Women's Justice Center), a place where lawyers and judges can get training and then take on women's cases pro bono.

But then came a pivotal moment for this new mind-set. Three professors objected to the plan, stating that Dowd was a negative influence on students because of his missteps in the parking-ticket business. Dowd was incensed and considered not creating the center. "But the objective of creating something unique and doing something valuable was bigger than my pride," he says. Once again, he didn't walk away from a fight. He did start the center, and it still runs today, with a full-time staff. "He sees past a single event in a person's life and doesn't let people get defined by their mistakes," says Julie Blackman, a social psychologist who has worked with many of Dowd's clients. In effect, his work with the center's clients turned out to be his rebound as well. Dowd reapplied to the bar early and was readmitted in 1994. He has since built a healthy solo practice defending battered women and white-collar criminals.

Dowd sets down his glasses and considers how others autopsy his past. "If my obituary is worth more than a paragraph, I doubt I can avoid some mention of that whole event," he says. "We all have crises. If we're lucky, they don't become public."

CIENA: IT'S ALWAYS RISKY BUSINESS

How do you hang on to your best people—and keep the faith of your directors and investors—when you take a business risk that doesn't pan out? You take on even more risk and be clear with everyone that part of winning big in business is reckoning honestly with the potential for setbacks and reversals.

That's the lesson that Steve Chaddick, 49, senior vice president of systems and technology at Ciena Corp., learned from a wild two-year ride at one of the new economy's highest-flying companies. Ciena was one of the first companies to stake a claim in the optical-networking sector. Chaddick's team was first to market with what is now a critical technology: dense wave division multiplexing (DWDM). Carriers such as Sprint and WorldCom quickly became converts to the technology, which essentially increases bandwidth-transmission capacity across fiber-optic cables. In 1997, Ciena enjoyed the best-performing IPO of the year, more than doubling its share price. Meanwhile, senior executives snared a merger deal with Tellabs, an old-line telecommunications carrier in the Chicago area. Chaddick was on the merger team that spent more than four months shuttling back and forth between Chicago and Ciena's Maryland headquarters to sort out details and cultural matches with Tellabs.

But literally minutes before the two companies' shareholders were scheduled to vote on the merger, AT&T (without testing the products) decided not to close an expected contract to use Ciena's more-advanced DWDM offerings. Ciena's stock price collapsed, from more than $55 to barely more than $31. The company's business was fine: It was on track to make its revenue estimates, even without the AT&T contract. Regardless, three weeks later, Tellabs called Ciena to say that the merger was off. The stock price plunged again—this time to $8. "We were stunned and angry about the situation," Chaddick says.

Faced with such a difficult situation, lots of public companies would have retreated—cutting costs, scaling back their ambitions. But Chaddick and the leaders of Ciena harnessed their anger to take on an even bigger target: building a full-scale optical network themselves. As a result, not a single engineer left Chaddick's team. Then Ciena took another risk. It decided to acquire two companies that had the customers and the technology that Ciena needed in order to grow. By early 1999, Ciena had acquired Lightera Networks and Omnia Communications to create a full-service optical network with an optical-switching system. "People thought we were nuts," Chaddick says. "My philosophy is, 'Don't be afraid to think big.'"

To be sure, rebounding from a disaster does not mean mistake-proofing your company. It means acknowledging that there will be more setbacks in the future. Case in point: the Omnia acquisition. One of Omnia's technologies promised to help the company move its increased bandwidth closer not just to businesses but also to homes. But the architecture was flawed. So Chaddick and his team shelved the technology. "Most business cultures aren't capable of accepting error," Chaddick says. "We teach from the top down that sometimes, we will be wrong."

But Chaddick and his colleagues have been right far more often than they have been wrong. Ciena is now winning contracts from customers like Qwest Communications International. Two years ago, Ciena was in the DWDM market. Today, it's in four markets. Its customers have nearly tripled in number since 1998. And its stock price (adjusted for a split) has been higher than $300 per share. "This has been an impressive revival from the dead," says Paul Silverstein, senior communications and networking analyst at Robertson Stephens. "The fact that they were a cohesive group helped a lot."

Chaddick doesn't think of Ciena's staggering comeback as a revival from the dead—he views it as a sensible way to respond to a business challenge. "There are only two ways to act," he says. "Make bold moves, knowing that some will work and some won't. Or make no moves, which guarantees that you'll be an also-ran."

Rekha Balu (rbalu@fastcompany.com) is a *Fast Company* senior writer. We're still waiting for her first big setback.

RESILIENCE RULES

Andrew Shatte and his colleagues at Adaptiv Learning Systems, a consulting firm based in King of Prussia, Pennsylvania, teach people at such companies as Ford and Nortel Networks how to stay resilient in the face of adversity. It's an important skill for leaders to have at any time, but in a period of challenge and change, it is especially crucial. Here are some of the principles that they teach.

1. **Explain yourself.** Dealing effectively with a problem or a setback starts with how you explain it—to yourself and to those around you. "Too many people learn negative or helpless ways of thinking," Shatte says. "But they can unlearn them and adopt more resilient ways of thinking. Once you're aware of your explanatory style, listen for a pattern. Ask yourself why this happened, and listen to what you say." Some people tend to explain setbacks as temporary, while others view them as permanent. Do you tend to cast blame on others, or do you explain everything as your fault? Each style needs to be offset with logic and perspective.

2. **Don't overreact.** "In most rough situations, people tend to describe what went wrong in terms of 'always' and 'everything,'" Shatte says. For instance, when a boss criticizes part of a presentation, or report, many people say to themselves, "My reports are always bad," or, "I bet I'm one step away from getting canned." Shatte and his colleagues teach people to counter those standard overreactions with a more accurate evaluation. Most of the time, things aren't as bleak as we make them out to be.

3. **Act fast, but don't rush to judgment.** It's important to be honest when you run into a setback—but it's also important to be sure you understand what's really going on. Adaptiv worked with a European company that was selling whiskey in a country that preferred vodka. The country also had an active black market. Whiskey sales had hit the skids. The company's executives blamed the sales team. Everyone knew there was a problem, and everyone rushed to judgment about the cause. The real problem, it turns out, involved the sales force's lack of training. Armed with the proper analysis, both sides worked the problem.

4. **Keep it in perspective.** Ask yourself: What's the worst thing that can happen? What's the best outcome that we can hope for? And then keep pressing yourself about the accuracy of those scenarios. "People most need to work on being accurate and candid about what has happened," Shatte says. "Then they can take strides to remedy the situation."

Contact Andrew Shatte by email (ajshatte@adaptivlearning.com).

LEADING OTHERS IN A GLOBAL, DIVERSE WORLD

In this section, we bring together several articles that form a clear picture of the globalization and diversification of the workplace. Survival in today's business environment often requires a bold move toward globalization, not only in terms of customer base, but also in terms of employing workers from around the world who are also located across the world. If organizations want to tap the best and brightest to lead them, they must seek out people from a diverse array of backgrounds and cultures. The first article is a thought piece that describes how winning in a global economy requires the creativity that comes from diversity. The second article provocatively discusses the special challenges that women leaders face in contemporary business contexts. The last piece highlights the accomplishments of Ted Childs who is the head of workforce diversity at IBM. The stories he tells of the challenges of bringing diversity to a largely homogeneous organization are mind numbing.

Mighty Is the Mongrel

**WHAT DOES IT TAKE TO WIN IN THE GLOBAL ECONOMY?
A COMMITMENT TO MIXING PEOPLE, EXPERIENCES, AND IDEAS.
COMPANIES AND COUNTRIES THAT EMBRACE DIVERSITY TO
STIMULATE CREATIVITY WILL BE THE ONES THAT OWN THE FUTURE.**

Diversity defines the health and wealth of nations—as well as of companies and the people inside them. The mixing of races, ethnic groups, and nationalities—at home and abroad—is at a record level. In a world of deepening connections, individuals, organizations, and entire countries draw strength and personality from places as near as their local neighborhood and as far away as a distant continent. Mixing is the new norm. The hybrid is hip. Mighty is the mongrel.

This is no passing fashion. Rather, it is a deep change. Say good-bye to the pure, the straight, the smooth. Forget the original, the primordial, the one. Mixing trumps isolation. It spawns creativity, nourishes the human spirit, spurs economic growth, empowers nations. Racial, ethnic, and national categories no longer impose fixed barriers or unbending traditions. These categories do not vanish. Instead, they join the many pieces inside a kaleidoscope, presenting a different image from one instant to the next.

Nothing can stop the rise of mongrels—of people who mock the very idea that union requires homogeneity or that victory depends on smothering dissent in a blanket of uniformity. Rich nations will go mongrel because it is right and good. They will go mongrel because it is the only antidote to stagnation, the only durable source of innovation, the only viable way to preserve their traditions while embracing change.

And what goes for countries goes for companies as well. The conditions for creating wealth have changed in ways that play to the strengths of hybrid individuals, organizations, and nations. And those who wish to profit from changing economic conditions must view hybridity as their first and best option.

The ability to apply knowledge to new situations is the most valued currency in today's economy. More than ever, creativity rewards those who exercise it, so curiosity about the source of creativity has never been higher. How creativity comes about is a riddle, but a few things seem clear. Highly creative people don't necessarily excel in raw brainpower. They are misfits on some level. They tend to question accepted views and to consider contradictory ones. Not coincidentally, such an appreciation for paradox defines the mongrel mentality.

The implications of this asynchrony are plain to see: Divergent thinking is an essential ingredient of creativity. Diverse groups produce diverse thinking. Ergo, diversity promotes creativity. This logic applies to corporations, research teams, think tanks, and other groups of creators. Those who rely on diverse people are more likely to innovate than those who rely on platoons of similar people.

To be sure, hybridity poses risks. A hybrid person may lose himself in a jumble of affiliations. A hybrid nation may botch the process of reinvention. Still, the price of such errors seems lower than the cost of circling the ethnic wagons and either shutting out people who are different or forcing them to become "one of us." Never before have so many people married across racial and ethnic lines. Never before have so many people left their homelands for work or pleasure. Never before have so many people touched or tasted the clothes, foods, musical styles, and ideas of cultures not available to them in their youth. These people are not becoming phantoms or dilettantes. Rather, they are part of an outpouring of human creativity that is being driven by radical mixing.

What follows, then, are portraits in the new power of hybrids, in the triumph of mongrels. In meeting these mongrels, we are meeting ourselves—and our future. "You cannot spill a drop of American blood," Herman Melville wrote in 1849, "without spilling the blood of the whole world." More than ever, Melville's declaration applies not only to America, but to all nations.

INNOVATION: "I FEEL LIKE I BELONG ANYWHERE"

Radha Basu's job spans the world. Literally. From her base in Cupertino, California, she manages teams of Hewlett-Packard software writers who work in California and Colorado, in Australia, England, Germany, India, Japan, and Switzerland. Born and educated in India, she earned a computer-science degree in the United States, became a naturalized U.S. citizen, and notched her first experience as an international manager in Germany. "I feel like a global person," she says. "I feel like I belong anywhere."

Her feeling is appropriate, given the realities of business today. In many industries, gone are the days when a single location produced an entire project or product. The need to finish products and services quickly—and in forms varied enough to satisfy local differences—means that designers often must work around the clock. This "following the sun" approach works best when tasks are split between continents. And, as the search for talent gets more heated, global managers must be technically adept but culturally sensitive, familiar with corporate rules but flexible enough to bend those rules when necessary. Above all, they must get their message across to people who are working across many time zones—15 time zones, in Basu's case.

Basu has thrived at Hewlett-Packard. In 1985, after two years in Germany, she was sent to India to set up a software unit in that country. Hewlett-Packard was among the first multinationals to tap Indian software prowess by setting up local operations, and Basu would become a formative figure in India's now-booming code sector. The assignment thrilled her: She had long wanted to give something back to her homeland.

Basu's four years in India were rocky. Her Anglo and European colleagues at Hewlett-Packard considered her to be ideal for the job, but local Indians resented her for leaving their country and returning as the standard-bearer of a U.S. company. But by the time she left India, in 1989, Hewlett-Packard's India offices employed 400 people and comprised one of the company's most successful offshore units. Basu's husband, meanwhile, launched one of India's first public computer networks.

A decade later, Basu maintains close ties to India. Besides helping to hire local software developers, she came up with a plan to help found a half-dozen companies in Bangalore and Madras by having Hewlett-Packard contract with them for services. Some of those companies even set up shop in Hewlett-Packard's facilities in order to save money and to obtain proper support from the very start.

To be sure, Hewlett-Packard could have hired people from those companies directly, but Basu has long felt that "you don't have to own all of the organization in order to succeed." The idea of a big company serving as a seedbed for local entrepreneurs appeals to her—especially since, in many places, people with good ideas but no track record can't get funding. "This is a new way of empowering people," says Basu. "And not just in India. The idea applies just as well to Brazil, China, the Czech Republic, and other developing countries with lots of technical talent."

The interconnectedness of hybridity, innovation, and growth still eludes most Americans. In the new economy, ideas and innovation—the chief currency of hybrids—are at the heart of commercial success. The costs of assembling the minds required to develop a conceptual product are small compared with the potential rewards of setting a standard or creating a "killer" application. So canny employers are often willing to pay the finest foreign talent even more than they pay local talent—not underbidding for foreign talent, as nativists fear, but often overbidding.

That is a principle by which Basu has worked for 17 years. "We use our diversity to great advantage," she says. The mathematics of creativity means that casting a wide net for key people is a necessity. But the value of diversity involves more than just numbers. Strangers instinctively question things that natives take for granted. They are in a position to stimulate new perspectives because, to put it simply, many things strike them as odd or stupid. That's why it's great for any tribe to have a smart stranger injected into it. Under the right conditions, the newcomer aids the group—an effect that is increased if the group is already mongrelized, because then resistance to the outsider will be lower.

IDENTITY: ROOTS ARE NOT A ZERO-SUM GAME

The shiny steel machine bellows like a whale. Donald Jagau, his long hair wrapped in a net, leans over the belly of the machine and shifts the position of a small circuit board that is inching along a conveyor belt. Holding a gas torch in his gloved hand, he burns some excess solder off the machine's scrubber. Sweat runs down his forehead, gathering in a pool above his plastic goggles. It is 90 degrees in the sealed, brightly lit "hot-air" room. But Jagau steps lightly. He's used to the heat. He grew up in the jungles of Borneo, where the heat is worse.

One day in the summer of 1995, while cutting down a tree in the thick forest surrounding his village, Jagau heard an announcement on his portable radio. A U.S. company was looking for workers to hire and train for skilled jobs in one of the first high-tech factories in Kuching, Malaysia. The only requirement was a knowledge of basic English and a high-school degree. Jagau had both. He also had a desire to earn more than he could by cutting down trees and growing rice in nearby paddy fields.

The U.S. company, Hadco, makes printed circuit boards. It already had a factory in Silicon Valley, but it needed a foreign location to cut costs. It chose Kuching, which is an hour's flight from Penang, Malaysia's high-tech center. The move meant lower costs, but it also meant recruiting an entire workforce from scratch. To guarantee that new employees understood how to run an advanced electronics plant, the company planned to send about 100 of them to its factory in the United States for an 11-month apprenticeship.

It took Jagau three hours, traveling by riverboat, van, and bus, to reach Kuching. He got the job.

In California, Jagau thrived. His easy manner and infectious laugh won over Americans—and put at ease, too, the many Mexican immigrants who worked in Hadco's factory. He had a knack for understanding the way machines work. In training classes, he said little but understood a lot. After work, in a bungalow that he shared with five other Malaysians, he made detailed drawings of the arcane machines that were used in the factory. He pored over manuals written in dry English; he memorized daily routines.

Jagau was about to begin living simultaneously in two worlds. In California, he could pretend that he wasn't a Bidayuh, plucked out of the jungle by some mysterious American corporation and transported to Disneyland. He could imagine himself as a member of any of the dozen nationalities that were represented in the factory. He belonged there, as much as the Mexicans or the Vietnamese belonged there. His English was even better than that of most of the other immigrants. But back in Kuching, he could not escape his past—his ties to the Bidayuh, to his parents, and, most of all, to his wife, Lucy. "I am modern; she is not," he told me as we made the short walk from the factory to his bungalow. He had an email account, and the person he cared most about had never heard a dial tone.

Returning to Malaysia, Jagau resumed work at Hadco, whose factory was ready to launch. He and Lucy lived in a tiny shack. But at the factory, he ate breakfast—often pancakes, which he had grown to like in the United States. After breakfast, he put on his work clothes, and the fun started. He was good at his job. His machine enveloped his mind; it was no surprise that he often dreamed about it. After six months, Hadco asked him to begin training others. The company even began hiring people on his say-so—people from his village or from neighboring villages.

It is easy to paint Jagau as an Asian Horatio Alger, a creature of a U.S. multinational. Cynics paint such corporate behemoths as bloodsuckers, but I have seen countless examples of how they can transform the material and psychological lives of their employees. And not just in developing countries: The best multinationals are agents of change that create insurgents within the societies that they invade or, at the very least, that foster centers of excellence. Those insurgents then fan out across a society, carrying a greater sense of professionalism and more powerful technical skills than people who operate in a strictly local economy.

Jagau is my favorite example of this phenomenon, if only because he has traveled further—from his childhood until now—than anyone I know. He is a multinational corporate asset. And, as that asset, he has not only seen California but also traveled to London and Edinburgh for training on new machinery. Jagau has moved into the world of achievement, where his sense of self derives from what he has accomplished and what he owns.

The trappings of modern life, though, do not diminish Jagau. His experiences in America, his mastery over one aspect of a bewildering technological jungle, his rising material life in Kuching, his growing sense of self-worth—all of these factors make Jagau more, not less, than he was before. To him, affiliations can be piled up like chips on a card table. They are not enemies of his inherited identity. Even as his horizons broaden, he retains his passion for his village, his parents, and his Bidayuh past.

Roots are not a zero-sum game. One attachment does not lessen another. Indeed, people can have both roots and wings. They can be proud of their background but unafraid of adding to their identity. By having both roots and wings, they help to preserve the groups to which they belong while at the same time realizing their individual freedom and exposing their groups to nourishing outside influences. Hybrid lives, therefore, are good for individuals and good for the groups to which they belong. In short, hybridity pays. And, in the present economic moment, hybridity pays well.

STRATEGY: THE COSMOPOLITAN CORPORATION

Hybrids are everywhere, but multinational corporations are hybrid hothouses. The best corporations set the pace in diversity. Their mission is to match people and needs, regardless of nationality, race, or ethnicity. And the best managers want employees to retain their differences in order to make the most of their uniqueness and the most of the creative tension spawned by those differences. Employers don't want hollow harmony. They want a cosmopolitan corporation.

Hybrid teams are the new corporate ideal. Indeed, careers are now made or broken over diversity. The triumph of English as the language of business has made it easier for corporations to hire the best and brightest from around the world and then to mix those people together. International mergers have also spurred the trade in managers, which in turn promotes mixing. The mongrelization of management goes all the way to the top. An unprecedented number of foreign-born CEOs run major companies in the United States, Britain, and several other countries, according to a study by Denis Lyons, an executive recruiter in New York City. "The dawn of the millennium is ushering in a true global marketplace for CEOs," he writes.

As chief executives circulate, they form a global fraternity not unlike the aristocracy of the Middle Ages, whose members followed booty and glory regardless of national borders. To be sure, CEOs are a special case, but they are also the model for the business hybrid. In technical fields already, borders are becoming less and less meaningful. In engineering, physics, code writing, and all types of design, people carry their roots with them like the 16th-century explorers who sailed ships on behalf of wealthy patrons. U.S. corporations get their pick. The Chinese or Indian engineer who works in the United States is a cliché, but less is known about the American architects, salespeople, and shopping-mall developers who serve foreign corporations. Some live abroad; others shuttle back and forth. For these folks, a "day at the office" can mean a trip to another continent.

At the best companies, building diverse teams has become a routine part of business and a central piece of strategy. McKinsey & Co., the global consultancy, illustrates this trend. In the 1970s, most of its consultants were American, and its foreign contingent came from about 20 countries. By the mid-1980s, Americans still accounted for more than half of all McKinsey consultants, although the company drew from a wider range of foreign countries—perhaps 30 in all. In the 1990s, the trend accelerated. By 1999, McKinsey's chief partner was a foreign national (he hails from India); only 40% of its 4,800 consultants were American; and its foreign-born consultants came from more than 40 countries.

The diversity at McKinsey means that there's no dominant group—no identity mold. And the company's "United Nations" profile isn't merely a reflection of where its customers are. The idea isn't to assign Indians to Indian customers, say, or French nationals to French customers. That's old thinking. New thinking presents the hybrid team as a positive agent. The members of McKinsey's 40-odd nationalities aren't necessarily where they "should" be. "If you let a meritocracy prevail, you're bound to get a lot of diversity," says Rajat Gupta, McKinsey's chief partner.

McKinsey encourages an appreciation for difference by having each of its offices evaluated annually by a consultant from somewhere else in the world. The head of its San Francisco office may review Dusseldorf. Paris may review Mexico City. This process acts as a check and balance by preventing too much coziness from forming between partners in a country or region. But a side benefit of such evaluations is that they raise cultural sensitivity and promote the intermingling of traits. "There's an obligation to see things from other points of view," says one McKinsey partner. "That's hardwired into this place."

Cosmopolitan corporations don't localize overseas operations; they seek a dynamic blend among strangers. That's quite different from what passes for diversity at some U.S. companies that practice "ethnic" marketing—such as hiring a black to manage accounts in Harlem, or a Hispanic to handle the south-Texas region. Ethnic marketing is blithely presented as a form of multiculturalism, but it smacks of tokenism and is based on a dubious business model.

Rather than try to pigeonhole customers, the hybrid enterprise acts as if they are all mongrels. Hybrid marketers don't seek one-dimensional terms to describe customers. Their approach contradicts the premise of ethnic marketing, which is to put people in boxes. Ethnic marketing may work for a time, but it won't endure. It will end up chasing the shifting borders of identity and alienating potential customers. Market researchers will end up talking about the specific buying habits of, say, "second-generation Bolivian-Japanese males married to fourth-generation Russian-Arab women who have a university degree and fewer than two children."

Hybridization also takes place at lower corporate levels, as the experience of Donald Jagau suggests. In the new corporate ethos, not only are employees entitled to their differences—they should revel in them. By pouring their authentic identities into their jobs, employees become more creative and effective. Corporations are discarding the old assumption that all employees must think and act the same— that they must bring the same tools, attitudes, and values, or even the same language, to work.

A modem factory in Morton Grove, Illinois is typical. The factory's 1,200 workers speak 20 different languages, forming an industrial Tower of Babel. It's a miracle that the plant runs at all. Pragmatism rules. The owner of the plant, 3Com, takes a simple approach. "Managers don't even try to accommodate cultural quirks—probably an impossibility anyway," notes one observer. "They just make it clear that they expect newcomers to adapt to the factory's methods." On the plant floor, employees must mingle and cooperate, but in the lunchroom, they can cluster in their ethnic and linguistic groups if they wish.

Often, a team requires such specialized talents that it can be assembled only virtually, or by drawing members from locations around the world. Speed is another factor. Scattering members of a team across time zones makes around-the-clock progress possible. One set of team members can write code during the day, and while those workers sleep, colleagues on the other side of the planet can test the code. When members of the first group arrive at work the next morning, they can see a list of their mistakes—and that hastens the process of improvement.

Such global teams are on the rise—and not only because of time pressures and skill shortages. Corporations find that the line between "local" and "global" blurs when they are designing many products and services. No master recipe controls the balance between local and global elements. Since the balance constantly shifts, many companies hybridize their teams.

Consider Philips, the world's largest consumer-electronics company outside of Japan. In the 1990s, the Amsterdam-based company transformed its approach to design under the leadership of Stefan Marzano, an Italian who believes that creativity is stimulated by unusual combinations of people. He hybridized a Dutch-heavy team and built an operation with offices in 20 countries, including France, India, Singapore, Taiwan, and the United States. Among his staff of 500, he counted 33 nationalities.

Marzano didn't just look for a mix of ethnicities and nationalities. An architect by training and a professor at a design school in Milan, he also expanded the definition of "designer" and moved beyond the traditional boundaries of industrial engineering. He hired anthropologists, psychologists, sociologists, and architects. He loaded up on young people—another means of achieving fresh thinking—and drove down to 33 years the median age of the people in his division. Finally, he added another creative dimension to his staff by increasing the number of women on it to 40%.

By the late 1990s, Marzano's retooling had turned Philips into a trendsetter for consumer-product design. The company introduced splashy colors and aerodynamic styling to its line of traditionally black, boxy products. Philips didn't stop at aesthetics: Relying on original field research on how people around the world brush their teeth, take their coffee, and even chop their vegetables, company designers now influence how appliances work—and how consumers behave.

CHANGE: GET THE BEST PEOPLE, WHEREVER THEY ARE

The benefits of hybridization can be great, but conversion takes practice. It isn't easy for a mature corporation, with scant diversity, to go hybrid quickly. Because national identification seeps into the crevices of all corporations, many of them behave more like "national champions" than like global competitors. Headquarters retains its national character and is largely cut off from outsiders. Such corporations don't even realize that they need to hybridize. Some leaders of U.S.-based companies, because they rely on a diverse workforce or because their founders are foreign, hybridize organically. Others, like the managers at McKinsey, pragmatically pursue that end, gearing their training, tactics, and strategies toward it. But many corporate leaders believe that it's just too daunting to mongrelize their talent.

It is not. A company can consciously strive to raise the level of mixing among its employees—and in a way that creates not more opportunities for assimilation into a dominant style but a kaleidoscope of styles and interests. Yet the ideal of hybridity has been misunderstood even by people who decry the limitations of a national approach to business culture. Kenichi Ohmae, the longtime chief of McKinsey's Japanese consulting practice, advised companies in a 1990 book to "create a system of values shared by company managers around the globe to replace the glue a nation-based orientation once provided." He added, "Country of origin does not matter."

If naively followed, such advice diminishes people. A person's origins matter. Rather than promote creativity, a complete identification of an employee with his employer's transnational network robs him of what local identities have to offer. Indeed, many executives are leery of abandoning national identity—because the alternative seems worse: an empty globalization that produces a workforce without soul. Surely, it is better to embrace both roots and wings and to craft ways for the local and the global to drive performance together. But how?

The German pharmaceuticals company Schering AG is wrestling with this very question. Schering employs 56% of its 22,000 workers outside its home country—chiefly in the United States and Japan, where its subsidiaries have traditionally operated quite independently of one another. A major difficulty is that few American or Japanese employees work in Schering's sprawling Berlin headquarters, and just a handful of non-Germans rank among its top 100 executives. By contrast, hundreds of Germans work in foreign units. To be sure, some Americans and Japanese visit Berlin frequently, but the company's core remains dominated by Germans who shape its priorities, from research to marketing.

Enter Dieter Schmeier, a 29-year veteran of Schering and a native German. As top managers wrestled with the company's lack of diversity in its main operations, Schmeier, an organizational psychologist, stepped back from the problem. He enrolled in a management program at Harvard. For four months, he lived in a dorm with eight other executives, and he and they were expected to tackle class assignments together. Two of them were from the United States, and one each came from Australia, Canada, China, India, the Philippines, and South Africa.

Schmeier had never been part of such a diverse team and was skeptical of the value of mixing people so thoroughly. The routine seemed hard—and not only because he had to work in English, the native language of nearly everyone else in his group. He also found that the Americans (and, to a surprising degree, the Australian, Canadian, and Indian participants) reached decisions very quickly—even too quickly. "They are hip shooters," he says. "We [Germans] are more analytical. We're more logical and systematic."

As the months went by, Schmeier began to realize that Harvard was "very clever to bring together people with very different backgrounds." His outlook on mixing began to shift—from disbelief that mere cohabitation could do much to promote understanding to positive attraction to the ideal of mixing. He understood what many Americans take for granted: the power of diversity.

Schmeier's insight fired his imagination: Could Schering do, on a grander scale, what Harvard had done? When he returned to Germany, he was a man possessed: Mixing matters, he told people.

They started to listen. Schering's board asked Schmeier to draw up a plan for hybridizing the company. He made a radical proposal that boiled down to this: Get the best people, wherever they are and no matter what country they are from. This idea represented a dramatic change from company practice. Schering limits job contests by country. Thus, when a marketing post in Berlin comes open, only Germans learn of it. Similarly, only Japanese employees would be up for a Tokyo job. The system effectively makes mixing impossible.

Schmeier wanted that system scrapped. He argued that Schering should not only open up competition for its jobs but also circulate more of its foreign talent. Nearly 95% of its executives working outside their home country were German. As a result, not only couldn't Americans win rotations into Germany; they couldn't win rotations anywhere. "We have to change this imbalance," Schmeier urged. "It's absolutely necessary."

Schmeier made another key point: Employees should circulate more frequently, despite the extra cost. Drawing on his Harvard experience, he insisted that it was through a critical mass of associations with strangers that people really grow—that reaching a threshold of experience in several places is more important than simply getting to know one new place. "If they stay too long in one country," he says, "then the idea to make a person multicultural gets lost. Then we will be helping a German become an American or a Frenchman. That's not the idea."

The board approved Schmeier's plan. Yet many barriers remain. Employees must be encouraged to move. Their new jobs must be attractive. Middle managers must grow enthusiastic about the vision, because, in the end, they make most hiring decisions. They are the ones who must work alongside strangers after decades of working only with their own kind. Schmeier cannot predict how quickly this change will happen, although he believes that his company's future depends on it.

So he remains possessed of a vision of tomorrow caught in the claws of the present. "Today, if we have a vacancy," he says, "we maybe think of three names: Muller, Schmidt, Lagenstein. What we have in mind in future is to have a different set of names: Smith, Lee Ping, Rodriguez. That is the idea."*

G. Pascal Zachary (gregg.zachary@wsj.com) is a London-based senior writer for the "Wall Street Journal." This article is drawn from his forthcoming book, "The Global

Me" (Public Affairs, July 2000). (Radha Basu left Hewlett-Packard in 1999 to become CEO of Support.com, an Internet-solutions company in Redwood City, California.)

UNITED STATES OF DIVERSITY

People can argue about what makes a 50-mile stretch of northern California so successful. But certainly no one can argue that Silicon Valley is a monoculture. It has become a poster child for the power of mongrelization; the mixing of people is central to its success. "If you subtracted that," says Anna Eschoo, a member of Congress who represents the area, "the Valley would collapse." Indeed, at least one-third of the Valley's scientists and engineers are immigrants. They come from Europe, Latin America, the Middle East, and, in particular, Asia. Since 1980, Chinese and Indian immigrants alone have founded 2,700 companies, which in turn employ 58,000 people.

Silicon Valley is not an aberration. Throughout the United States, hybridity pays off in higher-quality ideas, in greater flexibility, and in closer ties to places and people around the world. The United States offers the best example of what happens economically when an entire business class exploits hybridity. The new economic paradigm turns hybrids into a signal economic weapon. And, because the United States has more hybrids than anywhere else, it gets a bigger bang from hybridity than any other country.

But the idea is spreading. Edgar van Ommen, managing director of Sony's unit in Berlin, believes in the "principle of United Nations." His prime directive is to recruit the best people for his team, regardless of their nationality. Sure, that makes life tougher for managers. But what's the alternative? For the most idea-driven enterprises, a focus on one nationality is too limiting. Ommen grew up in Austria, married a German, holds a Dutch passport, and keeps a second home in Bangkok. Two-thirds of the 60 people on his team come from outside Germany; they represent more than a dozen nationalities. "The engineering of a concept is a lot easier because each person shows a different emotion as to what's being presented," Ommen says. "Maybe the Turkish lady likes it, but the Sri Lankan doesn't." To think great thoughts, he says, employees must contribute their "whole being," not just their mind. Heated argument may spur fresh ideas. Passion matters.

BY MARGARET HEFFERNAN   FROM *FAST COMPANY* ISSUE 61, PAGE 58

The Female CEO ca. 2002

HERE ARE THE FIVE NAKED TRUTHS ABOUT WOMEN IN BUSINESS. TOGETHER THEY ADD UP TO ONE BIG MESSAGE: THE FUTURE OF BUSINESS DEPENDS ON WOMEN.

Memo
To: All You Businessmen
From: Margaret Heffernan
Re: Can't We Just Work Together?
CC: All Us Businesswomen

Hey, guys! What's the deal with you? You know how important women are—to your businesses as coworkers and as customers and to your lives as, well, fellow human beings—and yet you still can't figure out a reasonable way to work and live with the more than 50% of the world that happens to be us. Well, I think I can help—just by telling you five naked truths about why women still get screwed in the world of business.

But first, I want to tell you a story—and it happens to be a true one.

I was riding on the elevator at work when the doors opened and a young woman got on. After a few seconds of the usual silence, she looked at me and said, "Excuse me. Are you Margaret?"

"Yes," I answered, not knowing what to expect next.

"I just wanted to meet you and shake your hand," she said. "I've never seen a female CEO before."

It's a true story, and it doesn't date from the Middle Ages—or even from last millennium. It happened in Boston in the year 2000 in the offices of CMGI. And what made it remarkable was that it wasn't unusual: Most men and women in business have never seen a female CEO—much less worked with one.

And it looked like we were doing so well! (Or at least that's what we told one another.) More women than ever before hold senior executive positions and sit on corporate boards. Legislation protects pay, maternity leave, and employment rights. The top financial-services firms are busy developing new products and services for a generation of professional women who manage substantial portfolios, who use their tremendous buying power with sharp business acumen, and who will outlive their husbands by a good number of years.

Every one out of four women earns more than her husband. Women control about 80% of household spending and, using their own resources, make up 47% of investors. Women buy 81% of all products and services, buy 75% of all over-the-counter medications, make 81% of retail purchases, and buy 82% of groceries.

Women account for 80% of household spending. Eighty percent of the checks written in the United States are signed by women. Forty percent of all business travelers are women. They are responsible for 51% of all travel and consumer-electronics purchases. Women influence 85% of all automobile purchases. They also head 40% of all U.S. households with incomes over $600,000 and own roughly 66% of all home-based businesses. Women have been the majority of voters in this country since 1964.

Small wonder, then, that car companies and electronics companies are honing their products' designs with women in mind. It makes sense for *Fortune* magazine to convene an annual conference of powerful women and then to feature Oprah on its cover. Then there's Meg and Carly, Pat and Anne—exhibits A through D to make the case that it's only a matter of time before women reach a state of total equality. And you don't hear women whining anymore, do you?

Well, it all depends on who you talk to. I've spent the past year talking to women, hearing funny, sad, outrageous stories. Those women aren't whining. They're not even complaining. But they do tell a different story than the one that we'd all like to believe.

For example: The wage gap between male and female managers actually widened in the prosperous years between 1995 and 2000. In the communications industry, for instance, a woman earns 73 cents for every $1 a man takes home. Five years earlier, she made 86 cents. The widest pay gap, of course, is between parents. Fathers simply make a lot more than mothers do. Only 4% of the top earners at *Fortune* 500 companies are women. Women fill only 7.3% of the total line positions held by corporate officers. Where women do hold executive positions, they are more often in management jobs that have relatively lower status—and hence less power. In the past 10 years, the percentage of business-school applicants who are women has not risen at all. It has remained stuck at around 38%. Meanwhile, women are leaving corporate America in droves. And by the way: Between 1992 and 2000, the number of sexual-harassment claims increased by 50%.

What's going on?

During the past 10 years, I have run five businesses, including old-economy and new-economy businesses in both the United States and the United Kingdom. I've hired, fired, and managed hundreds of women (and men) in every discipline and at every level. During the past year, I've interviewed many more women about their careers and their lives—and about the connections or gulfs between the two. What I've learned is just how wrong the conventional wisdom is. Here's the naked truth about women in business today.

1. TOXIC BOSSES STILL CREATE UNFRIENDLY WORK ENVIRONMENTS.

"Neutron Jack" Welch and "Chainsaw Al" Dunlap may have inspired men, but macho leadership styles continue to alienate women. The Boom Boom Room of Smith Barney was more luxurious than the cubicles of software startups, but I've talked to too many women in both environments who have been—and who continue to be—subjected to routine sexual harassment. I've even unwittingly hired some of the perps—liberated guys who definitely know better.

The truth is, the macho exhilaration of coding through the night holds no charm for female engineers. For women executives, racing rental cars around the hotel parking lot is not a cheap thrill. But you will find women enduring these events—sometimes even competing to join them—because they know that it's where the important information always surfaces. When women are asked to name the most significant factors that are holding them back from advancement, the top two answers are "exclusion from informal networks of communication" and "male stereotyping and preconceptions of women."

And it's not just about sex. There's also the money: Men still routinely underpay women and think nothing of it. For years I was the only woman CEO at CMGI. But it wasn't until I read the company's proxy statement that I realized that my salary was 50% of that of my male counterparts. I had the CEO title, but I was being paid as if I were a director.

Of course, I was already accustomed to environments that were riddled with stereotypes. At one point in my career, I received the following email: "I am concerned that you are building a company with too much of a female orientation. We are very strong in female subject promotions and very weak on the male subjects. Your employee population and Board of Directors composition seem to reflect this, as well. For instance, we seem to be strong on promoting gossip, cooking, stars, TV dramas, etc., but much lighter on the major sporting events, business, financial markets, science, autos, etc."

I saved that email. What amazed me about it was that man's preconceptions about "female" and "male" interests. Apparently, women aren't interested in sports, cars, or money.

Here's the bottom line: Toxic bosses claim to like women. But they like them strictly as ornaments, not as power players. Toxic bosses aren't overtly, outrageously sexist—except in occasional emails. And they're not even impossible to work for. But they do poison the atmosphere and pollute the environment. They do create alienating, macho cultures in which it's tough for women to have much fun. Somehow, they can never quite get over their feeling that women in business are charming, submissive, fun to have around, and nice as eye candy—but never quite "one of us."

Which is why women are leaving big companies as fast as they can. By 2005, there will be about 4.7 million self-employed women in the United States, up 77% since 1983. The increase for men? Just 6%. Women leave because they want to work differently and because they don't want to have to add the second job of becoming a change agent to their existing job. Women don't want to redecorate the company. They want to build something new, different, and theirs—from scratch.

2. WOMEN'S CHOICES ARE LIMITED: WHAT'LL IT BE? GEISHA, BITCH, OR GUY?

Everywhere I go, I hear women tell me that in order to progress, women must assimilate. They have to learn to act like a guy. Carly Fiorina's grim stare from the cover of *Business Week,* complete with cropped hair and dull-gray suit, suggests that assimilation works.

It just doesn't look like much fun. "Of all of the female lawyers who joined my firm when I did, only one remains," one female Boston attorney told me. "And she's just like a guy. I left because I didn't want to play the game."

Not surprisingly, none of the women I've spoken with really wants to be a man. And their stories have made me rethink my own. At one of the companies I ran, a core part of my job was to negotiate agreements with the labor unions. One of the union bosses took me out to lunch at a Chinese restaurant. He used the opportunity to order the most gruesome items on the menu: webbed chicken feet, ducks' tongues, lambs' testicles. The challenge was obvious—and I rose to it. I wasn't about to let him intimidate me; I ate it all. But where I used to tell that story with pride, I now realize that, in a way, I fell into his trap. A far better response to his test would have been to simply order my own dishes, food that I preferred. I should have refused to do the guy thing.

The alternative roles aren't any better. Geishas get jobs because they've got great legs, dress well, or in some way decorate the boss's office. They endure routine flattery—"You're such a treasure!"—and in the process, they end up trivialized. Assertive women get labeled as bitches. There's even a program in California for "bully broads," women whose assertiveness scares men and whose companies send them off to finishing school to learn how to temper their "challenging" behavior. *The Taming of the Shrew* comes to business.

"You can be a mistress, a daughter, a wife, a mother—or a guy," a high-ranking female property executive told me. Offered such an impoverished range of roles, it's not surprising that women choose the company of other women, creating our own jobs and job descriptions inside organizations that allow us a wider degree of personal expression.

3. YOU CAN'T HAVE IT ALL.

If men and women were truly equal at work, then both genders would hold roughly equal expectations of what is possible—and what isn't. But the truth is, they don't. When it comes to MBAs, fewer women than men get married. And fewer women MBAs have families. On Wall Street, 66% of men with MBAs have families, while 55% of women with MBAs do. The message here is simple: Men and women have very different views of what is manageable—because they have very different management roles.

Women who do have families ultimately find that they have to make other trade-offs, such as giving up private time, friends, hobbies—or ambition. I found that as I gave myself over to my job, I inevitably put my health at risk. It was a choice I had to make: either take time to exercise or give that time to my children.

Women have to give up something, because in dual-income families, women still do most of the child care and the housework. All too often, women collude in their own oppression. They let their mates off easy, holding steadfastly to the sense of power and self-esteem that comes from doing it all—and doing it well. "I like choosing what to cook for everyone," one British woman executive told me. "I like making the lunches and organizing the birthday parties. Does doing it all de-skill my husband? Well, yes. I guess it does."

The most stubbornly optimistic of us still maintain that we can have it all—just not all of it at once. As every woman in the world will tell you, "We all need a wife." But even more than a wife, what every woman I've spoken with yearns for is a life— a whole life, one in which women can be the same people at work that they are at home, with different tasks but with consistent values and styles.

4. WOMEN'S NEW MISSION: CHANGE THE GAME.

Women's goals used to be to get into management, to get onto the boards of *Fortune* 500 companies, to become CEO. There's a new goal. The aim now is more radical and more ambitious: It is to change the game entirely. Young women pursue a different model, play by different rules. "I love my career, but there are other things in life," one up-and-coming businesswoman told me. "I don't want to be CEO," another said. "I want a whole and healthy life—and even a recession isn't going to scare me into accepting something that isn't me."

When I think back to my career as a CEO, I have to ask: Why did I stay at a place where I was underpaid and subjected to absurd, sexist stereotypes? And when I had a baby, why was I only willing to give myself 10 days of maternity leave? Why would I choose to live like that? The answer I keep coming back to is this: I did those things because I had enough autonomy to create a different kind of culture for all of the people who worked for me. Much more than men, women are painfully aware of the antihuman—and certainly antiwoman—realities that define the contemporary workplace. We feel the harsh conditions, suffer the belittling indignities, battle the sexist innuendos. And we genuinely long for the opportunity to create different structures and different cultures where people can thrive, places where men and women alike can stop faking it and instead unleash their hearts and minds on businesses that respect their capabilities, their commonalities, and their differences.

The truth is, I've heard from plenty of men who talk about having to deal with the idiotic legacy of old-fashioned male stereotypes. Men may not suffer financially and politically the way women do. But the cultural artifacts of a workplace that still operates like a 1950s old-boy network is as frustrating for men as it is for women.

Changing the game starts with honesty. One of my employees at CMGI came to me after a planning meeting at which the refrain was, "Don't tell Margaret." When she had the temerity to ask why I should be kept in the dark, she was told that I was "too honest." The men in the meeting who were advising her were afraid of what might happen if employees really knew what was going on. And they assumed that once I knew, I would share the information with others. What I learned from the story was this: Those men knew, at least intuitively, just how powerful the truth can be. Which is what I told my employee. I said, "There's no more powerful weapon for change than honesty." What she told me in response was, "Now I realize why I love working here. I've always been trusted with the truth, I always knew that I'd get straight answers. This is the first time that I've ever felt really respected at work."

When I talk with women, I'm always struck by their honesty, their directness, and their lack of posturing. Honesty has a way of releasing energy, the kind of energy that business desperately needs to embrace. Time after time, I've witnessed the paralysis that sets in when people are afraid to tell each other the truth. I've come to believe that it's part of the way that men relate to each other in the workplace. For all of their macho posing, most men are simply conflict averse. They don't really want to have an honest disagreement. And so they dodge one another, play turf games, engage in endless rounds of infighting and shadowboxing. They do anything they can to avoid sitting down with one another and telling the truth.

I've encountered CEOs who are unwilling to ask questions, because they're afraid of the answers. I've come into contact with CEOs who are unwilling to tell their direct reports that they are being replaced, because those CEOs are immobilized by the fear of bare emotions, terrified of unscripted conflict. I've seen deals hang in midair, because no one had the honesty to say out loud what everyone was thinking privately: *This is really stupid* and *It will never work.* And so millions of dollars and countless hours of work hover somewhere between intent and execution, with people in the know hoping that the whole mess will simply go away—but remaining unwilling to address the problem head-on.

Everyone I've spoken with on this matter—male and female alike—knows exactly what I'm talking about when I describe the awkward silence that sets in at corporate meetings when it becomes clear that the emperor has no clothes. Isn't that the most plausible explanation for what went on at Enron? The problem isn't that we don't know the truth. The problem is that we're afraid to speak the truth. Well, the truth is, women are much more likely than men to be truth tellers.

5. WOMEN WORK DIFFERENTLY FROM MEN.

This is the great unspoken truth, the new orthodoxy that every woman I have encountered acknowledges—although usually only in private or with a group of other women. Their caution betrays a fear that is commensurate with the truth: the fear that an acknowledgment of difference will come to mean an acceptance of inequality. A fear that "different from" will morph into "less than."

I don't believe that this is true. I don't believe that we can make meaningful progress as long as we willingly live a lie. More important, the new generation of women won't accept business on its old, dishonest terms.

The *Legally Blond* generation is not interested in compromise or assimilation. It wears its femininity with pride and seeks success on its own terms. If that success can't be found within traditional businesses or business schools, then these young women simply won't go there. "If I don't fit into GE or Ford or IBM," one bright young woman told me, "that's not my problem. That's their problem." Rather than fight the system, this next generation of women simply dismisses the system. Instead, these women seek places to work that value individuals—whether as customers or as employees. They seek places that are transparent and collaborative, that respect relationships as the bedrock of all good businesses. What women want are companies that look a lot more like a network than a pyramid, companies where fairness is a given, companies that value what's ethical above what's expedient.

At the same time, this next generation of women is too practical, pragmatic, and tough-minded to be dismissed as ideologues. If they can't find these kinds of companies, then they'll simply build them. What I love about the voices of these women is how they sound: They're not angry, strident, or arrogant—they're profoundly hopeful. These young women may not have seen many female CEOs, but that's just fine. In fact, it's wonderfully liberating. Unintimidated by precedent and unconstrained by convention, these women feel free to create their own style.

Not long ago, I attended yet another conference on business, competition, and where we are in the ongoing evolution of organizations. Needless to say, the speakers were almost all men. But one of them, a senior executive at a major multimedia company, caught my attention. He stood up in public in front of his peers and said, "Our way of doing business is broken."

Oddly enough, I found that admission enormously heartening. That executive said what most of us women already know: that the old command-and-control structures, inspired by or inherited from the military, simply aren't effective. And they are definitely not fun or inspiring. As I watch my female colleagues leave traditional business structures, as I see them flourish, as I notice how well networks protect women through a recession and how brutally men suffer from the harsh cutbacks and relentless downsizings that rumble through corporate hierarchies, it strikes me that women are building a parallel business universe. It's one in which companies work differently, one in which lives are lived honestly—a world of work where lives are integrated, not delegated.

If our way of doing business is indeed broken—and if the collapse of Enron, Andersen, Global Crossing, Kmart, and others are just the symptoms—then we had all better hope that this parallel universe is almost complete. We may need it sooner than we thought we would. And it sure looks like a lot more fun.

Margaret Heffernan (margaret_heffernan@hotmail.com) is writing a book on the naked truths about women in business.

BY KEITH H. HAMMONDS   FROM *FAST COMPANY* ISSUE 36, PAGE 258

Difference Is Power

LOTS OF COMPANIES TALK A GOOD GAME WHEN IT COMES TO THE PROPOSITION THAT DIFFERENT IS BETTER. TED CHILDS, IBM'S VICE PRESIDENT OF GLOBAL WORKFORCE DIVERSITY, WALKS THAT TALK.

"No matter who you are, you're going to have to work with people who are different from you. You're going to have to sell to people who are different from you, and buy from people who are different from you, and manage people who are different from you," says the thin, balding, black guy at the front of the auditorium, who demands to be taken seriously. "This is how we do business. If it's not your destination, you should get off the plane now."

This is management hardball, as well as gripping theater. Even though it's 9 PM (13 hours into their workday), the 60 newly promoted or recently hired first-level managers at IBM Learning Center, in Armonk, New York, are rapt. They understand that they underestimate J.T. "Ted" Childs Jr. at their own risk.

At least twice a month, Childs, IBM's vice president of global workforce diversity, lays some version of his stump speech on managers who have flown in from across the country. The speech is not standard corporate fare. Childs's lectures, uninterrupted and captivating, last for two hours. He brags, harangues, warns, and chides. During the third hour, he typically takes questions—then leaves his trainees to buzz among themselves into the night.

His lesson? Accepting, encouraging, and promoting diversity at IBM and beyond is good business. "We've moved beyond the moral imperative to the strategic imperative," he instructs. "What I want most is what's hardest to get: for business to see the link between diversity and competitiveness. Because if we don't understand that, we're not going to win."

Ted Childs is perhaps the most effective diversity executive on the planet. IBM has long been lauded for its progressive employment policies. And for just as long, it's also been known as a place where mostly white guys in mostly starched shirts hold all the cards. Since 1995, though, IBM has acquired a different look, largely because of Childs's strategic campaign to overhaul the company's practices pertaining to hiring and promoting women, ethnic minorities, and other groups that are underrepresented at IBM.

Between January 1996 and December 1999, the number of women executives at IBM worldwide has soared from 185 to 508. By the end of 1999, the number of minority execs working for IBM in the United States hit 270, up from 117 in 1995. "I'm intensely proud of that," Childs says. Both women and ethnic minorities are still scarce among the company's top 50 managers. But in March, for the third time in 15 years, Catalyst, an advocacy group for women in business, awarded IBM with a corporate-achievement award.

Childs, 55, grew up in Springfield, Massachusetts. He aspired to study at Amherst College, but his mother, a schoolteacher, and his father, a chemical analyst, insisted that he enroll at a predominantly black school, as they had. "You need to be in a dormitory with black boys," his mother said. "You need to have that experience at least once in your life." Childs went to West Virginia State College, which is largely black, but he ultimately helped integrate the school's racially divided social life by inviting both black and white bands to perform at the annual homecoming dance.

These days, Childs sports a purple baseball cap with his monogram and the initials of his college fraternity, Omega Psi Phi, on it. Above his coat pocket are three adornments: a fraternity pin, a red AIDS ribbon, and a multicolored orb that symbolizes global diversity. Together, they reflect what is most important to him—the essence of Ted Childs.

Childs spoke with Fast Company about the importance of corporate diversity and about his strategy for changing the face of IBM.

What's the tough-minded strategic case for diversity?

I've been trying to refashion the discussion about diversity and equal opportunity. This started for me back in 1980, when I took a leave of absence from IBM to work as executive assistant to Benjamin Hooks, who was head of the NAACP at the time. That was a very profound experience for me. I watched executives from large consumer companies meet with Ben and kiss his ring. They'd get photographed with him, then send those pictures to magazines like "Ebony" and "Jet."

Eventually, I came to understand what those executives were up to: All communities—African-Americans, Hispanics, women—have purchasing power. In America today, the number of women-owned startups is increasing faster than the number of startups in general. Minorities in the United States have $1.1 trillion in buying power, which is roughly equivalent to the world's seventh-biggest GDP. By 2050, the United States will be 50% white; 25% Latino; and 25% Asian, black, and other minorities. So it's not a bad thing if those communities view a company as a good place to do business.

When I returned to IBM, people patted me on the head and said, "That's nice, Ted." Back then, we were selling big boxes to big companies, so we didn't really touch consumers and small businesses. But personal computers started getting us into people's homes and into small businesses—many of which were owned by ethnic minorities, women, gays and lesbians, and the physically handicapped. That evolution presented an opportunity to have a different sort of discussion about diversity.

IBM does business in more than 160 countries. And global companies like IBM won't do very well for very long if its employees all look alike. Diversity of thought and culture and geography and race and gender enables us to bring the best solutions to our customers. If we don't reach out and make diversity a competitive advantage, it will become a liability. If customers go inside our company, they should see people who look like them at all levels.

So this is about protecting jobs. But it's also about getting and keeping talent. This insatiable hunger for talent must be reflected in our diversity effort. Workforce diversity is all about getting talented people from every group to work for you. We have a great opportunity. We can't afford to keep people out.

I had seen the opportunity in diversity long ago, and about four or five years ago, I took that message to two plants in North Carolina to see how white men there would react. Those men had never heard diversity discussed that way before—as something that they could benefit from and that would protect their jobs if they supported it.

Most people think of IBM as a historically "button-down" culture. Is it hard to make your arguments in the context of such a conservative past?

That straight-laced reputation is a misconception in many ways. I can look back 75 years and find an appreciation for the power of diversity inside IBM. In 1924, company president Tom Watson Sr. created the first Quarter Century Club—a club for people who had worked at IBM for at least 25 years. Among the 42 eligible members were three women, all of whom had worked at IBM since at least 1899—21 years before women's suffrage. One African-American was also in the club, having been an employee in 1899—10 years before the founding of the NAACP. Our hiring policy for professional women in 1935 was equal pay for equal work. We had a woman vice president in 1943. We hired black salesmen—salesmen!—in 1946.

When Tom Watson Jr. became CEO in 1956, he hosted a meeting of senior managers in Williamsburg, Virginia. He had recently received a letter, which was more than four pages long, from a man who wanted to be an IBM salesman but couldn't get hired. The letter said something to the effect of "I'm a graduate of a big-10 university, and I have a law degree from an Ivy League school. After several interviews, I finally said to the last man who interviewed me, 'Look, can you tell me why you fellows won't hire me? Because I have to give my wife an explanation. Is it my Jewish name?' And, of course, the gentleman said, 'No, we just think you're overqualified.'"

After reading the letter to senior management, Mr. Watson said that he never wanted a person's race or religious beliefs to factor into who gets hired and who doesn't. He just wanted people who could do the job. He told the managers in the room, "I want to know who on our team was involved in this situation, because whoever was shouldn't work here anymore."

That heritage was the foundation for what we're doing now.

Heritage is one thing, but progress is another. You've spent five years on a campaign inside IBM...

Real change takes time. In 1995, eight executive task forces were assembled—one each for African-Americans, Asians, disabled people, gays and lesbians, Hispanics, Native Americans, white males, and women—to look at IBM through the eyes of that constituency. Executives from each of the groups led their respective task forces. We also assigned a senior vice president—one of the CEO's direct reports—to sponsor each group.

The task forces were charged with answering three questions: What is necessary for your group to feel welcomed and valued at IBM? What can we do, in partnership with your group, to maximize your group's productivity? What can we do to influence your group's buying decisions, so that IBM is seen as a solution provider? I chose July 14, Bastille Day, as the task-force launch day because it's considered to be a day of social disruption. We were looking for some constructive disruption at IBM.

Lou Gerstner began the first meeting of task-force chairs. He spoke for 20 minutes about what he wanted, reinforcing his commitment to Team IBM. He said that he didn't want anyone to create divisiveness. Then he left. When I was sure that he was gone, I said, "Look, you're all here because I handpicked you. And you all know I fought for this, so I don't want any misunderstandings. I want to remind you of something. Many of you have bitched to me privately, saying such things as 'I'm a woman, and I had to go through this,' or 'I'm black, and I have to live with this.' Well, now you've been given a license to help us all understand those issues. And if nothing else, be motivated by what you've encountered during your career that you didn't think was fair. Make this a better place for the kids who will be your predecessors, so that maybe they won't encounter those same problems."

How have you encouraged people to represent their constituencies without turning IBM into a collection of special-interest groups?

We've taken steps to minimize that possibility. We continue to talk about the concept of Team IBM, and, once a month, I lead a meeting of all task-force chairs, during which I ask, "What are you working on? What are your issues?" I say, "Look, I want these meetings to be substantive. I want everyone to know what everyone else is working on. Because we need to be going forward as Team IBM, not as the black group, not as women, and not as gays and lesbians. We need to be going forward as a team with recommendations that will make this a better company. So think about what we can do to make IBM a better place for your constituency—and a better place for all people."

Because these executives were senior people in the company, they had enormous credibility. I knew that they weren't going to drive this project off a cliff. But at the first meeting, the chair of the white-male task force made a telling comment: He said that his group's members had concluded that their primary objective was to make sure that the other seven groups didn't see them as the problem. He made the comment humorously, so everybody laughed. But we also saw the value of his comment, and we knew that the guy who spoke was very thoughtful. He also said, "We recognize the issues here, and we want to be part of the solution. And part of our vision of the solution is that there will be more people who don't look like us in senior-management positions." That provided a foundation for enormous thought—and enormous cooperation.

What have these groups accomplished?

We scheduled their preliminary presentations for December 1, the anniversary of Rosa Parks's refusal to give up her seat on a bus. The groups each came back with two or three things that they thought were important for the company to address. Consistent throughout was a focus on the talent pipeline, employee development, and making sure that we had good, detailed recruiting strategies in place. That our development programs and our mentoring programs were at work. That we were sending crisp, clear messages to people about how they are valued. That we were sending clear messages to men that work-life is an issue for everyone, not just for women.

The white-male group presented a wonderful agenda. First, its leader said, if we are serious about diversity, then we need to take more ownership of it—ownership at the senior levels of the business. Second, if we are serious about the universal pertinence of work-life issues, then we need to start having discussions that address everyone, instead of just women. Third, if we are serious about diversity, then we ought to address the subject on a nationwide basis, not just within IBM.

One presentation that I was particularly eager to hear (to find out how it would be received) was the one from the gay and lesbian group, because I knew that its members' most important issue involved domestic-partner benefits. I thought it would be a benchmark discussion because some of the other constituencies had difficulty with those issues. But nothing exploded.

You were expecting more controversy?

When IBM was thinking about offering domestic-partner benefits, I was the one who led a discussion among senior management. Some employees worried that such a benefit would bring in more AIDS cases, which would drive up the cost of our premiums. So we had an outside firm examine our insurance expenses. And that company discovered that the cost of treating a catastrophic illness, such as cancer, or of dealing with a serious accident is typically higher than the cost of treating someone with AIDS. We pointed out that what increases medical costs most at IBM is childbirth.

We also pointed out that the group with the most education, the highest computer-literacy rate, and the largest disposable income, as a whole, is the gay community. So do we want to ignore that kind of a market? The diversity game is played from the neck up, which means that you have to use your brain.

In 1996, IBM announced that it was adding domestic-partner benefits, after which I spoke at an employee meeting. It was the first time in my career that I had been heckled, which actually intrigued me. People were upset about this policy. Finally, I said, "I think you guys are right. We shouldn't hire gays, and we shouldn't sell to them either. We should just walk away. It's a matter of principle. Walking away is going to cost some jobs, but the principle is important. Now, which one of you wants to be first to give up your job?"

Of course, no one moved.

Honestly, though, it's hard to imagine that those task forces have had an impact on something as complex, something as human, as barriers to diversity inside a company. What's the connection between their work and genuine results?

Let's take the women's task force, for instance. The senior-executive sponsor for that group was Ned Lautenbach, who at the time was senior vice president for worldwide sales and distribution. That's a major chunk of IBM's employee population. Before those task forces, Lautenbach's staff members would give him a slate of candidates from which they wanted him to choose someone to fill an executive position. He would generally approve the slate.

Well, he stopped doing that; he started rejecting the slates. He would ask, "Why are no women on the slates? I want to see women on the slates. And if these women are qualified to be on the slates, what's going to happen if we pick them for executive jobs? Is something bad going to happen?" He would ask logical questions to find out why people thought that a man would be best qualified for a particular job. And frequently, there wasn't a reason.

Somebody in power who was reviewing jobs had to push for fairness, and that person was Lautenbach. Before the first Global Women Leaders Conference, in

1998, Lautenbach wrote a letter to general managers around the world. He told them, "I want you to get back to me by September with your strategies for addressing our global-diversity challenges. And to help you, we're going to host our first Global Women Leaders Conference."

I added a couple of sentences to the letter, and after Lautenbach signed it, I got nervous. I went back to him and said, "I want to make sure that you read the entire letter, that you didn't just trust me and sign it." And I pointed out my addition, which read, "I want you to talk to our women leaders about the barriers to their advancement. I don't care about the opinions of the men." He said, "I read it. It's going to put starch in some collars, isn't it? But we've got to let these guys know that we're serious."

I wanted the men to understand that they were not going to determine what the issues were. They had to allow themselves to be influenced on the issue of the advancement of women by the views of the women. And that has happened. Since 1996, we've gone from one to 13 women executives in Asia; and we've gone from 5 to 46 in Africa, Europe, and the Middle East. Men are listening to women.

In 1998, I spoke about diversity to a group of employees that IBM had just contracted with. A few weeks earlier, women from that group had set up a women's network. I told them, "That's great, and I'm going to announce it at the town meeting." The women were worried because they thought that it would upset their male bosses. They wanted to keep it quiet. I said, "Trust me."

At the meeting, I said, "I'd like to congratulate the women here who have established a new women's network. And I'd especially like to congratulate their managers, who had the foresight to let this happen. You embody the values that we stand for at IBM." And I never heard about any problems.

IBM still isn't very diverse at the top. Why not?

That's true. Among our top 50 executives, we have only 2 African-Americans, 3 Asians, one Hispanic, and 4 women. But change is under way. Glass ceilings exist here. But they exist at the entry level. If you fill the pipeline with qualified, talented people, they will break through. We have an extraordinary pipeline, but we have to focus on that pipeline. We have to look down, not up.

The task forces are continuing their work. This year, each one will hold an executive forum. About 150 women are expected to attend this year's Global Women Leaders Conference, in July. In May, 700 people participated in an IBM Women in Technology Conference. Plans are also under way for a black-executives forum, a disabled-executives forum, a gay-and-lesbian-executives forum, a Hispanic-executives forum, a male-executives forum, and a Native American-executives forum. I recently went to Japan to speak to 1,600 women IBM leaders, at their second meeting. That's historic stuff for Japan. Pre-1995, that never would have happened.

I think this train is moving. We can argue that the pace is too slow. But I've been to a lot of places that I wouldn't have visited 10 years ago—including Lou Gerstner's office and the Oval Office. We're on a journey. It's not over.

Keith H. Hammonds (khammonds@fastcompany.com) is a *Fast Company* senior editor. Contact Ted Childs by email (childsjt@us.ibm.com).

LEADERSHIP OF THE FUTURE

In this final section, we look toward the future. The world is changing, organizations are changing, and consequently leadership must periodically reinvent itself. We have no crystal ball, but we can learn from expected trends in demographics, economics, and social dynamics. The first piece showcases Harvard University Ron Heifetz's thought-provoking ideas about the leader of the future. It is followed by Tom Peters' list of 50 reasons why leadership is going to get weirder, tougher, and even more turbulent in the next few years. The final piece discusses personal challenge and equates effective leadership with what it means to be a successful human being. Leaders need to look in the mirror before they can expect others to follow them confidently.

The Leader of the Future

HARVARD'S RONALD HEIFETZ OFFERS A SHORT COURSE ON THE FUTURE OF LEADERSHIP.

It's hard to imagine discussing "the leader of the future" without having a discussion with Ronald Heifetz—one of the world's leading authorities on leadership. Heifetz, 48, director of the Leadership Education Project at Harvard University's John F. Kennedy School of Government, is a scholar, a teacher, and a consultant. His course at Harvard, "Exercising Leadership," is legendary for its popularity with students and for its impact on them. His students (many of them in mid-career) include leaders from all walks of life: business executives, generals, priests and rabbis, politicians. His clients have included senior executives at BellSouth, who brought him on to conduct a two-year program on leadership in a fast-changing world, and the president of Ecuador, who is struggling to lead that nation through tough economic times.

What makes Heifetz's approach to leadership so compelling is that he is so honest about what real leadership demands. The book that rocketed him to prominence was called Leadership Without Easy Answers (Belknap/Harvard University Press, 1994). The role of the leader is changing, Heifetz argues. The new role is "to help people face reality and to mobilize them to make change." And making change is painful: "Many people have a 'smiley face' view of what it means to lead. They get a rude awakening when they find themselves with a leadership opportunity. Exercising leadership generates resistance—and pain. People are afraid that they will lose something that's worthwhile. They're afraid that they're going to have to give up something that they're comfortable with."

So why bother to lead? "There are lots of things in life that are worth the pain," he says. "Being a leader is one of them." In a series of conversations with Fast Company, Heifetz offered ideas, advice, and techniques for the leaders of the future.

HOW LEADERS SEE

There is so much hunger for leadership in business today. Everyone wants better leaders. What do great leaders do?

The real heroism of leadership involves having the courage to face reality—and helping the people around you to face reality. It's no accident that the word "vision" refers to our capacity to see. Of course, in business, vision has come to mean something abstract or even inspirational. But the quality of any vision depends on its accuracy, not just on its appeal or on how imaginative it is.

Mustering the courage to interrogate reality is a central function of a leader. And that requires the courage to face three realities at once. First, what values do we stand for—and are there gaps between those values and how we actually behave? Second, what are the skills and talents of our company—and are there gaps between those resources and what the market demands? Third, what opportunities does the future hold—and are there gaps between those opportunities and our ability to capitalize on them?

Now, don't get the wrong idea. Leaders don't answer those questions themselves. That's the old definition of leadership: The leader has the answers—the vision—and everything else is a sales job to persuade people to sign up for it. Leaders certainly provide direction. But that often means posing well-structured questions, rather than offering definitive answers. Imagine the differences in behavior between leaders who operate with the idea that "leadership means influencing the organization to follow the leader's vision" and those who operate with the idea that "leadership means influencing the organization to face its problems and to live into its opportunities." That second idea—mobilizing people to tackle tough challenges—is what defines the new job of the leader.

Most companies have a remarkable tendency to underestimate their external threats and to overestimate their own power. Why is it so hard for leaders to convince people to face reality?

Companies tend to be allergic to conflict—particularly companies that have been in operation for a long time. Being averse to conflict is understandable. Conflict is dangerous: It can damage relationships. It can threaten friendships. But conflict is the primary engine of creativity and innovation. People don't learn by staring into a mirror; people learn by encountering difference. So hand in hand with the courage to face reality comes the courage to surface and orchestrate conflicts.

Leaders of the future need to have the stomach for conflict and uncertainty—among their people and within themselves. That's why leaders of the future need to have an experimental mind-set. Some decisions will work, some won't. Some projects will pay off, some won't. But every decision and every project will teach you and your organization something about how the world is changing—and about how your company compares with its competition.

In other words, facing reality means facing up to mistakes and failures—especially your own failures. In the mid-1990s, Bill Gates made a big decision about the Internet. He decided that the Net wasn't going to be all that important. Then he changed his decision, because the people whom he was listening to contradicted his earlier decision. In the mid-1980s, Ken Olsen, the cofounder of Digital Equipment Corp., decided that personal computers weren't going to be all that important. He didn't change his decision very quickly, and Digital suffered as a result. These days, leaving any big decision in one person's hands is like playing Russian roulette. It's much safer to run multiple experiments. You never know which ideas are going to flourish and which ones are going to die.

If everything is subject to change, how can leaders help people keep their bearings?

Not everything is subject to change. If the role of the leader is first to help people face reality and then to mobilize them to make change, then one of the questions that defines both of those tasks is this: What's precious, and what's expendable? Which values and operations are so central to our core that if we lose them, we lose ourselves? And which assumptions, investments, and businesses are subject to radical change? At the highest level, the work of a leader is to lead conversations about what's essential and what's not.

Examples from politics abound. The civil-rights movement posed several questions: What's most precious about America? What values do we stand for? Do we stand for freedom and equal opportunity? Or do we stand for how we are living today? By posing those questions in such terms, Martin Luther King Jr. and the movement's other strategists generated conflict within the hearts and minds of many people around the country. People faced an internal contradiction between the values they espoused and the way they lived. Millions of people had to decide for themselves what was precious about their country and what was expendable about the supremacist lessons that they had learned.

Now, that is a very difficult inner conversation for anyone to have. Imagine how hard it was for Lew Platt, CEO of Hewlett-Packard, to lead conversations about breaking up that company—and about leaving the HP name with the computer business rather than with the test-and-measurement business, which is where William Hewlett and David Packard got their start. I wasn't privy to those conversations, but my guess is that they were quite emotional. You can understand the business logic: HP's technology is so established in the test-and-measurement world that the company can survive a name change in that business without losing market share. The HP name isn't what's precious. Even so, if you grew up in that business, immersed in the legend of Hewlett and Packard's innovation in a garage, it might seem awfully precious.

HOW LEADERS LISTEN

With leaders, the sense of sight—vision—is closely linked to the sense of hearing. People who love their boss often say, "She's a great listener." What does it mean to be a "great listener"?

Most leaders die with their mouths open. Leaders must know how to listen—and the art of listening is more subtle than most people think it is. But first, and just as important, leaders must want to listen. Good listening is fueled by curiosity and empathy: What's really happening here? Can I put myself in someone else's shoes? It's hard to be a great listener if you're not interested in other people.

Think about some of the best-known leaders in the airline business: Jan Carlzon at SAS (Scandinavian Airlines System) in the early 1980s, Colin Marshall at British Airways in the early 1990s, Herb Kelleher at Southwest Airlines today. These executives are always flying on their own airlines' planes. They're always talking with customers. They're always encouraging ticket agents and baggage handlers to be creative about helping customers to solve problems. They're in "dynamic listening" mode, asking questions all the time—and not getting seduced into trying to provide all of the answers. If you're the boss, the people around you will invariably sit back and wait for you to speak. They will create a vacuum of silence, and you will feel a compelling need to fill it. You need to have a special discipline not to fill that vacuum.

What else does it take to be a great listener?

Great listeners know how to listen musically as well as analytically. As president, Jimmy Carter relied on "rational discourse" to weigh the pros and cons of various initiatives. He would have people prepare papers, and then he would sift their views in private. Doing it that way enabled him to listen to their arguments analytically but not musically. What do I mean by that? Jimmy Carter did not enjoy being in meetings with people who were posturing, arguing, haggling. But there's an enormous amount of information in the haggling, and that information tells us quite a lot about the values, the history, and the personal stakes that people bring to an argument. It's difficult for someone who's lost the last six arguments to say in a policy paper, "I've lost the last six arguments. If I don't win the next one, what am I going to tell my people?"

But in a conversation, the tone of voice and the intensity of the argument give clues to that subtext. Listening musically enables leaders to get underneath and behind the surface to ask, "What's the real argument that we're having?" And that's a critical question to answer—because, in the absence of an answer to that question, you get superficial buy-in. People go along in a pseudo-consensus, or in a deferential way, but without commitment.

If curiosity is a prerequisite for listening, what's the enemy?

Grandiosity. Leaders need to check their sense of self-importance. But you shouldn't think that grandiosity arises from bad intentions. It usually grows out of the normal human need to feel important. I don't know any human being who doesn't want to feel important, who doesn't want to matter to other people. And those of us who have a strong need to be needed—I happen to have that need, so I know a lot about it—spend our lives solving other people's problems. It makes us feel needed: "Surely you have a problem that I can solve." But that orientation creates its own kind of problem. The more we demonstrate our capacity to take problems off other people's shoulders, the more authority we gain in their eyes—until, finally, we become a senior executive or a CEO. And, by then, the tracks have been laid so deeply inside our brain that it becomes hard to stand back, hard to listen, hard to learn from others. Our normal need to feel important—"Let me help you"—has been transformed into grandiosity: "I have all the answers."

HOW LEADERS FAIL

Why do so many people dislike their bosses? Why do so many of us not respect our leaders?

For decades, I've been interested in that question—because it sounds like a paradox: "Our leadership isn't exercising any leadership." Why do so many people feel that way about those who lead their companies or their communities? One reason is that people in positions of authority are frequently asked not to exercise their leadership. Instead of mobilizing their constituents to face tough, frustrating challenges, they are asked to protect those constituents from having to make adjustments. It's very hard for a congressman to go to his district and say, "Good news: The Cold War is over. Time for 10,000 of you to lose your jobs." He has been elected to his post to protect people from challenges that will require adjustments to their way of life.

That's why leadership is dangerous. Sure, you have to protect people from change. But you also have to "unprotect" them. It's dangerous to challenge people in a way that will require changes in their priorities, their values, their habits. It's dangerous to try to persuade people to take more responsibility than they feel comfortable with. And that's why so many leaders get marginalized, diverted, attacked, seduced. You want to be able to stir the pot without letting it boil over. You want to regulate disequilibrium, to keep people in a productive discomfort zone.

How do you keep people in a "productive discomfort zone"?

Attention is the currency of leadership. To a leader with formal authority, attention comes naturally. Fidel Castro can give a two-hour speech, and people will pay attention. So can Nelson Mandela. The president of the United States can give a State of the Union address that lasts an hour and 15 minutes. The big questions for that kind of leader are "How do I use that attention? What do I focus it on? When does a broad agenda become too broad? How do I push the organization without alienating my core constituency?" You have to remember: Drawing attention to tough challenges generates discomfort. So you want to pace the rate at which you frustrate or attempt to change expectations.

That means distinguishing between "ripe" and "unripe" issues. A ripe issue is one in which there is a general urgency for action. An unripe issue is one in which there is local urgency—a readiness to change within just one faction. The work that it takes to ripen an unripe issue is enormous—and quite dangerous. It needs to be done, but it's different from working a ripe issue.

Lyndon Johnson exercised wonderful leadership in helping to ripen civil rights as an issue. Six weeks after Kennedy's assassination, he called Roy Wilkins, executive secretary of the NAACP, and said, "When are you going to get down here and start civil rights?" Then he gave Wilkins counsel on how to lobby Everett Dirksen, the senate minority leader. Johnson was ripening an unripe issue: He couldn't get out front on the Civil Rights Act of 1964, but as an authority figure, he could provide counsel and cover for leaders without authority—leaders who could then disseminate a sense of urgency. He did the same thing with King. Basically, he said, "If you open the door, if you create the political will, I'll drive through that opening." Johnson was asking King to ripen the issue for him. He was expected to be president for all the people. So, unless King and other civil-rights leaders generated the necessary political will, he couldn't move on that issue. He was prevented from exercising leadership by virtue of his authority.

What about grassroots leaders—people without formal authority?

Again, it starts with attention. People who lead without authority, who lead from below, must draw attention to the issues that they raise without drawing too much attention to themselves. Grassroots leaders often generate "sticky" attention—attention that sticks to them personally, rather than to their agenda. To use a different metaphor, it's never comfortable to be a lightning rod. The easiest way for an organization to neutralize the disturbance that you represent is to neutralize you.

There's a second big difference between people who lead with authority and people who lead without authority. If you're leading without authority, other people's attention spans are going to be short whenever you try to communicate with them. Forget two-hour speeches—most people aren't willing to give you more than 30 seconds! So you have to use their attention wisely. You have to make your interventions short, simple, intelligible, and relevant.

I've met many in-the-trenches leaders who blame the people above them when they fail to make progress on their agenda: "I know where we have to go, but my boss doesn't get it. He's standing in the way." That's usually a complete misdiagnosis of the situation. Don't attack your boss. Look at the situation from his or her point of view. You should treat his or her attitude as a barometer of stress in the organization.

Let's say there's a well-meaning person—we'll call him Max—who has an imaginative idea, an idea with plenty of merit. Max speaks up in the middle of a meeting, off the agenda, and offers his inspired intuition. What the boss notices is how Max's colleagues fidget, roll their eyes, demonstrate their impatience. That's because they're all saying to themselves, "I've got an agenda item that I need to get covered, because my troops are expecting me to bring home the bacon. And there goes Max with his enthusiasms again." The boss immediately picks up on that attitude and takes Max down.

Now, the boss isn't the problem. Max is the problem. Max has to find a smarter way to intervene in behalf of his agenda. He has to understand the dilemma that he's creating for the boss, and he has to figure out how to help the boss resolve that dilemma. Remember: Most bosses are already operating near the limit of how much distress they can tolerate—of how much disequilibrium, confusion, and chaos they can stomach. Naturally, they're inclined to suppress additional disturbances. So Max needs to understand the pains of change that he represents and to choose his tactics accordingly.

HOW LEADERS STAY ALIVE

Leadership is hard—on the people who work with leaders as well as on leaders themselves. How do leaders maintain the stamina, the energy, and the passion that they need to keep pushing ahead?

I'm working on this question with a Kennedy School colleague, Martin Linsky. We're writing a book for leaders that will be called Staying Alive. To sustain yourself over the long term, you must learn how to distinguish role from self. Or, to put it more simply: You can't take things personally. Leaders often take personally what is not personal and then misdiagnose the resistance that's out there.

Remember: It's not you they're after. It may look like a personal attack, it may sound like a personal attack—but it's the issues that you represent that they're after. Distinguishing role from self helps you maintain a diagnostic mind-set during trying times.

There's a second point: Because we get so swept up in our professional roles, it's hard to distinguish role from self on our own. That's why we need partners who can help us stay analytical. And we need two different kinds of partners. We need allies inside the organization—people who share our agenda. And we need confidants inside or outside the organization—people who can keep us from getting lost in our role.

Leaders also need a sanctuary, a place where they can go to get back in touch with the worth of their life and the worth of their work. I'm not necessarily talking about a physical place or an extended sabbatical. I'm talking about practical sanctuaries—daily moments that function as sanctuaries. One sanctuary that I recently developed for myself involves getting an email that's sent out by a rabbinic friend, who's a mystic and a biblical scholar. Every day, he sends out an interpretation of one word from the Bible. It's just a few screens long, but as I'm going through my email every day, I take a few minutes to read this thing, and it roots me in a different reality, a different source of meaning.

I'm not peddling any particular kind of sanctuary; we all have to find our own structures. Unfortunately, though, people who get swept up in fast-moving companies often treat their partners and their sanctuaries as expendable luxuries rather than as necessities: "I don't have time to have lunch with my friend"; "I don't have time to go to the gym in the morning, or to pray or meditate." I live in Boston. No one would live in Boston without owning a winter coat. But countless people think that they can exercise leadership without partners or without a sanctuary. To stay alive as leaders—to tend the wounds that we inevitably receive when we raise tough questions—requires maintaining these structures in our lives.

You make leadership sound so hard, so demanding. Do you worry that more people are going to start opting out?

Recognizing the challenges of leadership, along with the pains of change, shouldn't diminish anyone's eagerness to reap the rewards of creating value and meaning in other people's lives. There's a thrill that comes with the creation of value—and of course there's money and status—and those rewards are surely worth the pain that comes with the territory. There are lots of things in life that are worth the pain. Leadership is one of them.

William C. Taylor (wtaylor@fastcompany.com) is a founding editor of *Fast Company*. You can reach Ronald Heifetz by email (ronald_heifetz@harvard.edu).

Rule #3: Leadership Is Confusing as Hell

YOU THINK THE PAST FIVE YEARS WERE NUTS? YOU AIN'T SEEN NOTHIN' YET! IT'S ONLY GOING TO GET WEIRDER, TOUGHER, AND MORE TURBULENT. WHICH MEANS THAT LEADERSHIP WILL BE MORE IMPORTANT THAN EVER—AND MORE CONFUSING (SEE RULE #3).

Ladies and gentlemen, the captain has turned on the "fasten seat belt" sign. Please return to your seats immediately! Make sure that your tray tables are in the upright and locked position, and please return your seat backs to their full, upright position. Now brace yourselves: We're headed for some turbulent times!

Not that the past five years weren't demonstrably nuts. They were. But they were nuts in a generally recognizable way. Never mind all of that easy-to-come-by venture capital and the ATM approach to IPO cash. What really matters is how the past five years challenged us all to rip off our neckties, shed our standard-issue business suits, and, most important, lose our Model T-type business thinking.

But that was the past five years. For the next five years, we're going to go from nuts to flat-out freakin' crazy. For the next five years, it's business on a wartime footing—a high-stakes, high-risk, high-profile event that is filled with uncertainty and ambiguity. And clear-cut performance outcomes matter more than ever before. You can still invent your own career, be your own brand, and promote your own project—you just gotta sprint and deliver.

Think of pre-1990 as the Age of Sucking Up to the Hierarchy. The Age of the Promise 'Em Everything Pitch lasted from 1995 to 2000. The next five years will be the Age of No-Bull Performance. Which means that we're going to see leadership emerge as the most important element of business—the attribute that is highest in demand and shortest in supply. And that means that over the next five years, we're going to have to reckon with a new, unorthodox, untested, maybe just plain freaked-out list of leadership qualities: 50 ways of being a leader in freaked-out times.

1. Leaders on snorting steeds (the visionary greats!) are important. But great managers are the bedrock of great organizations. LEADERSHIP became sooooo coooool in the 1990s. Crank out THE VISION. Harangue the troops. Stand tall in the saddle. Management? That was for wusses, wimps, and dead-enders.

Well, I aim to amend all of that. Vision is dandy, but sustainable company excellence comes from a huge stable of able managers. If you don't believe me, then go read *First, Break All the Rules: What the World's Greatest Managers Do Differently*

(Simon & Schuster, 1999), by Gallup execs Marcus Buckingham and Curt Coffman. Here's a boiled-down version of what they found: Great managers are an organization's glue. They create and hold together the scores of folks who power high-performing companies.

Stop being conned by the old mantra that says, "Leaders are cool, managers are dweebs." Instead, follow the Peters Principle: Leaders are cool. Managers are cool too!

2. But then again, there are times when this cult-of-personality stuff actually works! Okay, here goes the zig-zag, paradoxical path of leadership in freaked-out times. It's true that there are times of genuine corporate peril when no one other than a larger-than-life visionary leader can get the job done.

As far as I'm concerned, the first business leader who was able to establish a cult of personality around his tenure was Lee Iacocca. When he took over as Chrysler's chairman and CEO in 1978, that company was on its deathbed. Chrysler turned to him the way the country turns to charismatic leaders in times of war—which is exactly how Iacocca characterized Chrysler's competitive situation. The Japanese, Iacocca said, were eating our lunch, and he was going to be the wartime leader to rally the troops. The point is, there are times when you really do need to turn to a leader who offers a broad, popular, galvanizing vision—someone who can symbolize a new approach to business.

3. Leadership is confusing as hell. If we're going to make any headway in figuring out the new rules of leadership, we might as well say it up front: There is no one-size-fits-all approach to leadership. Leadership mantra #1: It all depends. Years ago, Yale professor of organization and management and professor of psychology Victor Vroom developed a model that was later adapted and popularized by Ken Blanchard. Their point: We need to think about situational leadership—the right person, the right style, for the right situation.

I saw it at McKinsey & Co. when I went to work there. The firm had gotten offtrack operationally, so the partners elected Alonzo McDonald to be the managing partner. They didn't do this because they liked him (he wasn't the cuddly sort), but because he was the right guy to fix what was broken. McDonald did precisely what the partners wanted him to do but were unwilling to do themselves: He busted the weak performers, tightened up the control systems, and put the firm back on profitable ground. After which the partners said, "Enough!"—and booted him straight to the White House to be assistant to president Jimmy Carter and director of the White House staff. Motto: The situation rules. Leader for all seasons? In your dreams!

4. When it comes to talent, leadership doesn't income-average. It's a favorite one-liner these days: There is no "I" in team. What crap! Is there anyone who really thinks that Phil Jackson won six NBA championships with the Chicago Bulls by averaging Michael Jordan's talent with that of the rest of the team? Yes, teamwork is important. No, teamwork doesn't mean bringing everyone with exceptional talent down to the level of the lowest common denominator.

Bottom line: Stellar teams are invariably made up of quirky individuals who typically rub each other raw, but they figure out—with the spiritual help of a gifted leader (such as Phil Jackson at Chicago or Los Angeles)—how to be their peculiar selves and how to win championships as a team. At the same time.

5. Leaders love the mess. One leader who deserves to be celebrated? That fabulous third-grade teacher your Charlie has—the one who sees each of her 23 charges as unique-quirky souls who are in totally different places on their developmental paths toward becoming their cool-peculiar selves. The third-grade teacher whom you should avoid at all costs? The one who's got everything under control, with all of the kids sitting at their desks, completely unable to express themselves. There's no mess—and no creativity, no energy, no inspired leadership. You want leadership? Go find a fabulous third-grade teacher, and watch how he "plays" the classroom.

6. The leader is rarely—possibly never?—the best performer. I once read that the three greatest psychological transitions an adult human being goes through are marriage, parenthood, and her first supervisory job. In each of these situations, people learn to live and to succeed primarily through the success of others. Which is why there is no more important decision that a company makes than the selection of its first-line managers.

Who are those people? Take a look at the former players from the world of sports who become the best coaches and managers. Last summer, Tommy Lasorda coached the U.S. Olympic baseball team to a gold medal, finally defeating the Cubans. In his career with the Los Angeles Dodgers, Tommy L. was a terrific manager. His own career as a player? It lasted for three at bats.

The best leader is rarely the best pitcher or catcher. The best leader is just what's advertised: the best leader. Leaders get their kicks from orchestrating the work of others—not from doing it themselves.

7. Leaders deliver. If you're aiming to be a real leader during the next five years, then you need to mimic the pizza man: You'd better deliver! For the past five years, ideas and cool have counted (which was important). What counts now? Performance. Results.

8. Leaders create their own (peculiar?) destinies. During the next five years, there won't be room for paper pushers. Only people who make personal determinations to be leaders will survive—and that holds true at all levels of all organizations (including entry level).

Surprisingly, we've seen this phenomenon take place most often where most people least expect to find it: in the military. First, war is the ultimate improv venture. The most improvisational, least hierarchical situation that I've ever been in was my 16-month stint in Vietnam. But second, real-life experience in the Army or in the Navy teaches you that you must have leaders at every level. So too in today's corporate wars. In this new world order, the real battle starts when the computer gets knocked out, the captain gets killed, the lieutenant is gravely wounded, the sergeant is hesitant, and suddenly the 18-year-old Iowa farmhand finds himself leading a platoon into combat. And the life and death of the company or the team or the project hangs in the balance. That's leadership at all levels, which boot camp teaches a lot better than business school.

9. Leaders win through logistics. Vision, sure. Strategy, yes. But when you go to war, you need to have both toilet paper and bullets at the right place at the right time. In other words, you must win through superior logistics. Go back to the Gulf War. After that war ended, the media stories focused on the strategy that was devised by Colin Powell and executed by Norman Schwartzkopf. For my money, the guy who won the Gulf War was Gus Pagonis, the genius who managed all of the logistics.

It doesn't matter how brilliant your vision and strategy are if you can't get the soldiers, the weapons, the vehicles, the gasoline, the chow—the boots, for God's sake!—to the right people, at the right place, at the right time. (Right now, Amazon.com and a hundred of its dotkin are learning—or failing to learn—the Gus Pagonis lesson.)

10. Leaders understand the ultimate power of relationships. Here's a mind-blowing proposition: War—or business on a wartime footing—is fundamentally a woman's game! Why? Because when everything's on the line, what really matters are the relationships that leaders have created with their people. I recall a Douglas MacArthur biographer who claimed that the one piece of advice that MacArthur most valued (which was passed on to him by one of his military forbearers) was "Never give an order that can't be obeyed." But women already know that. They tend to understand the primacy of massive IIR (investment in relationships), which is one reason why the premier untapped leadership talent in the world today rests with women!

11. Leaders multitask. Which element is in the shortest supply today—and tomorrow and tomorrow? Time. The future belongs to the leader who can juggle a dozen conundrums at once. And who is he? I mean she? I just glanced at a lovely book called *Selling Is a Woman's Game: 15 Powerful Reasons Why Women Can Outsell Men* (Avon Books, 1994), by Nicki Joy and Susan Kane-Benson. Take this quick quiz, the authors urge: Who manages more things at once? Who usually takes care of the details? Who finds it easier to meet new people? Who asks more questions in a conversation? Who is a better listener? Who encourages harmony and agreement? Who works with a longer to-do list? Who's better at keeping in touch with others? Now that's what I call multitasking! And again: Let's hear it for women leaders!

12. Leaders groove on ambiguity. Message 2001: Wall Street is nuttier than a fruitcake! All of that stuff they teach us in Economics 101 about rational expectations? In the past year, we've seen those "rational" boys and girls of Wall Street fall in and out of love with whole sectors of the economy the way teenagers with overactive hormones swoon and dive over movie stars. But when Wall Streeters do it, real leaders in real companies feel real effects.

The next five years are going to be an economic roller-coaster ride. That means that business leaders are going to be challenged repeatedly not just to make fact-based decisions, but also to make some sense out of all of the conflicting and hard-to-detect signals that come through the fog and the noise. Leaders are the ones who can handle gobs and gobs of ambiguity.

13. Leaders wire the joint. The good-old-boy's network provided a direct way of operating: I'm a vice president, you're a vice president. I want your order, I call you up, I take you out for a drink or a game of golf, and, man to man, I get your order.

It doesn't work like that anymore—not when power is diffuse, alliances are ever changing, and decision-making channels are fluid, indirect, and muddy. The game today: Soft-wire the whole joint. The way to make the sale today—or to have influence on any high-impact decision—is to build, nurture, and mobilize a vast network of key influencers at every level and in every function of the operation.

14. Leadership is an improvisational art. The game—hey, the basic rule book—keeps changing. Competition keeps changing. So leaders need to change, to keep reinventing themselves. Leaders have to be ready to adapt, to move, to forget yesterday, to forgive, and to structure new roles and new relationships for themselves, their teams, and their ever-shifting portfolio of partners.

15. Leaders trust their guts. "Intuition" is one of those good words that has gotten a bad rap. For some reason, intuition has become a "soft" notion. Garbage! Intuition is the new physics. It's an Einsteinian, seven-sense, practical way to make tough decisions. Bottom line, circa 2001 to 2010: The crazier the times are, the more important it is for leaders to develop and to trust their intuition.

16. Leaders trust trust. My longtime business partner Jim Kouzes and his colleague Barry Posner nailed it with a one-word title to their recent book: *Credibility* (*How Leaders Gain and Lose it, Why People Demand It,* Jossey Bass Publishers, 1993). In a world gone nuts, we cry out for something or someone to rely on. To trust. The fearless leader may (make that, had better) change his or her mind with the times. But as a subordinate, I trust a leader who shows up, makes the tough calls, takes the heat, sleeps well amidst the furor, and then aggressively chomps into the next task in the morning with visible vitality.

17. Leaders are natural empowerment freaks. There are two ways to look at Jack Welch's legacy as a leader. The first is to say that he has created more value for his shareholders than any other comparable modern-day business leader. Which he has. He has also created more leaders than any comparable modern-day business leader.

When we think of Welch, we do not ordinarily think vision. (What is GE's vision? I haven't a clue! "We bring good things to life" ain't it.) We do think rigorous performance standards, empowerment ("WorkOut" in GE-speak), leadership, and talent development. Jack Welch, it turns out, is a great manager (see rule #1).

18. Leaders are good at forgetting. Peter Senge's brilliant insight 10 years ago was that companies need to be learning organizations. My campaign 2001: Companies need to be forgetting organizations. Enron Corp., which has repeatedly been tagged as the nation's most innovative corporation, is exhibit A as a world-class forgetting organization. It's not wedded to what it did yesterday. Enron chiefs Kenneth Lay and Jeff Skilling have figured out how to operate like a band of pirates. Got an idea? Don't dally. Go for it while it's an original! Doesn't work? Try something else. If that doesn't work, fuhgeddaboutit!

19. Leaders bring in different dudes. This is a corollary to forgetting. Many leaders are preoccupied with creating high-performance organizations. But to that, I say: Crazy times demand high-standard-deviation organizations! This isn't just weirdness for the sake of weirdness. This is weirdness for the sake of variety.

Winning leaders know that their organizations need to refresh the gene pool. That happens when leaders forget old practices and open up their minds to new ones. That also happens—and more effectively—when leaders bring in new people and new partners with new ideas. As a leader, do with your people what Cisco has done so effectively with technology: Acquire a new line of thinking by acquiring a new group of thinkers.

20. Leaders make mistakes—and make no bones about it. Nobody—repeat, nobody—gets it right the first time. Most of us don't get it right the second, third, or fourth time either. Winston Churchill said it best: "Success is the ability to go from failure to failure without losing your enthusiasm." Churchill blew one assignment after another—until he came up against the big one and saved the world.

As times get crazier, you're going to see more—and dumber—mistakes. When you make mistakes, you need to recognize them quickly, deal with them quickly, move on quickly—and make cooler mistakes tomorrow.

21. Leaders love to work with other leaders. Nortel CEO, president, and VC John Roth says, "Our strategies must be tied to leading-edge customers on the attack. If we focus on the defensive customers, we will also become defensive." Amen. (No: AMEN!) Leaders are known by the company they keep. If you work with people who are cool, pioneering leaders who have customers who are cool, pioneering leaders who source from suppliers who are cool, pioneering leaders—then you'll stay on the leading edge for the next five years. Laggards work with laggards. Leaders work with leaders. It really is that simple.

22. Leaders can laugh. Another corollary to the art of leadership and making mistakes: No one's infallible (except for the Pope). In order to survive in these wild times, you're going to make a total fool of yourself with incredible regularity. If you can't laugh about it, then you are doomed. Take it from me. (And if you are a humorless bastard, please do me a favor: Don't immediately march over to your VP of human resources and order, "Ve vill haff humor! Bring me ze funny people!" But do remember the madness of the times. Humor is the best tool you've got to keep your team from going mad. No bull!)

23. Leaders set design specs. You can't be a leader over the next five years and not be totally into design. Design specs are the double-helix DNA that sets the tone of the culture and establishes the operating ideas that embody the company. They are your distinguishing characteristics, your brand's brand. If you don't already know how, learn how to speak design. Apple CEO Steve Jobs calls design "soul." I say: Design specs = soul operating system.

24. Leaders also know when to challenge design specs. Here comes another bloody brain flip: In zany times, design specs (corporate character) must be open to constant reevaluation. What worked during the past five years may or may not work for the next five years.

The classic example we should all watch: What will Jeffrey Immelt do when he takes over "the house that Jack built" at GE? Want to know what kind of leader Immelt will turn out to be? The clearest signal will come from how he handles GE's design specs. In this Age of Madness, nothing is holy. Even at GE.

25. Leaders have taste. It's a big part of the often-subtle topic of design. There is such a thing as good taste. Maybe a better word is "grace." I love this quote from designer Celeste Cooper: "My favorite word is 'grace'—whether it's amazing grace, saving grace, grace under fire, Grace Kelly. How we live contributes to beauty—

whether it's how we treat other people or the environment." Leaders who would change our lives don't shy away from words like grace and beauty and taste.

26. Leaders don't create followers, they create more leaders. Too many old-fashioned leaders measure their influence by the number of followers that they can claim. But the greatest leaders are those who don't look for followers. Think of Martin Luther King Jr., Mohandas Gandhi, or Nelson Mandela. They were looking for more leaders in order to empower others to find and create their own destinies.

27. Leaders love rainbows—for totally pragmatic reasons. Another good word gone bad: "diversity." The case for diversity during the past 20 years has been that it was the "right thing to do." Well, in no-bull times, diversity isn't a good thing, it's an essential thing. It's a survival thing. The case for diversity is the case against homogeneity: When the world is undergoing sudden, unpredictable, dire change, you need to have a diverse gene pool. You need to have multiple points of view. In a heterogeneous time, homogeneity sucks!

28. Leaders don't fall prey to their own success. There are a lot of people who have made it really, really big over the past five years. Some of them actually think that they're responsible for their success, if you can imagine that. But in crazy times, leaders don't believe in their own press clippings. And they never, ever let their organizations get complacent! Read *The Paradox of Success: When Winning at Work Means Losing at Life: A Book of Renewal for Leaders* (G.P. Putnam's Sons, 1993), by John O'Neil. He talks about the good qualities that breed monsters. The first one on the list: Confidence breeds a sense of infallibility. Again: Amen.

29. Leaders never get caught fighting the last war. It's the age-old problem with bemedalled generals: They're always preparing to fight the last war. The lesson, embedded in history, applies to business. What business are you in? The only answer that makes sense today is, God alone knows! Did you win the war during the past five years? Were you an early adopter of Internet ways? Good for you! The only problem is that the Internet is still in diapers. The old giants are awakening to its potential. What's your next totally new act?

30. But leaders have to deliver, so they worry about throwing the baby out with the bathwater. Did I mention that these are paradoxical times? Well, they are. So here's the flip side to the other side: You must execute consistently, while fighting consistency. Years ago, in *Liberation Management: Necessary Organization for the Nanosecond Nineties* (A. A. Knopf, 1992), I called it the "ultimate leadership paradox." To be "excellent" (to deliver profits, provide quality, and satisfy customers), you must be consistent and build a stellar infrastructure-delivery capability. But the single-mindedness that allows you to hit earnings targets and quality goals is a disguised set of blinders that makes you vulnerable to new, oddball threats (consistency = focus = blinders). Love the bathwater! Throw the bathwater out! Go figure!

31. Leaders honor the assassins in their own organizations. There's only one reason why any human being ever makes it into the history books: because he or she remorselessly overthrew the conventional wisdom. Those are leaders. But truly great leaders, the ones who aim to leave a legacy, go to the next level. They consistently seek out and honor the people in their own organizations who want to overthrow their conventional wisdom. Great leaders honor the people who want to depose them, the assassins in their midst. Real leaders, repeat after me: All hail Brutus!

32. Leaders love technology. I mean love! L-O-V-E. Here's the equation for the next five years: Technology = architect of change. If you don't love (and I don't mean like or tolerate) the technology, it will change you and your company, but you will be the unwitting victim, not the partner of change. Look, you don't have to be a technologist. But you must embrace technology, care for it. It is your friend, your lover. It will be unfaithful at times. It will lead you down dark and dangerous alleys. No matter. It is remaking the world. And you must joyously leap aboard (that's the way love is).

33. Leaders wear their passion on their sleeve. There's absolutely no question in my mind: Leaders dream in Technicolor. They see the world in brighter colors, sharper images, and higher resolution. Leadership, in the end, is all about having energy, creating energy, showing energy, and spreading energy. Leaders emote, they erupt, they flame, and they have boundless (nutty) enthusiasm. And why shouldn't they? The cold logic of it is unassailable: If you do not love what you're doing, if you do not go totally bonkers for your project, your team, your customers, and your company, then why in the world are you doing what you're doing? And why in the world would you expect anybody to follow you?

34. Leaders know: Energy begets energy. Every successful company, every successful team, and every successful project runs on one thing: energy. It's the leader's job to be the energy source that others feed from. But sometimes the leader has no energy. Sometimes the situation is bleak, and the outcome is in doubt. And I say: Fake it! For it is at that critical juncture that having energy is the most essential. So if you gotta fake it, then fake it! Once you kick-start the energy cycle, nature takes over. The energy will start to flow. Benjamin Zander said it best: The job of the leader is to be a "dispenser of enthusiasm."

35. Leaders are community organizers. Let's hear three raucous cheers for Saul Alinksy! (Haven't heard of him? Quick! Go to Amazon.com and buy *Rules For Radicals: A Practical Primer for Realistic Radicals* [Random House, 1971]. Read it immediately!) It doesn't matter if you're recruiting talent, making a sale, or forging a partnership. Everything you do is the exact equivalent of grassroots organizing.

Your title may say that you are the leader, but you're running for office every day. Want to pull off that Internet-enabled business-process redesign? You've got to get the frontline commitment, the votes! You've got to get your customers to vote for you, your suppliers to vote for you, your employees to vote for you. How do you get them to do more than just show up? You enlist them and win their votes one damn day at a time.

36. Leaders give respect. There's another great book with a one-word title: *Respect (An Explanation,* Perseus Books, 1999), by Sara Lawrence-Lightfoot. The heart of her message: "It was much later that I realized Dad's secret. He gained respect by giving it. He talked and listened to the fourth-grade kid in Spring Valley who shined shoes the same way he talked and listened to a bishop or a college president. He was seriously interested in who you were and what you had to say." Care. Respect. Leaders care about connecting—because it moves mountains.

37. Leaders show up. Legendary, all-powerful sports agent Mark McCormack offers a potent lesson on leadership in one of his books. He insists that, even in the Internet Age (or is it especially in the Internet Age?), it's a worthwhile show of commitment and respect (see rule #36) to travel 6,000 miles round-trip to consummate a five-minute face-to-face meeting. Hatim Tyabji, who was then the soft-spoken, charismatic CEO of Verifone, once traveled from South Africa to Colorado—on his way to Norway—to give a one-hour presentation at a conference of just 30 people. Why? Because three months prior to that engagement, before all of the other trips had even been booked, he had promised to be there. I guarantee that people paid uncompromising attention to his one-hour talk, because he showed uncompromising leadership by showing up.

38. Leadership is a performance. According to HP big cheese Carly Fiorina, "Leadership is a performance. You have to be conscious about your behavior, because everyone else is." Leaders spend time leading—which means that they spend time and exert ceaseless effort making sure that they come across with the right message in the way that they walk, talk, dress, and stand. Leadership is not only about action. It's also about acting.

39. Leaders have great stories. A performance (see rule #38) needs to have a script. Howard Gardner wrote about that in his book, *Leading Minds: An Anatomy of Leadership* (BasicBooks, 1995). Effective communication of a story is a key—perhaps the key—to leadership.

Why? Because stories are the real thing. They are how we remember, how we learn, and how we visualize what can be. If you want to involve your colleagues in the future performance of your business, then don't just present them with the numbers. Tell them a story. Numbers are numbing. Stories are personal, passionate, and purposeful.

40. Leaders give everyone a cause. Corollary to rule #39: What's the point of our story? If you want people to care—really to care—enlist them in a cause that they can care about: being part of the team that will go down in history for inventing the most amazing personal computer that the world has ever seen (Apple's Mac); achieving customer loyalty so intense that it becomes the stuff of legends (Nordstrom); executing a strategy with such precision that proud, old competitors are publicly humbled in the market (Home Depot).

People enlist on behalf of a cause. They do the impossible for a cause. For a business, however, they just work. What's your cause?

41. Leaders focus on the soft stuff. People. Values. Character. Commitment. A cause. All of the stuff that was supposed to be too goo-goo to count in business. Yet, it's the stuff that real leaders take care of first. And forever. That's why leadership is an art, not a science.

If leadership were just about hitting your numbers, about driving the troops to meet their quotas, then leadership would just be a math problem. But leadership is a human mystery.

In these times, as the numbers get harder to hit (or even to understand), and as frustration abets the temptation to be a kick-ass, take-charge, top-down leader, we'll see very quickly who keeps an enterprise energized in the face of adversity and ambiguity. And we'll see who is faced with passive resistance, quiet rebellion, and random acts of insubordination.

42. Leaders think—make that know—that they can make a difference. Call it insane optimism. Call it rampant self-confidence. Call it plain stupid. Leaders are convinced that they are going to make a difference. It's not about egotism. It's about having a healthy, unquestioning feeling of mattering. And a leader who radiates (good word, "radiate") a sense of mattering attracts others who share that feeling. And out of that sharing comes a team of people who, by God, will damn well make a difference! Which comes first, the sense of mattering or the ability to matter? Ah, yet another layer to the alchemy of leadership.

43. Leaders always make time to work the phones. If you read the books on leadership, there's a strong undercurrent that says that leaders are people of action, charging about on great white steeds! Well, yes. But leaders are also great talkers. Leadership takes an almost bottomless supply of verbal energy: working the phones, staying focused on your message, repeating the same mantra until you can't stand the sound of your own voice—and then repeating it some more, because just when you start to become bored witless with the message, it's probably starting to seep into the organization. You can't be a leader these days and be the strong, silent type. You have to be an endless talker, a tireless communicator.

44. Leaders listen intently. Leaders talk. Leaders listen. That is, the other side of this coin is also true—again. Leaders listen to what the market is saying, to what the customer is saying, and to what the team is saying. No, you don't have to do everything that your constituents demand that you do. But just by showing that you're listening, really listening, you demonstrate the respect that you accord to them (there's that word "respect" again). Intent, tuned-in listening engenders empathy, creates connectedness, and, ultimately, builds cohesiveness. When the crap hits the fan, as it inevitably will, those are the qualities that will see you through. Listen while you can so that you can lead when you must.

45. Leaders revel in surrounding themselves with people who are smarter than they are. Now hear this: You will not have all of the answers. More important, you are no longer expected to have all of the answers. Nobody can have all of the answers! What you are expected to do is recruit people—at all levels of your organization—who do have the answers. These are the folks who lead you to make the right decisions about how to deal with an unglued world. These are, ultimately, the people you will be known by. Their accomplishments will be your signature, the measure of your tenure.

If you are confident enough to hire people who are more talented than you are, then you will be known as an audacious leader. If you hire only people who are not as talented as you are, then you will appear to be weak and insecure. And you will ultimately fail. So you decide. Do want to be the smartest person in the company? Or do you want to win—and leave a legacy?

46. Great leaders are great pols. Time for a reality check. Leadership is not for the lily-livered. Taking the responsibility to lead others into battle—whether it's at war or at work—isn't for the faint of heart. It's not just the casualties that you need to be able to stomach. It's the real world of organizational politics and inside deal making: doing what it takes to get things done. Dwight Eisenhower didn't become president because of his skills as a general, he became a general because of his skills as a politician. I'm not endorsing playing dirty. I'm just telling you that you can't pretend that the game won't get rough and that you can stay above the fray and still be an effective leader. Period.

47. Leaders make meaning. John Seely Brown, the former head of ceaselessly innovative Xerox PARC, nailed it, especially for these totally insane times: A leader's job isn't just to make decisions and to make products or services. A leader's job is also to make meaning. Why? Because in times like these, people depend on their leaders to absorb all of the chaos, all of the information, all of the change, and to find some meaningful pattern and compelling purpose in the midst of all of the splatter.

48. Leaders learn. The single worst thing that can happen to you as a leader? You exhaust your intellectual capital. Before you became a leader, you accumulated that capital by going to conferences and taking notes. You networked like a lunatic. You kept your eyes and ears open, and you came up with the totally original synthesis that propelled you into the front ranks of leadership. And then you got bogged down in the perpetual politics of implementation and started to dissipate all of that accumulated wisdom. And because you were so damn busy doing, you stopped learning. You became a broken record for yesterday's paradigm. (Hey, it boosted you into orbit.) You listened to yesterday's (closed) circle of "brilliant" advisors. You started to quote yourself! (As I said in *In Search of Excellence* in 1982...) This is only natural—if you let it happen. Leaders work double overtime to keep it from happening. Learn fast, or get left behind fast.

49. Leaders...? I left this one open: You tell me. What is the one key idea for leadership in whacked-out times that you would propose? You can go to TomPeters.com (http://www.tompeters.com/no49.htm) and contribute your idea there, or you can send your thoughts to me via email (tom@tompeters.com). What's the one-liner that captures the essence of leadership for you? What do you think leaders need to do to win in the next five years?

50. Leaders know when to leave. Much good work gets undone by those who stay beyond their expiration dates. And it's not just baseball players who do this. It's also CEOs of megacorps. How will you know? When you know an idea won't work before you even try it. When you see the same problem coming around on the merry-go-round, and you've solved it so many times that it's no longer interesting. When you became the leader by challenging conventional wisdom, and now you represent the status quo. When you stop doing numbers one through 49 on this list. At that point, go back to number one. Start over.

Tom Peters, author, speaker, learner, and listener, says that leadership is the scarcest commodity. What do you think? Contact him by email (tom@tompeters.com).

BY POLLY LABARRE   FROM *FAST COMPANY* ISSUE 32, PAGE 222

Do You Have the Will to Lead?

PHILOSOPHER PETER KOESTENBAUM POSES THE TRULY BIG QUESTIONS: HOW DO WE ACT WHEN RISKS SEEM OVERWHELMING? WHAT DOES IT MEAN TO BE A SUCCESSFUL HUMAN BEING?

Who hasn't stared out an airplane window on yet another red-eye and thought, What exactly is the point of this exercise? Or sat through a particularly senseless meeting and wondered, How in the world did I get here? Or wrestled with a set of strategic choices—all of which seem hard and unpleasant—and said, What happened to the fun part of being in business? According to Peter Koestenbaum, those uncomfortable questions—those existential quandaries—are at the root of issues that great leaders deal with all the time, and they influence every decision that must be made.

A classically trained philosopher with degrees in philosophy, physics, and theology from Stanford, Harvard, and Boston University, Koestenbaum has spent half a century pondering the questions that give most of us headaches: Why is there being instead of nothing? What is the ultimate explanation of the universe? What does it mean to be a successful human being? After fleeing pre-World War II Germany with his parents, Koestenbaum was raised in Venezuela; later, he emigrated to the United States to pursue his studies. He taught at San Jose State University for 34 years, and during that period he focused on creating a "practical philosophy"—a philosophy that is linked to education, psychology, and psychiatry. His many books include "The Vitality of Death" (Greenwood, 1971), "The New Image of the Person" (Greenwood, 1978), and "Managing Anxiety" (Prentice Hall, 1974). One of his books, "Leadership: The Inner Side of Greatness" (Jossey-Bass, 1991), has been translated into several languages, and Koestenbaum is now at work on a new book, tentatively titled "Diamond Reverse Engineering."

More than 25 years ago, Koestenbaum traded the cloistered halls of academia for the front lines of the global economy. It's not unheard-of for this philosopher, now a tireless 71-year-old with thick glasses and a flowing beard, to visit clients across three continents in a single week. His agenda: to apply the power of philosophy to the big question of the day—how to reconcile the often-brutal realities of business with basic human values—and to create a new language of effective leadership. "Unless the distant goals of meaning, greatness, and destiny are addressed," Koestenbaum insists, "we can't make an intelligent decision about what to do tomorrow morning—much less set strategy for a company or for a human life. Nothing is more practical than for people to deepen themselves. The more you understand the human condition, the more effective you are as a businessperson. Human depth makes business sense."

Koestenbaum's wisdom makes sense to leaders at such giant organizations as Ford, EDS, Citibank, Xerox, Ericsson, and even one of Korea's chaebols. All of these companies have welcomed him into their offices to roam free as a resident sage, company therapist, and secular priest. His involvement with them ranges from one-on-one coaching sessions to decade-long engagements featuring intensive leadership seminars. At Ford, Koestenbaum contributed to the company's 2,000-person Senior Executive Program throughout the 1980s. In more than a decade at EDS, he led seminars and coached hundreds of top executives, including then-chairman Les Alberthal. He also coached Alexander Krauer, a prominent Swedish industrialist, when Krauer was chairman of Ciba-Geigy. Picking up on that momentum, another leading Swedish industrialist, Rolf Falkenberg, founded the Koestenbaum Institute to disseminate the philosopher's teachings across Scandinavia.

"Everything I do," says Koestenbaum, "is about using themes from the history of thought to rescue people who are stuck." His logic: Change—true, lasting, deep-seated change—is the business world's biggest and most persistent challenge. But too many people and too many companies approach change by treating it as a technical challenge rather than by developing authentic answers to basic questions about business life. "We've reached such explosive levels of freedom that, for the first time in history, we have to manage our own mutation," declares Koestenbaum. "It's up to us to decide what it means to be a successful human being. That's the philosophical task of the age. Nothing happens unless you make it happen. As a leader, everything is your responsibility, because you always could have chosen otherwise."

In an interview with Fast Company, Koestenbaum explains how age-old questions apply to the new world of work.

Why does being a leader feel so hard today?

Because reckoning with freedom is always hard—and the powerful paradoxes of the new economy make it even harder. We're living in a peculiar time: It's marked by a soaring stock market, the creation of tremendous wealth, an explosion in innovation, and the acute alienation that occurs when the global economy hits the average individual. What I call the "new-economy pathology" is driven by impossible demands—better quality, lower prices, faster innovation—that generate an unprecedented form of stress. People feel pressure to meet ever-higher objectives in all realms of work, wealth, and lifestyle—and to thrive on that pressure in the process.

This condition is exacerbated by the pornographic treatment of business in media and culture. The message is, You're living in the best country in the world at the best time in history; you have an amazing degree of freedom to do what you want, along with an unprecedented opportunity to build immense wealth and success—and to do it more quickly than ever before. Of course, the average individual has as much of a chance of launching a skyrocketing IPO as he or she has of becoming a movie star.

What's even more disturbing is that the ascendancy of shareholder value as the dominant driving force in business has resulted in a terrible insensitivity to basic human values. That's the real "stuck point" for leaders: How do we cope with a brutal business reality and still preserve human values? How do we handle competition without becoming either the kind of fool who allows it to crush us or the kind of fool who forgets people?

Resolving that paradox requires something like an evolutionary transformation of who we are, how we behave, how we think, and what we value. We've reached such an incredible level of freedom that, for the first time in history, we have to manage our own mutation. It's up to us to decide what it means to be a successful human being. That's the philosophical task of the age.

In some sense, of course, that has been the task of every age. There's nothing in today's economic disruptions that equals the horror of World War II. According to some estimates, nearly 100,000 people were killed during every week of that war. In 1935, when I was a seven-year-old boy, I once stood in the Alexanderplatz, a square in Berlin, and watched Hitler parade by in his Mercedes, just a few feet away. I'll never forget the mothers with babies in their arms, the children holding up swastikas. That leaves a mark on you that can't be erased—and it leaves you with questions that you have to confront: Who am I to have witnessed such acts? How am I to live meaningfully in a world such as this?

The new economy just happens to be the form that our existential challenge takes today. As always, the real obstacle is existence itself.

 That's a heavy burden to place on leaders. They must not only guide organizations but also wrestle with basic philosophical questions.

There's a terrible defect at the core of how we think about people and organizations today. There is little or no tolerance for the kinds of character-building conversations that pave the way for meaningful change. The average person is stuck, lost, riveted by the objective domain. That's where our metrics are; that's where we look for solutions. It's the come-on of the consulting industry and the domain of all the books, magazines, and training programs out there. And that's why books and magazines that have numbers in their titles sell so well. We'll do anything to avoid facing the basic, underlying questions: How do we make truly difficult choices? How do we act when the risks seem overwhelming? How can we muster the guts to burn our bridges and to create a condition of no return?

There's nothing wrong with all of those technical solutions. They're excellent; they're creative; they're even necessary. But they shield us from the real issues: What kind of life do I want to lead? What is my destiny? How much evil am I willing to tolerate?

Reflection doesn't take anything away from decisiveness, from being a person of action. In fact, it generates the inner toughness that you need to be an effective person of action—to be a leader. Think of leadership as the sum of two vectors: competence (your specialty, your skills, your know-how) and authenticity (your identity, your character, your attitude). When companies and people get stuck, they tend to apply more steam—more competence—to what got them into trouble in the first place: "If I try harder, I'll be successful," or "If we exert more control, we'll get the results we need."

The problem is, when you're stuck, you're not likely to make progress by using competence as your tool. Instead, progress requires commitment to two things. First, you need to dedicate yourself to understanding yourself better—in the philosophical sense of understanding what it means to exist as a human being in the world. Second, you need to change your habits of thought: how you think, what you value, how you work, how you connect with people, how you learn, what you expect from life, and how you manage frustration. Changing those habits means changing your way of being intelligent. It means moving from a nonleadership mind to a leadership mind.

What are the attributes of a "leadership mind"?

Authentic leaders have absorbed the fundamental fact of existence—that you can't get around life's inherent contradictions. The leadership mind is spacious. It has ample room for the ambiguities of the world, for conflicting feelings, and for contradictory ideas.

I believe that the central leadership attribute is the ability to manage polarity. In every aspect of life, polarities are inevitable: We want to live, yet we must die. How can I devote myself fully to both family and career? Am I a boss or a friend? A lover or a judge? How do I reconcile my own needs with those of my team? Those paradoxes are simply part of life. Every business interaction is a form of confrontation—a clash of priorities, a struggle of dignities, a battle of beliefs. That's not an invitation to wage an epic battle of good versus evil or right versus wrong. (Chances are, your boss is less of an SOB than he is an agent of the cosmos.) My point is, you have to be careful not to bang your head against the wrong door. Polarities are in the nature of things. How we act, how we respond to those polarities—that is where we separate greatness from mediocrity.

That doesn't mean that we don't have to make decisions. Tough choices are a daily requirement of leadership. Leaders have to hire and fire, to sign off on new strategies, and to risk investments—all of which can lead to stress and guilt. The presence of guilt is not a result of making the wrong choice but of choosing itself. And that is the human condition: You are a being that chooses.

A young, ambitious guy whom I worked with at Amoco got a double promotion that required a transfer to Cairo. He went home to his new wife and young baby and said, "Great news, we're moving to Cairo." Appalled, his wife said, "You're moving alone. I'm going home to my mother." That was the first test of leadership in that family. There was no viable compromise: If he relinquished his promotion, he would resent his wife for ruining his career; if she just went along with the move, she would hate him for squashing her ideals for her baby and herself. What to do?

After some discussion, they might have been tempted to believe that maturity required them to deny their feelings and to sacrifice on behalf of each other. But that actually leads to illness, depression, and the end of affection. Instead, they went back to the fundamentals: Is it my career, or is it our career? Is it your baby, or is it our baby? Are we individuals, or do we operate as a team? What are our values? That marriage had to grow up by the equivalent of five years in about two weeks. They ended up going to Cairo, but their relationship had been transformed: She understood that his career was important to her; he recommitted to his values as a participant in the family. What matters is not what they ended up choosing, but how, and why

They took the courageous step to redefine, from the inside out, who they truly were. The how is what gives you character. The what, which at first appears paramount, is ultimately of no emotional significance.

Managing polarity teaches us that there are no solutions—there are only changes of attitude. When you grapple with polarities in your life, you lose your arrogant, self-indulgent illusions, and you realize that the joke is on you. To get that message makes you a more credible human being—instantly.

It's one thing for a leader to embrace the contradictions of the new economy. But how does he or she persuade colleagues to go along with this kind of thinking?

The best leaders operate in four dimensions: vision, reality, ethics, and courage. These are the four intelligences, the four forms of perceiving, the languages for communicating that are required to achieve meaningful, sustained results. The visionary leader thinks big, thinks new, thinks ahead—and, most important, is in touch with the deep structure of human consciousness and creative potential. Reality is the polar opposite of vision. The leader as realist follows this motto: Face reality as it is, not as you wish it to be. The realist grapples with hard, factual, daily, and numeric parameters. A master in the art of the possible, the realist has no illusions, sees limits, and has no patience for speculation.

Ethics refers to the basic human values of integrity, love, and meaning. This dimension represents a higher level of development, one ruled not by fear or pleasure but by principle. Courage is the realm of the will; it involves the capacity to make things happen. The philosophic roots of this dimension lie in fully understanding the centrality of free will in human affairs. Courage involves both advocacy—the ability to take a stand—and the internalization of personal responsibility and accountability.

The real challenge of leadership is to develop all four of these often-contradictory modes of thinking and behaving at once. Leaders tend to operate on two dimensions at most—which has more to do with a lack of insight into human nature than with corrupt intent. Reality dominates, and the second-most-common attribute is ethics: Consider the statement "People are our most important asset." Unfortunately, those are often empty words—not just because too few people make the connection between profits and human values, but also because there is no adequate understanding of what it means to be a human being in a brutally competitive environment. "Vision" might be one of the most overused words in business, but in fact vision—in the sense of honing great thinking and fostering the capacity for ongoing inventiveness—is rarely practiced. And courage is demonstrated even more rarely.

When we talk about courage, we usually mean having guts or taking risks. But you talk about courage as if it were an almost mythic quality—one that lies at the heart of leadership success.

It goes back to the beginning of our discussion. Aristotle believed, correctly, that courage is the first of the human virtues, because it makes the others possible. Courage begins with the decision to face the ultimate truth about existence: the dirty little secret that we are free. It requires an understanding of free will at the archetypal level—an understanding that we are free to define who we are at every moment. We are not what society and randomness have made us; we are what we have chosen to be from the depth of our being. We are a product of our will. We are self-made in the deepest sense.

One of the gravest problems in life is self-limitation: We create defense mechanisms to protect us from the anxiety that comes with freedom. We refuse to fulfill our potential. We live only marginally. This was Freud's definition of psychoneurosis: We limit how we live so that we can limit the amount of anxiety that we experience. We end up tranquilizing many of life's functions. We shut down the centers of entrepreneurial and creative thinking; in effect, we halt progress and growth. But no significant decision—personal or organizational—has ever been undertaken without being attended by an existential crisis, or without a commitment to wade through anxiety, uncertainty, and guilt.

That's what we mean by transformation. You can't just change how you think or the way that you act—you must change the way that you will. You must gain control over the patterns that govern your mind: your worldview, your beliefs about what you deserve and about what's possible. That's the zone of fundamental change, strength, and energy—and the true meaning of courage.

Does developing the will to transform mean that you can actually will others to change?

Taking personal responsibility for getting others to implement strategy is the leader's key polarity. It's the existential paradox of holding yourself 100% responsible for the fate of your organization, on the one hand, and assuming absolutely no responsibility for the choices made by other people, on the other hand. That applies to your children too. You are 100% responsible for how your children turn out. And you accomplish that by teaching them that they are 100% responsible for how they turn out.

So how do you motivate people? Not with techniques, but by risking yourself with a personal, lifelong commitment to greatness—by demonstrating courage. You don't teach it so much as challenge it into existence. You cannot choose for others. All you can do is inform them that you cannot choose for them. In most cases, that in itself will be a strong motivator for the people whom you want to cultivate. The leader's role is less to heal or to help than to enlarge the capacity for responsible freedom.

Some people are more talented than others. Some are more educationally privileged than others. But we all have the capacity to be great. Greatness comes with recognizing that your potential is limited only by how you choose, how you use your freedom, how resolute you are, how persistent you are—in short, by your attitude. And we are all free to choose our attitude.

Polly LaBarre, a Fast Company senior editor, is based in New York City. Contact Peter Koestenbaum by email (pkipeter@ix.netcom.com) or on the Web (http://www.pib.net).

FEAR AND TREMBLING IN THE NEW ECONOMY

You don't need a philosopher to tell you that anxiety is one by-product of what Peter Koestenbaum calls "the brutality and promise" of the new economy. But you do need a philosopher to explain how anxiety rules the human condition—and how it can serve as a powerful, productive force in your life. The best thinker for the job, says Koestenbaum, is Soren Kierkegaard, a Danish philosopher who did as much for the analysis of anxiety as Freud did for the analysis of the subconscious. Here's a short course from Koestenbaum on the value of anxiety.

Anxiety generates knowledge. "As Kierkegaard explains it, anxiety is the natural condition. It's a cognitive emotion that reveals truths that we would prefer to hide but that we need for our greater health. In an essay called 'The Concept of Dread,' Kierkegaard draws a connection between anxiety and free will. We cannot prove that free will is true—because we freely choose the meaning of truth in the first place. But our anxiety tips us off to the existence of our freedom: It reminds us of our huge responsibility to choose who we are and to define our world."

Anxiety leads to action. "Kierkegaard wrote that the most common form of despair occurs when one does not choose or 'will' to be oneself—when a person is 'another than himself.' The opposite of despair is 'to will to be that self which one truly is.' That's the experience of anxiety. It is choosing life in the face of death; it is the experience of thought becoming action, reflection becoming behavior, and theory becoming practice. Anxiety is pure energy."

Anxiety makes you a grown-up. "Anxiety is the experience of growth itself. In any endeavor, how do you feel when you go from one stage to the next? The answer: You feel anxious. Anxiety that is denied makes us ill; anxiety that is fully confronted and fully lived through converts itself into joy, security, strength, centeredness, and character. The practical formula: Go where the pain is."